THE

CHARTER AND ORDINANCES

OF THE

CITY OF RICHMOND,

WITH THE

AMENDMENTS TO THE CHARTER.

PUBLISHED BY AUTHORITY OF THE

COMMON COUNCIL OF THE CITY OF RICHMOND.

RICHMOND:
V. L. FORE, PRINTER, 1315 MAIN STREET.
1867.

CONTENTS.

CHARTER OF THE CITY OF RICHMOND.

ORDINANCES OF THE CITY OF RICHMOND.

TITLE 1.

OF THE CITY GOVERNMENT.

TITLE 2.

OF THE REVENUE OF THE CITY.

TITLE 3.

CITY DEBT.

TITLE 4.

CITY PROPERTY.

TITLE 5.

HEALTH.

TITLE 6.

POLICE.

TITLE 7.

NUISANCES.

TITLE 8.

THE POOR.

TITLE 9.

EDUCATION.

TITLE 10.

OFFICERS.

TITLE 11.

OFFENCES.

TITLE 12.

ENACTING AND REPEALING STATUTE.

APPENDIX.

ERRATA.

Page 90, line 11 from bottom, for "requisitions" read "regulations."

Page 149, line 10 from top, insert "be" before "made."

Page 171, line 16 from bottom, insert "a" before "military."

BOUNDARIES OF THE CITY OF RICHMOND.

AN ACT

TO EXTEND AND DEFINE THE BOUNDARIES OF THE CITY OF RICHMOND.

[Passed February 13, 1867.]

1. *Be it enacted by the General Assembly*, That the boundaries of the city of Richmond shall be extended and defined as follows: The said city of Richmond shall extend, on its southern boundary, to the line which now divides the counties of Henrico and Chesterfield, from a point in said dividing line which will be struck by the extension of the western line of the city limits, across the river, to said dividing line to a point in said dividing line, which will be struck by the extension of the eastern line of the city limits, across the river, to said dividing line; and shall include all the territory lying between the present southern limits of said city and the said dividing line and between said western and eastern lines extended as aforesaid.

2. The other boundaries of said city shall be as follows: Beginning at a point in the line which divides the counties of Henrico and Chesterfield, which will be struck by the extension southwardly of the western line of Hollywood Cemetery, and running thence northwardly to the southern line of the Clark's Spring property, now belonging to the city of Richmond; thence along said line and the extension of the same to a point one hundred and fifty feet west of the western line of Randolph

street; thence northwardly and on a line parallel with said Randolph street and one hundred and fifty feet from its western line to a point on said line, one hundred and fifty feet southward from the southern line of Dover street on the plank road, to a point one hundred and fifty feet west of the western line of a street on which Mr. John Carter resides, which is probably a continuation of Carter street; thence northwardly, crossing the plank road and on a line parallel with said Carter street, and one hundred and fifty feet westwardly from its western line, to the street or road which separates the farm of William C. Allen from the lands of the Richmond College, and continuing the same line through sundry lots and the lands of Nathaniel F. Bowe, to the northern margin of Bacon branch, one of the branches of Shockoe creek; thence down the northern margin of Bacon branch by its meanders to the point where the present northern boundary of the city crosses the said branch, at or near the extended line of Seventh street, on the map of the city; thence eastwardly with the present boundary line, passing the corner on said boundary, marked C on said map, to a point on the west side of the county road leading from Valley street in said city to Chelsea or Bowling Green; thence down the centre of said road southwardly to Seventeenth or Valley street; thence along said Seventeenth or Valley street southwardly to the country road leading from said Seventeenth or Valley street to Fairfield; thence up and along the centre of said road eastwardly to a point one hundred and fifty feet eastward of the east line of Gamble street, extended northwardly, as the said street is laid down on the plan of Brown, Page and Gamble, commonly called McKenzie's Garden; thence southwardly and parallel with the said Gamble, Federal or Purcell streets one hundred and fifty feet eastward of the eastern lines of said streets, to a point in said line one hundred and fifty feet north of Venable street, as marked on Adams' plan; thence eastwardly and on a line one hundred and fifty feet northward of the north line of Venable street and parallel therewith, to a point one hundred and fifty feet northward of the north line of Q street; thence along a line eastwardly and parallel with said Q street, and one hundred and fifty feet therefrom, to a point one hundred and fifty feet eastward of Thirty-first street; thence southwardly and parallel with Thirty-first street, and one hundred and fifty feet therefrom, to a point one hundred and fifty feet north of the northern line of Marshall street on said plan; thence eastwardly and on a line one hundred and fifty feet northward of the north line of Marshall street, and parallel therewith, to a point on said line one hundred and fifty feet eastward of Thirty-fourth street; thence southwardly on a line parallel with Thirty-fourth street, and one hundred and fifty feet therefrom, to a point in said line one hundred and fifty feet north of the northern line of Main street extended; thence eastwardly and on a line parallel with said Main street so extended, and one hundred and fifty feet therefrom, until the said line meets a point one hundred and fifty feet eastward of the eastern line of Fulton street in the town of Fulton; thence along said line in a southwardly direction, and parallel with said Fulton street, until it strikes a point in said line one hundred and fifty feet southwardly of the south line of a street known as Orleans street; thence westwardly and on a line one hundred and fifty feet south of the southern line of said Orleans street, and one hundred and fifty feet therefrom, to James river, and thence across said river, continuing the same course, to the dividing line between the counties of Henrico and Chesterfield.

3. The inhabitants of the district of country lying between the present boundary of the city and the new boundary hereby established, shall not be liable, in their persons or property within the said district, for the period of five years from the passage of this act, for any portion of the debt contracted by the city of Richmond prior to the commencement of this act, or of the interest due and accruing thereon.

4. All taxes levied and collected upon persons and property within the limits hereby added to the city of Richmond, shall, for the period of three years from the passage of this act, be applied to the improvement, protection and police of the district so annexed.

5. It shall be lawful for the sheriff or other collectors of the county of Henrico to collect and make distress for any public dues or officers' fees which shall remain unpaid, by the inhabi-

tants embraced within the limits of the extension of the corporation of the city of Richmond, at the time when this act shall commence and be in force, and shall be accountable for the same in like manner as if this act had never been passed.

6. The county levy for the year eighteen hundred and sixty-seven shall be collected within the limits added to the city of Richmond by this bill, by the authorities of Henrico county, and no taxes shall be collected from the persons or property within said limits by the authorities of the city of Richmond for the year eighteen hundred and sixty-seven.

7. The Council of the city of Richmond shall provide for the representation in the Council of the city of Richmond of the inhabitants of the territory embraced in said extension.

8. This act shall be in force from and after the first day of July, eighteen hundred and sixty-seven.

AMENDMENTS TO CHARTER.

AN ACT

TO AMEND THE ACT PASSED MARCH 18, 1861, ENTITLED AN ACT TO AMEND THE CHARTER OF THE CITY OF RICHMOND, AS AMENDED BY THE ACT PASSED FEBRUARY 24, 1866, ENTITLED AN ACT TO AMEND THE ACT PASSED MARCH 18, 1861, ENTITLED AN ACT TO AMEND THE CHARTER OF THE CITY OF RICHMOND.

[Passed March 19, 1867.]

SEC. 1.—§ 3. Mayor; Council, how many, how divided among wards; a court; name: to consist of Judge and other members; how many; how divided among wards; a Criminal court, name; held by Judge thereof.

§ 5. When Mayor, Council, Aldermen and Judge to be elected; their term of office; Judge of Criminal court to be appointed by Council; to appoint clerk.

§ 7. What officers appointed by court; their term of service.

§ 8. Qualification of voters in city elections.

§ 32. Council to divide city into five wards; may change the boundaries of wards, names of wards and streets; how Aldermen to be selected; when wards changed.

§ 80. Court of Hustings held by Mayor, &c.; terms; jurisdiction.

§ 81. Terms of court held by Judge; jurisdiction.

§ 82. Criminal court; jurisdiction; terms.

§ 83. How business of Court of Hustings distributed.

§ 84. Grand jury summoned to Criminal court; what laws applicable to the court.

§ 85. Criminals examined by court held by Mayor, &c., sent to Criminal court.

§ 86. Jurisdiction of Judge and court for partition, &c. Appeals, &c.; how taken &c.

§ 87. Commonwealth's Attorney for Circuit court of city to prosecute all cases in Criminal court; his compensation; in absence of Judge of either court who may hold court.

§ 88. What duties Commonwealth's Attorney for Court of Hustings shall perform; how records, &c., to be kept.

§ 89. Jurisdiction of city courts; how far it extends.

§ 90. What penalties Council may impose; how recoverable: jurisdiction of the Mayor, &c.; when his judgment final.

SEC. 2. When Council to put this act into effect; till done, jurisdiction of Hustings court unchanged.

SEC. 3—§ 99. Council may submit question of subscription to work of improvement, or guarantee of bonds, to vote of people.

§ 100. When city authorities to have jurisdiction over new territory.

SEC. 4. Act in force from its passage.

[NOTE.—The sections of the Charter amended by this act are not the same numbers as are affixed to them in the Charter as printed in this volume. Sections 23 and 58 of the act of March 18, 1861, having been repealed by the act of February 24, 1866, they have been omitted, and the sections have been numbered regularly without reference to them. From section 22 to 57 the sections in the Charter as printed are one in advance of the numbers in this act, and from section 57 they are two in advance. The Charter was printed before this act was passed.]

1. *Be it enacted by the General Assembly of Virginia,* That sections three, five, seven, eight, thirty-two, eighty, eighty-one, eighty-two, eighty-three, eighty-four, eighty-five, eighty-six,

eighty-seven, eighty-eight, eighty-nine and ninety, of the act passed March eighteenth, eighteen hundred and sixty-one, entitled 'An act to amend the charter of the city of Richmond,' be amended and re-enacted so as to read as follows:

"§ 3. For the said corporation there shall be a Mayor; there shall be a board called the Council of the city of Richmond, which shall be composed of not less than fifteen nor more than twenty-five members, of whom not less than three nor more than five shall be for each ward; and there shall be a court which shall be called the Court of Hustings for the city of Richmond, and the members of said court shall consist of a Judge, the Mayor and not less than fifteen nor more than twenty-five other persons, of which other persons there shall in like manner be not less than three nor more than five from each ward; and there shall be a court which shall be called the Criminal court of the city of Richmond, which shall be held by the Judge thereof. The Council may from time to time prescribe how many persons shall compose the Council, and how many persons other than the Mayor and Judge shall compose the Hustings Court: provided, that the said members shall not be less than fifteen nor more than twenty.

"§ 5. There shall be an election annually in each ward of the said city on the first Wednesday in April for members of the Council; and there shall be an election in each ward on the first Wednesday in April in every fourth year from the year eighteen hundred and sixty-six, for a Mayor of said city, and for the members of the Court of Hustings other than the Judge thereof; and in the event of a failure to hold either of said elections on that day, then such election shall be held on such day as said Council may direct; and there shall also be elected by the qualified voters of said city at such times and places as the Council may prescribe, a Judge of the Court of Hustings for said city: provided, that no election for said Judge shall be held until a vacancy shall occur in the office of said Judge under the laws now in force; and there may also be appointed by the Council of said city a Judge of the Criminal court of the city of Richmond; and the judges aforesaid shall hold their office each for the term of eight years from their election; and the judges aforesaid shall each receive such compensation as may be allowed by the Council of said city, to be paid by said city: provided, that the election of the Judge of the Court of Hustings shall not take place within thirty days of any municipal or state election, and that the compensation of neither judge shall be diminished during his continuance in office. The manner of conducting elections of a judge under this section, of making return thereof, of his qualification, of ordering new elections to supply vacancies, and of deciding contested elections, shall be prescribed by the Council. The Judge of the Criminal court shall appoint a Clerk of said court, who shall hold his office for four years, and the salary of said Clerk shall be fixed and paid by the Council of said city. The Sergeant of said city shall attend the terms of the Criminal court of the city of Richmond, and shall act as the officer thereof. It shall be the duty of the Council of the city of Richmond to provide for the election, on some day after the first day of July, eighteen hundred and sixty-seven, of five members of the Council, in that portion of the county of Henrico which will be added to the city of Richmond by the act passed February thirteenth, eighteen hundred and sixty-seven, entitled 'An act to extend and define the boundaries of the city of Richmond.' And the said Council shall have authority to regulate and prescribe and enforce within that portion of the county of Henrico which will be added to the city of Richmond by the act aforesaid, between the date of the passage of this act and the first of July, eighteen hundred and sixty-seven, any sanitary rules and regulations which to the said Council may seem proper, similar to those prescribed and enforced within the city of Richmond.

"§ 7. At the May term of the Hustings court held by the Mayor, Recorder and Aldermen, in the year eighteen hundred and seventy, and at the May term of said court, held in every fourth year thereafter, there shall be appointed by said court a Sergeant and High Constable for said city, and at the May term of the Hustings court held by the Mayor, Recorder and Aldermen next before the expiration of the present term of office of the Attorney for the Commonwealth in said court and of the Clerk of said court; and at the May term of said court held in every fourth year thereafter there shall be appointed by said court an Attorney for the Commonwealth in said court and a Clerk of said court. In the event of a failure to hold a term of said court in the month of May, or to make any of said appointments, then such appointment or appointments shall be made at the next ensuing term of said court. The term of office of the Sergeant, High Constable, Attorney for the Commonwealth and Clerk shall commence on the first day of July next succeeding their appointment, and shall continue for four years.

"8. At such election in a ward every white male citizen of the commonwealth, of the age of twenty-one years or upwards, who has been a resident of the state for two years and of the city of Richmond for twelve months, and who resides in such ward, shall have a right to vote, and be eligible as a member of the Council or of the Court of Hustings.

[Amends § 31 as printed.]

"§ 32. The Council of the city shall, after the first day of July and before the first day of January next, divide the city in five or more wards; such division to take effect on the day before the first Wednesday of April, eighteen hundred and sixty eight. And the Council may thereafter from time to time change the names of the streets and wards, and may change the boundaries of the wards, or lay off the city into wards differently: provided, that no such alteration of the boundaries of the wards, or change in the number of wards, shall take effect until the day preceding the first Wednesday in April next after such alteration or change shall have been made by the Council. And if after such alteration or change shall have taken effect, there shall be residing in any ward more of the Aldermen than such ward shall be entitled to, then the Court of Hustings, held by the Mayor, Recorder and Aldermen, shall choose from among those persons the requisite number of Aldermen for such ward, and the others shall cease to exercise or have the powers of Aldermen. And if there should be any deficiency in any of the wards in the number of Aldermen to which such ward may be entitled, then said court shall proceed to elect the requisite number of Aldermen for such ward, who shall continue to hold their office and discharge the duties thereof as if they had been duly elected by the qualified voters of the city.

[Amends § 78 as printed.]

"§ 80. The Court of Hustings of the city of Richmond shall be held by the Mayor, Recorder and Aldermen of the city, or any four of them, and also by a judge, to be called the Judge of the Court of Hustings. A term of said court, not exceeding six days, shall be held by the Mayor, Recorder and Aldermen in every month, at such times and places as the Council may prescribe, at which shall be exercised all the jurisdiction, powers and duties of the Court of Hustings, except such as are expressly vested in and delegated to the said court, when held by a Judge thereof, and such as are vested in and delegated to the Criminal court of the city of Richmond.

[Amends § 79 as printed.]

"§ 81. There shall be four terms of said Court of Hustings for the city of Richmond, to be held by the Judge thereof, commencing on the first Monday in January, April, June and October of each year, at such place as the Council of said city may prescribe. At such terms the said court shall exercise exclusively the jurisdiction now vested in it over all attachments, appeals in civil cases, civil actions, motions and suits at law and in chancery; all matters concerning the probate of wills, the appointment, qualification and removal of fiduciaries, and the settlement of their accounts; and the court so held, or the Judge thereof, may appoint commissioners in chancery, commissioners to take depositions, receivers and any other officers or agents for conducting its business which a circuit court or judge may appoint in similar cases, and whose appointment is not otherwise provided for. The said court shall have appellate jurisdiction in cases in which the constitutionality or validity of an ordinance of the city is involved, and the said Court of Hustings, when held by the judge thereof, may at any time during a term adjourn for a period not exceeding fifteen days.

[Amends § 80 as printed.]

"§ 82. The Criminal court of the city of Richmond shall

have original jurisdiction of all felonies and misdemeanors committed within the territorial limits of its jurisdiction. The said court may exercise the power which a circuit court may exercise under section thirty-five, chapter one hundred and eighty-four, and section one, two and three of chapter two hundred and ten of the Code of eighteen hundred and forty-nine. The said Criminal court of the city of Richmond shall hold six terms in each year, commencing on the first Monday of January, March, May, July, September and November, and at such place as the Council of said city may from time to time appoint.

[Amends § 81 as printed.]

"§ 83 The business of said Court of Hustings, whether held by the Mayor, Recorder and Aldermen, or by the Judge, shall be distributed by law.

[Amends § 82 as printed.]

"§ 84. A grand jury shall be summoned to attend the terms of the Criminal court of the city of Richmond; which grand jury shall be charged by the Judge. All provisions of law concerning grand and petit juries, the taxation of costs and clerk's fees, applicable to circuit courts, shall apply to the said Criminal court of the city of Richmond."

[Amends § 83 as printed.]

"§ 85. All criminals examined by the Court of Hustings, when held by the Mayor, Recorder and Aldermen, if remanded for trial, shall be sent to the Criminal court of the city of Richmond, and all depositions and recognizances shall be thereto returned.

[Amends § 84 as printed.]

"§ 86. The said Court of Hustings, held by the Judge, and the said Judge, respectively, shall have the same power as a circuit court or a circuit judge in suits for partition or for sale of lands of persons under disability, and to award and try writs of injunction, habeas corpus, mandamus and prohibition, and shall exercise the same jurisdiction and powers as a circuit court or a circuit judge, in such cases, and as to all subjects incident to the matter or cases of which the court or judge has jurisdiction;

and orders awarding injunctions may be directed to the clerk of the court, and injunction bonds taken by him, in all such cases over which the said court has jurisdiction. Appeals, writs of error and writs of supersedeas from and to judgments, decrees and orders of the said court held by the judge, and from or to judgments or orders of the Criminal court of the city of Richmond, shall be taken and allowed as if they were from or to those of a circuit court or a circuit judge. But if they be from or to the judgments, decrees and orders of the said court when held by the Mayor, Recorder and Aldermen, they shall be taken to the Circuit court of the city of Richmond.

[Amends § 85 as printed.]

"§ 87. The Commonwealth's Attorney for the Circuit court of the city of Richmond shall prosecute in all cases in the Criminal court of the city of Richmond, and shall receive therefor the compensation fixed by the act passed February ——, eighteen hundred and sixty-six, for prosecutions in a circuit court, with any and all other fees allowed by law. During the absence of the Judge of said Criminal court or of the Judge of the Court of Hustings, or the inability of either from any cause to hold a term of his court, or to sit in any particular case, said court may be held by any circuit judge or by the other of said judges, and the compensation of such judge shall be fixed and paid by the Council of the city, and the judge of either of said courts may remove a cause from his court to any circuit court for the same causes and in the same manner as are prescribed by law for the removal of a cause from one circuit court to another.

[Amends § 86 as printed.]

"§ 88. The Attorney for the Commonwealth for the Court of Hustings of the city of Richmond shall perform the duties connected with any matter coming within the jurisdiction of the said court, whether held by the Mayor, Recorder and Aldermen or by the Judge thereof, which are required of the attorney of the commonwealth of a circuit court, and shall receive like compensation therefor. The records and proceedings of the said Hustings court and of the said Criminal court shall be kept as the records and proceedings of a circuit court are required to be kept, and the duties, liabilities, compensation and mode of proceeding against the clerks and other officers and agents of the said courts, and the Attorney's fees taxed, shall be the same as in like cases in a circuit court.

[Amends § 87 as printed.]

"§ 89. The Court of Hustings of the city of Richmond, whether held by the Mayor, Recorder and Aldermen or by the Judge thereof, and the Criminal court of the city of Richmond, shall have jurisdiction, as limited and prescribed by this act, within the corporate limits of said city, and within the space of one mile, on the north side of James river, without and around said city and every part thereof, including so much of said river to low water mark on the shore of the county of Chesterfield as shall be between two lines drawn due south from the eastern and western termination of the one mile aforesaid, and within said limits the said Judge of the Criminal court, the said Judge of the Hustings court, the said Mayor, Recorder and Aldermen shall each have the powers of a justice of the peace.

[Amends § 88 as printed.]

"§ 90. The Council may impose penalties for the violation of this act, or of the act of which it is amendatory, and for the violation of any ordinance of the city, not exceeding five hundred dollars for one offence. If the penalty be above one hundred dollars, it shall be prosecuted in the Criminal court of the city of Richmond. But any prosecution for a fine or penalty, either under this act or an ordinance of the city, if it be limited to an amount not exceeding one hundred dollars, and any other claim against the city or against a person within the jurisdiction of the courts of the city, if it does not exceed one hundred dollars, exclusive of interest, shall be cognizable in the Mayor's court, and the decision of the Mayor shall be final in all civil cases in which the matter in controversy, exclusive of costs, is not more than twenty dollars."

2. The Council of the city of Richmond shall proceed, as soon as it can conveniently and properly be done, to carry out the provisions of this act; but until the Criminal court of the city of

Richmond is organized, as provided for by this act, the jurisdiction of the Hustings court of said city shall remain as it now is.

3. Be it further enacted:

[This section added.]

"§ 99. The Council of the city of Richmond may at any time submit to the qualified voters of the city of Richmond, under and according to the forty-sixth, forty-seventh, forty-eighth, forty-ninth, fiftieth and fifty-first sections of chapter sixty-one of the Code of Virginia (edition of eighteen hundred and sixty), to ascertain whether the voters of the city of Richmond be in favor of subscribing to any work of internal improvement, or of guaranteeing the bonds of any internal improvement company commencing or terminating in the city of Richmond. And the Council of said city shall do and perform all the things in the premises which the county courts are required to do by the aforesaid sections of the sixty-first chapter of the Code. And the order of the Council submitting the question to the said voters, shall state the maximum amount proposed to be subscribed, or the maximum amount of the bonds proposed to be guaranteed, without any limit as to amount.

"§ 100. The authorities of the city of Richmond shall have civil and criminal jurisdiction over the persons and property embraced in the territory added to the city of Richmond by the act passed thirteenth of February, eighteen hundred and sixty seven, from and after the first of July, eighteen hundred and sixty-seven."

4. This act shall be in force from its passage.

THE CHARTER OF THE CITY OF RICHMOND.

AN ACT

TO AMEND THE CHARTER OF THE CITY OF RICHMOND, PASSED MARCH 18, 1861, AS AMENDED BY AN ACT PASSED FEBRUARY 24, 1866, ENTITLED AN ACT TO AMEND THE SAME.

SEC.

1. Boundaries of the city; corporate name; powers.
2. What transferred and vested in the corporation.
3. Mayor, Council, Aldermen, Judge.
4. All estates, rights, &c., under management of Council; all power, &c., to be exercised by Council or under its authority.
5. When Mayor, Council, Aldermen and Judge to be elected; their term of office.
6. When their term shall commence.
7. What officers appointed by the Court; their term of service.
8. Qualification of voters in city elections.
9. Elections to be held in each ward; notice of election.
10. Council to appoint commissioners; their duties; their powers.
11. Oath of commissioner; before whom taken.
12. When polls opened and closed; when may be kept open.
13. Officers to conduct the poll; how appointed; his oath; his duties; how poll to be taken and kept.
14. When officer shall close the poll; when and by whom it shall be certified.
15. Person voting more than once, all but one struck out; when and by whom.
16. Who shall certify persons voted for or elected.
17. Certificates, polls and tickets returned to Clerk of Council; who shall qualify as Councilmen; what Council shall certify as to Aldermen.
18. Council's power as to contested elections.
19. What Council to certify to the Court; what bonds Court to take.
20. Members of Council and Court and officers to hold till successors qualify.
21. When Council shall order a new election.
22. How vacancies in office may be filled.

SEC.

23. Members of the Council and officers not to act until they have taken oath of office.
24. Council to elect a President; his term of office; a President *pro tem.* What officer to sign proceedings; how meetings of Council called.
25. Eight members a quorum; a majority of those present necessary to do any act.
26. Council may grant compensation to Mayor and Aldermen.
27. Council may adopt rules and appoint clerks, &c.; may fine or expel members. To keep a record of their proceedings. The Clerk of Council keeper of the seal.
28. Council may pass by-laws, &c.
29. May appoint officers, and define their powers and duties.
30. Proceedings upon official bonds given by officers; what.
31. Council may change boundaries or names of wards, names of streets, and apportion Councilmen and Aldermen among the wards.
32. May have a survey of the city; how made and verified.
33. May establish markets, &c.
34. May erect workhouses, almshouses, &c. Shall have exclusive authority to manage the poor of the city.
35. May restrain, &c., drunkards, vagrants.
36. Who Council may exclude or send out of the city.
37. Council may erect buildings, provide cemeteries and public grounds.
38. May erect city prisons.
39. May guard against contagious and other diseases, erect hospitals, &c.
40. May guard against fires, organize fire companies.
41. May establish, &c., water works, &c.
42. May provide city watch.

Be it enacted by the General Assembly, That the territory contained within the limits prescribed by the act now in force, and by any act hereafter passed by the General Assembly, shall be deemed and taken as "The City of Richmond;" and the housekeepers and inhabitants within the said limits, and their successors, shall continue to be a corporation, with perpetual succession, by the name and style of "The City of Richmond;" and as such, and by that name, may contract and be contracted with, sue and be sued, plead and be impleaded, answer and be answered unto; and may purchase, take, receive, hold and use goods and chattels, lands and tenements, and choses in action, or any interest, right or estate therein, either for the proper use of the said city, or in trust for the benefit of any persons or association therein; and the same may grant, sell, convey, transfer and assign, let, pledge, mortgage, charge and encumber in any case and in any manner in which it would be lawful for a private individual so to do; and may have and use a common seal, and alter and renew the same at pleasure; and generally shall have all the rights, franchises, capacities and powers appertaining to municipal corporations in this commonwealth.

2. The corporation of "The City of Richmond" shall have all the estates, rights, titles and privileges, all the funds, revenues and claims, and all the powers, capacities, franchises and immunities which were vested in or conferred upon, or belonged or appertained to "The City of Richmond," or to the Mayor, Aldermen and Commonalty of the City of Richmond, by or under any act or acts of the General Assembly, heretofore passed, and not in conflict with this act.

3. For the said corporation there shall be a Mayor; there shall be a board called "The Council of the City of Richmond," which shall be composed of fifteen members, of whom, until the Council shall otherwise prescribe, five shall be for each ward; and there shall be a court which shall be called "the Court of Hustings for the City of Richmond;" and the members of said court shall consist of a Judge, the Mayor and fifteen other persons, of which fifteen persons, until the Council shall otherwise prescribe, there shall in like manner be five from each ward.

4. All the estates, rights, titles and privileges, and all the funds, revenues and claims of the city shall be under the care, management, control and disposition of the Council; and all

the corporate powers, capacities, franchises and immunities of the city shall be exercised by the Council, or under its authority, unless it be otherwise expressly provided.

[As amended by act of February 24, 1866.]

5. There shall be an election annually in each ward of the said city, on the first Wednesday in April, for members of the Council; and there shall be an election in each ward, on the first Wednesday in April next, and on the first Wednesday in April in every fourth year thereafter, for a Mayor of said city, and for the members of the Court of Hustings, other than the Judge thereof; and in the event of a failure to hold either of said elections on that day, then such election shall be held on such day as the Council may direct; and there shall also be elected by the qualified voters of said city, at such time and places as the Council shall prescribe, a Judge of the Court of Hustings for said city, who shall hold his office for the term of eight years, and shall receive such compensation as may be allowed by the Council; *provided*, that his election shall not take place within thirty days of any municipal or state election other than a state election for a judge, and that his compensation shall not be diminished during his term of office. The manner of conducting his election, of making return thereof, of his qualification, of ordering new elections to fill vacancies in his office, and of deciding contested elections, shall be prescribed by ordinance of the Council.

[As amended by act of February 24, 1866.]

6. The term of office of members of the Council and of the Mayor and other members of the Court of Hustings, except the Judge thereof, shall commence on the Saturday after the election.

[As amended by act of February 24, 1866.]

7. At the next May term of the Hustings Court held by the Mayor, Recorder and Aldermen, and at the May term of said court held in every fourth year thereafter, there shall be appointed by said court a Sergeant and a High Constable for said city, and at the May term of the Hustings Court held by the Mayor, Recorder and Aldermen next before the expiration of the present term of office of the Attorney for the Commonwealth

in said court, and of the Clerk of said Court, there shall be appointed by said Court an Attorney for the Commonwealth in said court and a Clerk of said court. In the event of a failure to hold a term of said court in the month of May, or to make any of said appointments, then such appointment or appointments shall be made at the next ensuing term of said court. The term of office of the Sergeant, High Constable, Attorney for the Commonwealth and Clerk shall commence on the first day of July next succeeding their appointment, and shall continue for four years.

8. At such election in a ward, any white male citizen of the commonwealth of the age of twenty-one years, who resides in such ward, and is qualified to vote in the city for members of the General Assembly, shall have a right to vote, and be eligible as member of the Council or of the Court of Hustings.

9. For such election the city shall continue divided (as at present) into three wards, until the Council shall lay it off into wards differently, or alter the wards. The said election shall be held at such place in each ward as shall have been prescribed by the Council; the President or Clerk of the Council publishing, previous to the election, notice of the time and place therefor, in two papers of the city for two weeks, or for such other time as the Council may direct.

10. For superintending said election the Council shall, previous thereto, appoint five persons in each ward as commissioners, any two or more of whom may act, to superintend the election in each ward. They shall admit all persons entitled to vote to do so, and reject the votes of all not entitled, and in all respects have the poll fairly taken, according to the charter and the ordinances of the city. They may swear any person to answer questions in relation to any right to vote which is claimed; and the name of any person offering to vote, but rejected by them, if required by the voter or any candidate, shall be entered in a separate list on the poll, with the names of the persons for whom he wished to vote.

11. Every such commissioner shall, before he enters upon the discharge of his duties, take an oath faithfully to execute the office of commissioner; which oath may be administered by

the Mayor or any justice of the city, or by the person appointed to conduct the election; and a certificate of said oath shall be returned to the Clerk of the Council, and be preserved in his office.

12. The poll shall not be opened at any election sooner than sunrise, and shall be closed at sunset. But if the electors who appear at the place of voting cannot all be polled before sunset, or if it shall appear to the commissioners that many of those entitled to vote have been prevented from attending by rain, they shall keep the polls open for two days, including the first.

13. An officer to conduct the election in each ward shall be appointed by the Council; or if the Council fail to do so, or the officer appointed by it fail to attend, by the commissioners. And before he commences taking the poll, he shall take an oath or affirmation to the following effect: "I do solemnly swear, that in conducting the election about to be held, I will not attempt to influence the vote of any person, or be guilty of any partiality for any candidate or person voted for, and as far as depends on me, I will make a true return of the result of the election, according to law. So help me, God." Under the superintendence and control of the commissioners, it shall be the duty of the said officer, after taking the oath or affirmation herein prescribed (a certificate whereof shall be returned to the Clerk of the Council), to cause the polls to be opened publicly for the election in the ward for which he is appointed; to proclaim and see recorded the votes admitted by the commissioners; to preserve order and remove force. The said officer shall employ such writers, and at such rate of compensation as the Council may direct; or in the absence of such direction, such writers, and at such rate as he shall think fit; and they shall respectively take an oath, to be administered by said officer, to record the votes faithfully and impartially. He shall deliver to each writer a poll-book for those officers as to which such writer is to record the votes. The writers shall enter the name of each voter in a column, to be headed with the words, "Names of Voters;" and opposite the name of the voter, a mark or numeral under the name of each person for whom he votes for any of said offices. The said votes shall be given as prescribed by

the fourth section of the third article of the Constitution; but at the time a vote is given, the officer shall receive of each voter a paper or ticket (with his name written on it) which shall specify the names of the persons for whom he votes and for what office.

14. After the names of all the persons offering to vote before the time for closing the election shall have been thus entered, the officer shall conclude the poll. Immediately on the conclusion thereof, the correctness of the poll shall be certified by the commissioners superintending the election, and by the officer conducting the same.

15. If a person vote more than once in the same election, all his votes except one shall be stricken from the poll. This shall be done in an election for members of the Council, or of the Court of Hustings, by the officer conducting the election for the ward in which such election is held; and in the election of other officers, by the officers conducting the elections in the several wards. It shall be done upon an examination of the poll to be had as soon as practicable after they are closed; and the officer or officers shall at the same time attach to the poll a list of the votes stricken therefrom, and the reasons therefor.

16. The officer conducting the election in a ward shall then ascertain, declare and certify what persons are elected in said ward as members of the Council; or, if an equal number of votes be given for persons of whom one or more, but not all, could lawfully be elected, he shall certify the name of each of said persons, and the number of votes given for him. He shall also ascertain and certify the name of each person voted for in such ward as member of the Court of Hustings, and the number of votes given for him. And the officers conducting the elections in the several wards shall, in respect to each of the other offices, for which an election is held, ascertain and certify the name of each person voted for for such office, and the number of votes given for him.

17. The certificates of said officers, with the polls and tickets, shall be delivered by them to the Clerk of the Council: whereupon, the persons appearing from said certificates to be elected in a ward as members of the Council for such ward, shall be

entitled, after taking the proper oath, to sit in the Council until the Council shall otherwise decide. The Council shall ascertain, and upon their journal enter what persons are elected from each ward as members of the Court of Hustings, and what person is elected to each of the offices for the city that are mentioned in the fifth and seventh sections.

18. The Council may decide between two or more persons having an equal number of votes for the same office, which of them is elected; it may pass upon the qualifications of persons voted for; it may prescribe the manner of determining contested elections in cases not specially provided for by this act; it may prescribe the fines to be imposed on persons who vote illegally; and in regard to any other question in respect to which it directs a poll, it may make such rules and regulations as it may deem fit.

[As amended by act of February 24, 1866.]

19. The Council shall certify to the Court of Hustings held by the Mayor, Recorder and Aldermen the names of the persons elected from each ward as members of said court, and the said court shall take from said Sergeant and Constable respectively a bond in such penalty as it may deem fit, conditioned for the faithful discharge of his duties. The Council shall cause the several persons elected to be notified of their election, and the persons elected members of the Court of Hustings shall elect from among themselves one person as Recorder and one as Senior Alderman of the city, and certify sucn election to said court. The other persons elected members of said court shall be Aldermen of the city.

20. The members of the Council for any ward, who may be in office at the time an election is held for their successors, shall continue in office until said successors, or a majority of them, are qualified. The members of the Court of Hustings elected from any ward, who may be in office at the time an election is held for their successors, shall also continue in office until said successors, or a majority of them, are qualified: And the Mayor and all other persons holding offices mentioned in the fifth and seventh sections, or appointed under ordinances of the city, shall (unless sooner removed) continue in office, after

their terms of service have expired, until their respective successors are qualified.

21. If the person who shall have received the highest number of votes for an office be adjudged by the Council to be ineligible, or if in case of a contested election the Council decide that neither of the parties to the contest is entitled to the office for which the election was held, or shall expel a member, it shall, in either of said cases, order a new election to fill the vacancy and prescribe the time therefor: And unless the Council otherwise direct, such new election shall be conducted and superintended by the same officers who conducted and superintended the previous election, and shall be under the like regulations.

[As amended by act of February 24, 1866.]

22. If, during the term for which any person may have been elected or appointed to any office herein mentioned, a vacancy occur in said office otherwise than is mentioned in the preceding section, or unless it be in the office of Judge of the Hustings Court, such vacancy may be filled by an appointment for so much of said term as may be unexpired. Such appointment shall be by the Court of Hustings, held by the Mayor, Recorder and Aldermen, if it be in the office of the Attorney for the Commonwealth, Clerk, Sergeant, High Constable, Recorder, Senior Alderman, or any other Alderman, and shall, in all other cases, be by the Council. The appointment, if the vacancy be in the office of Recorder or Senior Alderman, shall be from among the other members of the court; if in the office of any other Alderman, or of a member of the Council, from among the voters in the ward for which such Alderman or member of the Council was elected, and, if in any other office, from among those who may be eligible thereto.

23. Neither the members of the Council nor any of the officers mentioned in sections five and seven of this act, nor the officers appointed by the Council, shall be competent to act until they shall have taken the oaths or affirmations prescribed by the charter or the ordinances of the city, before the Mayor or some other justice of the city. And if any person elected as a member of the Council, or to any of said offices, shall not have taken

2

such oath or affirmation and filed a certificate thereof in the proper office, within such time as the Council shall prescribe, he shall be considered as having vacated his office.

24. The Council shall elect one of its members to act as President, who shall preside at its meetings, and continue in office for the year; and when from any cause he shall be absent they may appoint a President *pro tempore*, who shall preside during the absence of the President. The President, or the President *pro tempore*, who shall preside when the proceedings of a previous meeting are read, shall sign the same. The President shall have power at any time to call a meeting of the Council; and in case of his absence, sickness, disability or refusal, the Council may be convened by the order in writing of any three members of the Council.

25. Eight members of the Council shall constitute a quorum for the transaction of business; and no by-law, ordinance or regulation shall be binding unless the same shall have been passed by the votes of a majority of the members of the Council who are present.

26. The Council shall be authorized to grant compensation to the Mayor, Recorder and Aldermen of the city: the said compensation to be paid out of the funds of the city.

27. The Council shall have authority to adopt such rules, and to appoint such officers and clerks as they may deem proper for the regulation of their proceedings, and for the convenient transaction of their business; may fine members of their body for disorderly behaviour, and may, with the consent of two-thirds of the Council, expel a member. They shall keep a record of their proceedings, which shall at all times be open to the inspection of any voter of said city; and at the request of any member present, the ayes and noes on any question put shall be taken and entered on the journal. The Clerk of the Council shall be the keeper of the seal of the city.

28. The Council shall have authority to pass all by-laws, rules and ordinances (not repugnant to the constitution and laws of this state), which shall be necessary for the good ordering and government of such persons as shall from time to time reside or be within the limits of the said city, or shall be concerned in

interest therein, for the management of its property and the due and orderly conducting of its affairs, or which shall be necessary or proper to carry into full effect any power, authority, capacity or jurisdiction which is or shall be granted to or vested in the said city, or in the Council, the Court of Hustings, or any officer of said city, or which they shall deem necessary for the peace, comfort, convenience, good order, good morals, health or safety of said city, or of the people or property therein; and to enforce any or all of their ordinances, by reasonable fines and penalties, not exceeding for any one offence the sums limited in this act.

[As amended by act of February 24, 1866.]

29. The Council may appoint such officers as they may deem proper, in addition to those hereinbefore provided for, and define their powers and prescribe their duties and compensation, and may take from any of the officers, &c., appointed, bonds with sureties, in such penalties as to the Council may seem fit, payable to the city by its corporate name, with condition for the faithful performance of said duties. All officers appointed by the Council may be removed from office at its pleasure.

30. The parties to bonds taken in pursuance of the preceding section, their heirs, devisees, executors and administrators, shall be subject to the same proceedings on the said bonds for enforcing the conditions and terms thereof by motion or otherwise, before the Circuit Court of the city of Richmond or the Hustings Court of the city, when held by the Judge thereof, or any other courts held in the city which may succeed to their civil common law jurisdiction, that collectors of the county levy and their securities are or shall be subject to on their bonds for enforcing payment of the county levies.

31. The Council may change the boundaries of the wards and increase the number thereof, and may alter the names of wards and streets, and may apportion the members of the Council and Aldermen among the several wards, according to their population.

32. The Council may (if it shall be deemed expedient) cause to be made a survey and plan of the city, showing each lot, public street and alley, the size and number of the lots and the

width of the streets and alleys, with such explanations and remarks as the Council may deem proper. The said plan, upon being approved by two successive Councils, shall be entered upon the books of the Clerk of the Council, and shall afterwards be recorded in the office of the Clerk of the Court of Hustings of this city, and remain in said office. It shall be evidence of said lots, streets and alleys: provided that the lots laid down shall be only the lots laid down in the plan of the town, and not the divisions thereof since made: provided that the said survey and plan shall not be approved by either Council until they shall have referred the same to a committee and the accuracy of the said survey and plan is certified by said committee.

33. The Council may establish markets in and for said city; appoint clerks and proper officers therefor, prescribe the times and places for holding the same; provide suitable buildings therefor; and they may enforce such regulations as shall be necessary or proper to prevent huckstering, forestalling and regrating.

[As amended by act of February 24, 1866.]

34. The Council may erect or provide, in or near the city, suitable workhouses, houses of correction, and houses for the reception and maintenance of the poor and destitute. They shall possess and exercise exclusive authority over all persons within the limits of the city receiving or entitled to the benefits of the poor laws; appoint officers and other persons connected with the aforesaid institutions, and regulate pauperism within the limits of the city; and the Council, through the agencies it shall appoint for the direction and management of the poor of the city, shall exercise the powers and perform the duties vested by law in overseers of the poor.

35. The Council may restrain and punish drunkards, vagrants, mendicants and street beggars.

36. The Council may take measures to prevent the coming into the city from beyond the limits of the State of persons having no ostensible means of support, or of persons who may be dangerous to the peace and safety of the city; and for this purpose may require any railroad company or the captain or

master of any vessel bringing such passengers to Richmond, to enter into bond, with satisfactory security, that such persons shall not become chargeable to the city for one year, or may compel such company, captain or master to take them back from whence they came, and compel the persons to leave the city, if they have not been in the city more than thirty days before the order is given.

37. The Council may erect and keep in order all public buildings necessary or proper for said city; may provide in or near the city lands to be appropriated, improved and kept in order, as places for the interment of the dead, or as places for city grounds, and may charge for the use of ground in said places of interment, and may regulate the same; may prevent the burial of the dead in the city except in the public burial grounds; may regulate burials in said grounds, and may require the keeping and return of bills of mortality by the keepers or owners of all cemeteries, if the owners live or their office is located in the city; and may provide suitable magazines in or near said city for the storage of gunpowder or other combustible and dangerous articles.

38. The Council may cause to be erected within said city a city prison, and said prison may contain such apartments as shall be necessary for the safe-keeping and employment of all persons confined therein.

39. The Council shall have exclusive authority within the said city and the port thereof, to secure the inhabitants thereof from contagious, infectious or other dangerous diseases, to establish, erect and regulate hospitals in or near said city; to provide for and enforce the removal of patients to said hospitals, and for the appointment and organization of a Board of Health for said city, and invest it with the authority necessary for the prompt and efficient performance of its duties.

40. The Council may take such measures as shall be necessary or proper to prevent accidents by fire within the said city, or to secure the inhabitants thereof, and their property, as far as practicable, from injury thereby; and specially to establish, organize, equip and govern fire companies in said city, and to appoint a fire marshal and assistants, with any or all of the

powers which have been or may be vested by law in such officers, and to purchase fire engines or other apparatus, and to keep the same in good order.

41. The Council may establish or enlarge water works and gas works within or without the limits of the said city; may contract and agree with the owners of any land for the use or purchase thereof, or may have the same condemned for the location, extension or enlargement of their said works, the pipes connected therewith, or any of the fixtures or appurtenances thereof. They shall have power to protect from injury, by adequate penalties, the said works, pipes, fixtures and land, or any thing connected therewith, within or without the limits of said city, and to prevent the pollution of the water in the river, by prohibiting the throwing of filth or offensive matter therein above the said water works, within one mile above said water works.

42. The Council may provide for the appointment, organization, compensation and regulation of a city watch; may prescribe the duties and define the powers of the several officers, members and classes thereof, in such manner as will most effectually preserve the good order and peace of the said city, and secure the inhabitants thereof from personal violence, and their property from loss or injury.

43. The Council may establish, construct and keep in order, and may alter or remove landings, wharves and docks, on land belonging to the city; and may lay and collect a reasonable duty on vessels coming to and using the same; and may regulate the manner of using other wharves and landings within the corporate limits; may prevent or remove all obstructions in and upon any landings, wharves or docks. They may also appoint port wardens for the port of said city; prescribe the duties, and fix their fees or compensation.

44. The Council may establish a quarantine ground for the city; but if said ground shall extend below the eastern boundary of the city on the river, the assent of the county court of Henrico shall be first obtained.

45. The Council shall prescribe the duties of the Surveyor of the city and establish and regulate his compensation or fees

of office; and all surveys or other acts which shall be made or done by said Surveyor, shall be as valid and effectual as if the same were done by a Surveyor of a county.

46. The Council may open, close or extend, widen or narrow, lay out and graduate, pave and otherwise improve streets and public alleys in the city, and have them properly lighted and kept in good order; and they shall have over any street or alley in the city, which has been or may be ceded to the city, like authority as over other streets or alleys. They may build bridges in and culverts under said streets; and may prevent or remove any structure, obstruction or encroachment over or under or in a street or alley or any side-walk thereof; and may have shade trees planted along the said streets. And no company shall occupy with its works the streets of the city without the consent of the Council. In the meantime, no order shall be made, and no injunction shall be awarded by any court or judge to stay the proceedings of the city in the prosecution of their works, unless it be manifest that they, their officers, agents or servants are transcending the authority given them by this act, and that the interposition of the court is necessary to prevent injury that cannot be adequately compensated in damages.

47. The Council may authorize the laying down of city railway tracks, and the running of horse cars thereon, in the streets of the city, under such regulations as they may prescribe.

48. The Council shall not take or use any private property for streets or other public purpose without making to the owner or owners thereof just compensation for the same. But in all cases where the said city cannot by agreement obtain title to the ground necessary for such purposes, it shall be lawful for the said city to apply to and obtain from the court of the county of Henrico, or the Circuit Court thereof, if the subject proposed to be condemned lies in said county, or to the Court of Hustings held by the Judge thereof, or the Circuit Court of the city, if the subject lies within this city, for authority to condemn the same; which shall be applied for and proceeded with as provided by law.

49. The Council may, from their own body, or from among the citizens, appoint trustees of the Richmond Lancasterian

School, and make regulations for the government of the trustees and of the school. They may also establish other schools and regulate the system of education therein; and may provide or aid in the support of public libraries, to which citizens may resort; and may establish an Athenæum or Lyceum for the diffusion of knowledge by lectures or otherwise.

[As amended by act of February 24, 1866.]

50. The Council may, on the petition of the owner or owners of not less than one-fourth of the ground included in any square of the city, prohibit the erection in such square of any building or addition to any building, unless the outer walls thereof be made of brick and mortar, or stone and mortar, and to provide for the removal of any such building or addition which shall be erected contrary to such prohibition, at the expense of the builder or owner thereof; and may provide for the regular and safe building of houses in the city. And if any building shall have been commenced before said petitions can be acted on by the Council, or if a building in progress appears clearly to be unsafe, the Council may have such buildings taken down.

51. The Council may require and compel the abatement and removal of all nuisances within said city, at the expense of the person or persons causing the same, or the owner or owners of the ground whereon the same shall be. They may prevent or regulate slaughter-houses and soap and candle factories within said city, or the exercise of any dangerous, offensive or unhealthy business, trade, or employment therein, and may regulate the transportation of coal and other articles through the streets of the city.

52. If any ground in the said city shall be subject to be covered by stagnant water, or if the owner or owners, occupier or occupiers thereof shall permit any offensive or unwholesome substance to remain or accumulate therein, the Council may cause such ground to be filled up, raised or drained, or may cause such substances to be covered or to be removed therefrom, and may collect the expense of so doing from the said owner or owners, occupier or occupiers, or any of them, by distress and sale, in the same manner in which taxes levied upon real estate

for the benefit of said city, are authorized to be collected: provided that reasonable notice shall be first given to the said owners or their agents. In case of non-resident owners, who have no agent in said city, such notice may be given by a publication for not less than four weeks in any newspaper printed in said city.

[As amended by act of February 24, 1866.]

53. The Council may prevent hogs, dogs and other animals from running at large in the city, and may subject the same to such confiscations, regulations and taxes as they may deem proper; and the Council may prohibit the raising or keeping of hogs in the city.

54. The Council shall have the power to prevent the practice of flying kites, of firing guns, crackers or any combination of gunpowder or other combustible and dangerous materials, in the city, or the engaging in any employment or sport in the streets or public alleys thereof, dangerous or annoying to passengers; to prevent the riding or driving of horses or other animals, or the running of steam or horse-engines or cars, at an improper speed within the limits of said city, and wholly to exclude the said engines or cars, if they please: provided no contract be thereby violated.

55. The Council may require spirituous liquors, wine, oil, molasses, vinegar and spirits of turpentine, in casks, to be gauged and inspected; and may make such provision for the weighing of hay, fodder, oats, shucks, or other long forage, as will not be in conflict with the act passed the twenty-second of March, eighteen hundred and forty-seven, to prevent the authorities of said city from laying and collecting a tax on the bales of hay sent by the farmers of the state to said city. They may also provide for measuring corn, oats, grain, coal, stone, wood, lumber, boards, potatoes and other articles for sale or barter.

56. The Council may adopt measures to suppress riots, gaming and tippling houses and houses of ill fame; and upon persons who unlawfully sell by retail wine, beer, ale, porter, ardent spirits, or a mixture thereof, may impose fines in addition to those prescribed by the laws of the state. They may also adopt measures to prevent lewd, indecent and disorderly conduct or

exhibitions in the city, and to expel therefrom persons guilty of such conduct, who shall not have resided therein as much as one year.

57. The Council may grant aid to military companies and regiments organized within the city, to societies or associations for the advancement of agriculture and the mechanic arts, to scientific, literary and benevolent societies: provided such societies or associations are located in or near the city, or in the case of agricultural societies, shall hold their fairs in or near the city.

58. The Council may grant or refuse licenses to auctioneers, and require taxes to be paid on their licenses, in addition to any tax paid by them to the state; and may regulate sales at auction within the city, and require a per centum to be paid on such sales (except sales in the city under the judgment or decree of a court or magistrate of this state), and may require bond with security for the payment of such per centum.

59. The Council may grant or refuse licenses for theatrical performances in a public theatre, or for any public show, exhibition or performance elsewhere, and may require taxes to be paid on such licenses, and make regulations as to any such show, exhibition or performance.

60. The Council may grant or refuse licenses to owners or keepers of wagons, drays, carts, hacks and other wheeled carriages kept or employed in the city for hire; and may require the owners or keepers of wagons, drays and carts, using them in the city, to take out a license therefor, and may require taxes to be paid thereon, and subject the same to such regulations as they may deem proper.

61. The Council may grant or refuse licenses to hawkers and peddlers in the city, or persons to sell goods by sample therein, under such regulations as they may deem proper, and may require taxes to be paid on such licenses.

62. The Council may provide that no agent or sub-agent of any insurance company or office, whose principal office is located out of this city, shall establish or keep any office or transact the business of his agency within this city without obtaining a

license therefor; and may require payment of a tax on such license and a per centum on the premiums received by such agent or sub-agent, and bond with security for the payment of such per centum.

63. The Council may grant or refuse a license for keeping billiard tables, ten-pin alleys and pistol galleries, and may impose a tax on said license; or the Council may prohibit or regulate the keeping thereof in the city, under such penalties as the Council is authorized to impose.

64. On the petition of one-fourth of the freeholders of the city, the Council may by resolution direct a poll to take the sense of the freeholders of the city on the question whether the Council on behalf of the city shall subscribe to the stock of a company incorporated for a work of internal improvement in this state (which or any part of which is to be constructed in or near the city, or which connects with a road leading to the city), an amount not exceeding a certain maximum to be stated in the resolution. The resolution shall designate a certain time for the poll, not less than one month from its date, and shall be published for one month in at least two newspapers in the city. At the time designated, commissioners appointed by the Council shall, after taking an oath fairly to take and return the poll, proceed in the city in like manner as commissioners acting under the forty-seventh section of chapter sixty-one of the second edition of the Code, proceed in a county, except that the polls, instead of being of freeholders of the county and at the courthouse of the county, and at other places, shall be of freeholders of the city, and at the courthouse of the city, and other places at which elections are held in the wards; and instead of being returned to the clerk of the county court, shall be returned to the Clerk of the Council. If by the poll-books it appears that a majority of the freeholders of the city voting upon the question are in favor of the subscription, the Council may subscribe on behalf of the city for stock in said company to an amount not exceeding the maximum mentioned in said resolution.

65. The Council may subject any person or persons, who, without having obtained license therefor from the Council, shall do any act or follow any employment or business in said city,

for which the Council are or shall be authorized to grant licenses, to any fine or punishment which they are authorized to impose or inflict for the enforcement of their ordinances.

[As amended by act of February 24, 1866.]

66. For the execution of its powers and duties the Council may tax real estate in the city; all personal property therein; all free persons over sixteen years of age; all corporations located in the city, or having their principal office therein, not exempt by law from taxation; all moneys owned by, or credits due to, any person living in the city; all capital of persons having a place of business in the city, and doing business therein, and employed in said business, though the said business may extend beyond the city: provided that so much of said capital as is invested in real estate, or is employed in the manufacture of articles, outside of the city limits, shall not be taxed as capital; all stocks in incorporated joint-stock companies owned by persons living in the city, not exempt by law from taxation; incomes, interest on money, dividends of banks or other corporations owned by persons living in the city: provided that no capital, interest, income or dividends shall be taxed when a license or other tax is imposed upon the business in which the capital is employed, or upon the principal money, credit or stocks from which the interest, income or dividend is derived; nor shall a tax be imposed at the same time upon stock of a corporation and upon the dividends thereon.

[As amended by act of February 24, 1866.]

67. The Council may tax the keepers of ordinaries, houses of entertainment, boarding houses, public or private; public eating houses, coffee houses, lager beer, or other drinking saloons or cook shops; agents to rent out houses; agents to sell cattle, sheep or hogs; dealers in horses and mules; keepers of livery stables; brokers, lawyers, physicians and dentists; persons who keep a daguerreian, photograph or ambrotype gallery, and all who take pictures by light, or who sell or barter any patent or specific or quack medicine; all sellers of wine or spirituous or fermented liquors; all manufacturers, merchants, traders and shop-keepers, and any other person or employment

upon whom or upon which the state may at the time have imposed a license tax. And as to all persons or employments embraced in this section, the Council may lay the tax directly, or may require them to take out a license, under such regulations as may be prescribed by ordinance, and impose a tax thereon; but the taxes herein authorized shall be subject to the provisions stated in the next preceding section.

68. The Council may vest in the collector of the city taxes, and of assessments for the use of water and gas, any or all of the powers which are now or may hereafter be vested in a sheriff as collector of the state taxes; may prescribe the mode of his proceeding, and the mode of proceeding against him for the failure to perform his duties; and may authorize him to appoint assistants, under such regulations as they may prescribe.

69. No deed of trust or mortgage upon goods or chattels shall prevent the same from being distrained and sold for taxes assessed against the grantor in such deed, while such goods and chattels remain in the grantor's possession; nor shall any such deed prevent the goods and chattels conveyed from being distrained and sold for taxes assessed thereon, no matter in whose possession they may be found.

70. A tenant from whom payment shall be obtained by distress or otherwise of taxes due from a person under whom he holds, shall have credit for the same against such person out of the rents he may owe him; except where the tenant is bound to pay such tax by an express contract with such person.

71. Where a tax is paid by a fiduciary on the interest or profits of moneys of an estate laid out or invested either under an order of court or otherwise, the tax shall be refunded out of such estate.

72. There shall be a lien on real estate for the city taxes assessed thereon from the commencement of the year for which they are assessed. The Council may require real estate in the city, delinquent for the non-payment of taxes, to be sold for said taxes, with interest thereon, and such per centum as they may prescribe for charges; and they may regulate the terms on which real estate so delinquent may be redeemed.

73. The Council may, in the name and for the use of the

city, contract loans or cause to be issued certificates of debt or bonds; but such loans, certificates or bonds, shall not be irredeemable for a period greater than thirty-four years.

74. There shall be set apart annually, from the accruing revenues of the city, a sum equal to seven per cent. of the city debt existing at the commencement of this act. The fund thus set apart shall be called the "sinking fund," and shall be applied to the payment of the interest of the city debt and the principal of such part as may be redeemable. If no part be redeemable, then the residue of the sinking fund, after the payment of such interest, shall be invested in the bonds or certificates of debt of the city or of this state, or of the United States, or of some of the states of this Union, and applied to the payment of the city debt as it shall become redeemable.

75. Whenever, after the commencement of this act, there shall be contracted by the city any debt not payable within the next twelve months, there shall be set apart in like manner annually, for thirty-four years, or until the debt is paid, a sum exceeding by one per cent. the aggregate amount of the annual interest agreed to be paid thereon at the time of its contraction; which sum shall be part of the sinking fund, and shall be applied in the manner before directed.

76. The Council shall not appropriate any part of the sinking fund or its accruing interest, otherwise than is mentioned in the two preceding sections, except in time of war, insurrection or invasion.

77. All moneys received or collected for the use of the city shall be paid over, held and disbursed as the Council may order or prescribe.

78. The Court of Hustings for the city of Richmond shall be held by the Mayor, Recorder and Aldermen of the said city, or any four of them, except where otherwise provided, and also a judge, to be called the Judge of the Court of Hustings. A term of said court, not exceeding six days, shall be held by the Mayor, Recorder and Aldermen in every month, at such times and places as the Council shall prescribe, at which shall be exercised all the jurisdiction, powers and duties of the Court of

Hustings, except such as are expressly vested in and delegated to the said court when held by the judge aforesaid.

79. A term of the said court, not exceeding twenty days, shall also be held by the said judge in every month, except the month of August, at such time and place as the Council of the said city shall prescribe; at which term the said court shall exercise exclusively the jurisdiction now vested in it over all attachments, appeals in civil cases, civil actions, motions and suits at law and in chancery; all matters concerning the probate of wills, the appointment, qualification and removal of fiduciaries and the settlement of their accounts; and the court so held, or the judge thereof, may appoint commissioners in chancery, commissioners to take depositions, receivers, and any other officers or agents for the conducting of its business, which a circuit court or judge may appoint in similar cases, and whose appointment is not otherwise provided for by this act, or ordinances of the city. And the said court, when held by the judge thereof, may exercise the power which a circuit court may exercise under section thirty-five, chapter one hundred and eighty-four, and sections one, two and three of chapter two hundred and ten of the Code of eighteen hundred and forty-nine.

[As amended by act of February 24, 1866.]

80. The said court held by the judge shall have orginal jurisdiction of all felonies committed within the territorial limits of its jurisdiction; and if a prisoner, put on his trial for a felony, shall be found by the jury guilty of only a misdemeanor, the said court held by the judge shall have jurisdiction of the case; and it shall have appellate jurisdiction in cases in which the constitutionality or validity of an ordinance of the city is involved.

81. The business of the said court, as heretofore vested in it, whether held by the Mayor, Recorder and Aldermen, or by the judge, shall be distributed by law. But the judge may designate which of his terms shall be quarterly terms.

82. A grand jury shall be summoned as now prescribed by law, to attend the terms of the said court, held by the Mayor, Recorder and Aldermen in February, May, August and Novem-

ber. And a grand jury shall be summoned in like manner to attend the terms held by the judge immediately succeeding his quarterly terms, which grand juries shall be charged by the judge. All provisions of law concerning grand and petit juries, the taxation of costs and clerk's fees applicable to circuit courts, shall apply to the said court when held by the judge thereof.

83. All criminals examined by the said court, held by the Mayor, Recorder and Aldermen, if remanded for trial, shall be sent to the said court at its terms held by the judge, and all depositions and recognizances shall be thereto returned.

84. The said court held by the judge, and the said judge respectively shall have the same power as a circuit court, or a circuit judge, in suits for partition or for sale of lands of persons under disability, and to award and try writs of injunction, habeas corpus, mandamus and prohibition, and shall exercise the same jurisdiction and powers as a circuit court, or a circuit judge, in such cases and as to all subjects incident to the matters or cases of which the court or judge has jurisdiction. And orders awarding injunctions may be directed to the clerk of the court, and injunction bonds taken by him, in all such cases over which the said court has jurisdiction; appeals, writs of error and writs of supersedeas from and to judgments, decrees and orders of the said court held by the judge, shall be taken and allowed as if they were from or to those of a circuit court or a circuit judge. But if they be from or to the judgments, decrees and orders of the said court, when held by the Mayor, Recorder and Aldermen, they shall be taken to the circuit court of the city aforesaid as heretofore.

85. The Commonwealth's Attorney for the Circuit Court of the city of Richmond shall prosecute in all cases of felony in the said Court of Hustings held by the judge thereof. During the absence of the said judge, or his inability from any cause to hold terms of his court, the same may be held by any circuit judge, whose compensation shall be fixed and paid by the Council of the said city. And the said court, when held by the judge, or the said judge, may remove causes to any circuit court for the same causes and in the same manner as are prescribed by law for the removal of causes from one circuit court to another.

86. The Commonwealth's Attorney for the Circuit Court of the City of Richmond shall perform the duties connected with any matter or proceeding in the said Hustings Court held by the judge thereof, which are required of the attorney of the commonwealth in circuit courts, and shall receive the same fees or compensation therefor as is done in a circuit court. The records and proceedings of the said court held by the judge thereof shall be kept as the records and proceedings of a circuit court are required to be kept; and the duties, liabilities, compensation of and modes of proceedings against the clerk and other officers and agents of said court, held by the judge thereof, and the attorney's fees taxed, shall be the same as in like cases in the circuit court

87. The said Court of Hustings shall continue to have civil and criminal jurisdiction, and the Mayor, Recorder and Aldermen and Judge shall each have the powers of a justice of the peace, except as in this act limited, not only within the corporate limits of the said city, but also for the space of one mile on the north side of James river, without and around said city and every part thereof, including so much of said river to low water mark on the shore of the county of Chesterfield, as shall be between two lines drawn due south from the eastern and western termination of the one mile aforesaid, for matters arising within the same, according to the laws of the commonwealth.

[As amended by act of February 24, 1866.]

88. The Council may impose penalties for the violation of this act, or any of the ordinances of the city, not exceeding three hundred dollars for one offence. If the penalty be above one hundred dollars, it shall be prosecuted in the Court of Hustings of the city, at the terms held by the Mayor, Recorder and Aldermen; but any claim to a fine or penalty under this act, or under any ordinance of the city, if it be limited to an amount not exceeding one hundred dollars, and any other claim against the city or a person therein, if it does not exceed one hundred dollars (exclusive of interest), shall be cognizable in the Mayor's Court, and his judgment shall be final in all civil

cases where the matter in controversy, exclusive of costs, is not more than twenty dollars.

89. The Mayor, or when he is absent from the city, or so sick as to be unable to attend to his duties, or his office is vacant, the Recorder, or if he be absent from the city, or so sick as to be unable to attend to his duties, or his office is vacant, the Senior Alderman shall hold a court, which shall be called the Mayor's Court, every day except Sunday, in such place as the Council may designate, and take cognizance of such cases as may be brought before him under the laws of the state, and all cases arising under the ordinances or by-laws of the city, and where the jurisdiction is not taken away by the next preceding section of this act. And of the Recorder and Aldermen of the city, only the one who is authorized for the time being by this section to hold said court, shall have authority to discharge from custody a person who has been committed to the jail for felony.

90. The Mayor shall keep an office in some convenient part of the city. In addition to his powers as a justice of the peace, his jurisdiction shall extend to all breaches of the peace committed within the jurisdictional limits of the Hustings Court; and as to all infractions of the city ordinances, shall be final, except in cases in which the constitutionality or validity of such ordinances is involved.

[As amended by act of February 24, 1866.]

91. The Mayor shall be the head of police of the city, and shall have a general superintendence and control of said police, pursuant to the ordinances of the city. When he is absent from the city, or is so sick as to be unable to attend to his duties, or his office is vacant, the Recorder, or if he be absent from the city, or is so sick as to be unable to attend to his duties, or his office be vacant, the Senior Alderman shall exercise all the powers of the Mayor.

92. The police officers of the city, or such of them as the Council may designate for the purpose, shall, in criminal cases, have the same powers, duties and fees, and be subject to the same penalties that are prescribed by law as to constables; and in proceedings for violations of this act, or of any ordinance or

by-law of the city, said officers shall act to such extent and in such manner as the Council may direct.

93. No person shall be capable of holding at the same time more than one of the offices mentioned in the fifth and seventh sections of this act.

94. In all respects, except as to the collection of taxes, the Sergeant of the city shall have the powers and authority of, and shall perform the duties and receive the same fees, and be subject to the same liabilities and penalties, and be proceeded against in the same way as sheriffs. The High Constable of the city shall, in civil cases, have the same powers, duties and fees, and be subject to the same penalties as are prescribed by law as to other constables; and no constable of the county of Henrico shall within the corporate limits execute a warrant issued by a justice of the peace in a civil case, or an execution issued on a judgment obtained on such warrant. The said High Constable may, with the consent of the Court of Hustings held by the Mayor, Recorder and Aldermen, appoint one or more deputies, of whom the court shall enter of record that the person so appointed is a man of honesty and good demeanor. Any such deputy may be removed from office by his principal or by the said court. During his continuance in office he may discharge any of the official duties of his principal.

95. This act shall be construed in relation to the powers conferred upon the city as a remedial statute in favor of the city.

96. The printed copies of the ordinances of the city, published under its authority, and transcripts from such ordinances, or from the journal of the Council, certified by the clerk thereof, shall be received as evidence for any purpose for which the original ordinances or journal could be received and with as much effect.*

*The twenty-third and fifty-eighth sections of the act of March 18, 1861, were repealed by the act of February 24, 1866, and are therefore omitted.

THE

ORDINANCES OF THE CITY OF RICHMOND.

WHEREAS it is expedient that the general ordinances of the city of Richmond should be arranged in appropriate titles, chapters and sections; that the amendments thereto made since the last revision should be ingrafted therein, and that any inconsistencies should be corrected; therefore,

Be it ordained by the Council of the City of Richmond, in manner and form following, that is to say:

TITLE 1.

OF THE CITY GOVERNMENT.

CH. 1. Of the wards of the city.
CH. 2. Of elections.
CH. 3. Of the election of Judge of the Court of Hustings.
CH. 4. Of contested elections.
CH. 5. Of official oaths, bonds and seal of the city.
CH. 6. Of salaries of officers.
CH. 7. Of rules of the Council.
CH. 8. Of the Mayor's court.
CH. 9. Of the Messenger of the Council.
CH. 10. Of the Auditor and Chamberlain of the city.

CHAPTER I.

OF THE WARDS OF THE CITY.

SEC.
1. Boundaries of Jefferson Ward.
2. Boundaries of Madison Ward.
3. Boundaries of Monroe Ward.

1. Jefferson Ward shall include all that part of the city lying east of a line beginning at Mayo's bridge, running along the middle of 14th street, as at present laid out, to Broad street;

thence across Broad street to College street, and along the middle of College street to Marshall street; thence along the middle of Marshall street to 14th street; thence along the middle of 14th street to Shockoe creek; thence along said Shockoe creek to the eastern branch of said creek; and thence along said eastern branch to the corporation line.

2. Madison Ward shall extend from the said western boundary of Jefferson Ward to a line running along the middle of 4th street, from the corporation line to Arch street, and in continuation of the centre line of 4th street to the James river and Kanawha canal; thence up said canal to the middle of the street laid out between the Tredegar works property and Tate's old tan-yard; thence along the middle of said last mentioned street to James river.

3. Monroe Ward shall include all that part of the city west of said western boundary of Madison Ward.

CHAPTER II.

OF ELECTIONS.

1. Elections held under the charter and ordinances of the city shall be held at the time and conducted in the mode therein prescribed. And the Council shall at its regular meeting in March of each year, or as soon thereafter as practicable, designate the place in each ward where the said elections shall be held, of which notice shall be given for two weeks, twice a week, in two of the daily papers published in the city.

2. At the time mentioned in the preceding section the Council shall appoint five persons in each ward, as commissioners, any two of whom may act, to superintend the elections in each ward.

3. There shall also be appointed by the Council an officer of the police to conduct said elections, who shall employ as many writers as he shall deem necessary to keep the polls accurately, at the rate of compensation hereinafter fixed.

4. Each commissioner who shall act shall be entitled to receive as compensation three dollars per day, and the writers at the rate of five dollars per day; and the conductors shall certify the number of days that such commissioners and clerks are employed.

5. The conductor in each ward shall, under the directions of the Council, provide the necessary conveniences for receiving the vote of the city, and present his bill for the same to the Council for payment.

6. No compensation shall be allowed for refreshments for the clerks, commissioners or conductors.

7. If any conductor shall take the poll unfairly, or make a false certificate or return, or neglect to deliver the polls or make a return at the time and in the mode prescribed by the charter and ordinances of the city; or if such conductor, or any commissioner, whilst acting as such in any election, shall show undue partiality, he shall pay a fine of not less than twenty nor more than one hundred dollars; and the conductor shall be discharged from his office.

CHAPTER III.

OF THE ELECTION OF JUDGE OF THE COURT OF HUSTINGS.

SEC.
1. When office of judge vacant.
2. How vacancy in office to be filled.
3. When election to be held.
4. How, when and by whom election conducted.
5. Commission to be given to person elected.
6. Official oath to be taken.
7. Salary.
8. Appellate jurisdiction.
9. Compensation to judge holding court in absence of Hustings judge.
10. Where the court to be held.

1. The office of the Judge of the Court of Hustings of the city shall be vacant, not only when he dies or resigns, but also when he fails to qualify within thirty days next after he receives his commission.

2. When there shall be such a vacancy in the office of said

judge as is mentioned in the preceding section, the Council shall declare the fact, and have the same published in two or more papers published in the city, for two weeks, and shall, at the same time, require an election to fill the vacancy, to be held on a certain day, not less than one month nor more than three months next after the said publication.

3. Every election of the judge, not provided for in the preceding section, shall be held at the end of eight years from the commencement of his term, on such day as the Council may direct: provided, that such election shall not be within thirty days of any other city or state election, except an election for a state judge.

4. In every election of a judge there shall be opened in the several wards of the city, polls at the place prescribed by the Council. The commissioners appointed to superintend the city elections, at the last preceding election for Councilmen, shall act at, and in relation to, elections under this ordinance, and shall have the like powers and perform the like duties as in case of the election for aldermen; and the ordinances in force at the time of said election shall be applicable to the case of the election of judge, except so far as the same are inconsistent with this ordinance.

5. When the Council shall have ascertained the person elected to the office of Judge of the Court of Hustings, and shall have inserted the fact of his election upon their journal, a commission, signed by the President and attested by the Clerk of the Council, with the seal of the city thereto, shall be delivered to him, which shall be to the following effect:

Whereas it has been ascertained and declared by the Council that at an election held in the city of Richmond, on the ——— day of ——, ——— has been duly elected Judge of the Court of Hustings of the city of Richmond for eight years, commencing from the —— day of ———.

Now, know all men by these presents, that by virtue of the laws of Virginia and the charter and ordinances of the city of Richmond, and of the election held on the —— day of ———, the said ——— is fully authorized and empowered to perform all the functions of Judge of the Court of Hustings of the city of Richmond during his continuance in office.

6. The said judge shall not act in his said office until he has taken the oath prescribed by the second section of chapter five, "concerning official oaths," &c.; and the certificate of his qualification shall be entered of record in his court at the first term thereof held by him.

7. The salary of the said judge shall be three thousand dollars per annum, payable quarterly.

8. In addition to the powers and authority vested in the said judge and the said court by the charter, the said Court of Hustings held by said judge, shall have appellate jurisdiction, to hear and determine appeals from the Mayor, in all cases in which the constitutionality or validity of any ordinance of the city shall be drawn in question, or where a fine shall be imposed, or the application for a fine shall be refused for a nuisance, or an order made or refused for abating it, if the alleged nuisance is caused by the pursuit of any trade or manufacture, or by the occupation of the streets and alleys of the city under a colorable and *bona fide* claim of title: and such appeal shall be as well for the city as for individuals or corporations, and shall be allowed in the same mode and upon the same terms as other appeals from the judgment of the Mayor are allowed.

9. When during the absence of the judge, or his inability from any cause to hold a term of his court, the same shall be held by a circuit judge, the said circuit judge shall receive for each day he shall hold said court, the sum of ten dollars; and the same shall be paid by the Auditor upon the certificate of the clerk of the court, stating the name of the judge, the term of the court, and the number of days the said court was held by the said circuit judge.

10. The said Court of Hustings shall be held by the judge in the City Hall of the city of Richmond, unless otherwise ordered by resolution of the Council; and the term of said court, held by the said judge, shall begin each month on the Monday immediately following the term of said court held by the Mayor, Recorder and Aldermen.

CHAPTER IV.

OF CONTESTED ELECTIONS.

1. Any person who shall vote more than once, or shall vote illegally in any election held under the charter of the city, shall be fined twenty dollars.

2. A person intending to contest the election of another to any office provided for by the charter of the city, shall present his petition to the Council, or file the same with the Chamberlain within five days after the election has been closed, and give notice of his intention to do so to the person whose election he contests. Said petition shall state the grounds on which the election is contested, and the petitioner and one other person of good character shall verify the same on oath or affirmation; and ten other persons shall certify that in their opinion the said petition is well founded.

3. If such petition shall be intended to contest the election of a person as Mayor, Judge or Alderman, and shall be presented to the Council or filed with the Chamberlain before the Council shall ascertain and enter upon their journal that such person is elected, the Council shall not proceed to ascertain and enter on their journal his election until such contest shall be either abandoned or determined.

4. All petitions contesting elections, and all other matter relating to elections, shall be referred to the committee on elections, if a reference to a committee shall be deemed necessary by the Council.

5. If the grounds on which the election is intended to be contested is the ineligibility to the office of the person who has been returned as elected, or as having received the greatest number of votes, the grounds on which such ineligibility is rested shall be stated in the petition, a copy of which petition

shall be delivered to the party having the return; and no other statement shall be necessary. But if the election shall be intended to be contested, on the ground that the person having the return has not received the greatest number of legal votes given, then, and in that case, each of the parties claiming to have received the greatest number of legal votes for the office, shall, within five days after the petition has been presented to the Council or filed with the Chamberlain, deliver to the other a list of votes he will dispute, with his objections to each stated specifically, and a list of the votes improperly rejected, for which he will contend. And he shall append to the list of votes he intends to dispute or claim, an oath to the following effect: "I do swear that I have positive information which leads me to believe, and I do believe, the persons above mentioned are not legally qualified (or are qualified, as the case may be) to vote in the ward of the city in which they voted (or in which they offered to vote, as the case may be)."

6. Each party shall, after the five days have expired, proceed to take all proper depositions to sustain or invalidate said election, upon reasonable notice to the adverse party; which depositions shall be delivered to the committee within twenty days from the day they are hereinbefore authorized to commence to take depositions in the case, unless the committee shall, for good cause shown, allow a further time, not exceeding ten days.

7. The committee shall as soon as the said twenty days, or the further time allowed, has expired, proceed to ascertain, upon the evidence thus furnished, and upon oral testimony, if the committee shall admit such testimony, and reduce the same to writing, the name of each person voted for for the said office, and the number of legal votes given for him; and shall report the same to the Council, and return therewith all the evidence before them.

8. The report of the committee shall state the grounds on which any vote objected to or contended for is rejected or admitted, and refer to the evidence on which the decision is founded.

9. If any party is dissatisfied with the report of the committee, he may make his objections before the Council after the

report is returned and before it is acted on; and he shall give notice of his objections to the party in whose favor the committee has reportêd, stating all his objections thereto; and if the other party has any objections to said report, he shall, within two days after receiving such notice, give to the party objecting to the report notice of his objections thereto. And the contest in the Council shall be confined to the objections thus made, unless a member of the Council shall be of the opinion that there is some other error in said report.

CHAPTER V.

OF OFFICIAL OATHS, BONDS, AND SEAL OF THE CITY.

1. Every person elected to the office of Mayor, Recorder or Alderman of the city, or a member of the Council thereof, shall within thirty days after his election, take an oath to perform the duties of his office honestly and to the best of his capacity.

2. Every person hereafter elected or appointed by the Council to any office, for the duties whereof he is allowed any salary, fees or compensation, shall, before he acts in such office, take an oath of office, which in every case wherein no other is specially prescribed, shall be as follows: "I swear that I will faithfully perform the duties of my office of —— to the best of my skill and judgment, so help me God." When such oath is not administered in the presence of the Council, a certificate of the fact of such oath having been taken shall be obtained by the person taking it, from the justice or other person administering it, and filed with the Chamberlain. If any person shall act in his office before taking the oath and filing the certificate as required by this section, he shall pay a fine of not less than one nor more than twenty dollars for each day on which he so acts.

3. Any oath required to be taken by the charter or ordinances of the city, unless otherwise specially provided, may be

taken before a justice or notary public, or any other person authorized by the laws of the state to administer oaths in the city.

4. If any person required to take an oath shall declare that he has religious scruples as to the propriety of taking an oath, he may make a solemn affirmation, which shall have in all respects the same effect as an oath.

5. If any person elected or appointed to any of the offices or posts referred to in the first and second sections of this ordinance, shall fail, for thirty days, to take the oath prescribed and file a certificate with the Chamberlain, when by this ordinance required to do so, and if security is required of the officer so elected or appointed, if he shall fail for the same time to give the same in the manner required by the ordinances under which his election or appointment is made, his office shall be declared to be vacant, and the Council, or the court, shall proceed to have the same filled in the mode provided by the charter and ordinances of the city.

BONDS.

6. Every bond required by any ordinance to be taken or approved by the Council, the court, or any other body or person acting under the authority of the city government, unless otherwise provided for, shall be made payable to "The City of Richmond," with surety deemed sufficient by the body or person before whom it is taken. Every such bond required of any person elected or appointed to any office, post or trust, unless otherwise provided for, shall be with condition for the faithful discharge by him of the duties of his office or trust, and shall be returned to the Auditor and preserved by him.

SEAL.

7. The seal of the city of Richmond shall continue to be the same in form and style as it was used prior to April, 1865. The Chamberlain of the city shall be the keeper of the seal.

8. Whenever the seal of the city shall be affixed to any paper, there shall be a tax thereon of two dollars, which shall be paid to the Chamberlain, except in such cases as are exempted by law.

CHAPTER VI.

OF SALARIES OF OFFICERS.

1. The several officers of the city hereinafter mentioned shall receive annually the following sums, that is to say:

The Mayor of the city, three thousand dollars.

The Recorder and Aldermen, eight hundred dollars to be divided among them in proportion to the number of days that the clerk of the court shall certify that they have attended on said court.

The Chamberlain, twenty-five hundred dollars.

The clerk in the Chamberlain's office, fifteen hundred dollars.

The Auditor, twenty-two hundred and fifty dollars.

The clerk in the Auditor's office, fifteen hundred dollars.

The Messenger of the Council, one thousand dollars. And for a servant to keep the building in order and make and keep up the fires, four hundred dollars.

The Engineer of the City, twenty-five hundred dollars.

The Superintendent of Streets, one thousand dollars.

The Assessor of the City Taxes, twenty-two hundred and fifty dollars.

The Superintendent of the Gas Works, twenty-two hundred and fifty dollars.

The Inspector of Gas Works, seventeen hundred and fifty dollars.

The Superintendent of Water Works, twenty-two hundred and fifty dollars.

The Assistant Superintendent of Water Works, fifteen hundred dollars.

The Superintendent of the Pump House, twelve hundred and fifty dollars.

The Assistant Superintendent of the Pump House, one thousand dollars.

The Clerk of the First Market, twelve hundred and fifty dollars; and for sweeping, whitewashing, &c., of building and grounds, seven hundred and fifty dollars.

The Clerk of the Second Market, twelve hundred and fifty dollars; and for sweeping, whitewashing, &c., buildings and grounds, six hundred and twenty-five dollars.

The Chief Engineer of the Fire Brigade, twelve hundred and fifty dollars.

The commanders of the fire companies, each two hundred and fifty dollars.

The engineer of the steam fire engine of Company B, one thousand dollars.

The engineer of the steam fire engine of Company C, nine hundred dollars.

The foremen of fire companies, each one hundred and eighty-seven dollars and fifty cents.

The firemen of the steam fire engine, each five hundred dollars.

The hostlers of the steam fire engine, each five hundred dollars.

The Clerk of Fire Brigade, two hundred and fifty dollars.

The other firemen, each one hundred and twenty-five dollars.

The Superintendent of the Almshouse, one thousand dollars. And he shall have, in addition thereto, the use of the house provided for the Superintendent, and his fuel, gas and water free of cost; and he shall have the privilege of taking supplies for his family from the provisions purchased for the almshouse at the prices given for them.

2. The salaries of the officers of the city shall be paid monthly, except the salary of the Assessor of the City Taxes, which shall be paid as provided by the ordinance concerning the assessment of taxes; and except that the payment to the Recorder and Aldermen shall be quarterly.

3. A person elected to any office under the charter of the city, who may be prevented from qualifying at the usual time by a contested election, shall, upon being declared duly elected and qualifying, be entitled to the salary from the time when he would have entered upon his office if there had been no contest.

4. All other officers and employees of the city shall receive the salaries or compensation provided by the ordinances of the city or resolutions of the Council under which their appointments have been made.

CHAPTER VII.

OF RULES OF THE COUNCIL.

SEC.
1. When Council shall meet—a quorum, how many.
2. How notice of meeting given.
3. The committees.
4. Priority of business.
5. Who may address Council orally.
6. Petitions, &c., to be respectful and in writing.
7. Petitions for remissions of fine or tax to be on oath; how referred and acted on.
8. Resolutions to be in writing; member's name recorded.
9. Member, how often and how long may speak.
10. Debate to be decorous and pertinent.
11. Presiding member to enforce rules as to time, and preserve order.

SEC.
12. Previous question, when it may be called.
13. Resolution or ordinance, when not to be passed on the day it is introduced; how ordinance may be amended.
14. Appointments to be by *viva voce* vote.
15. Members present must vote unless interested or excused.
16. Member entered present not to depart without leave.
17. When proceedings to be read, and by whom signed.
18. Question decided not to be brought up again—except.
19. Unfinished business, how disposed of.
20. Rule may be suspended by a vote of two-thirds.

For the regulation of the proceedings of the Council and the convenient transaction of its business, the following rules are adopted:

Rule I. The Council shall meet on the second Monday in every month, at four o'clock in the afternoon, and also shall meet at any other time to which it may adjourn or be regularly called. If eight members fail to attend within half an hour after the time appointed for a meeting, the Clerk shall enter in the journal the names of those attending, and the adjournment for want of a quorum.

Rule II. Before the time of any meeting of the Council the Clerk shall make out and sign a notice thereof to each member. The notices shall be placed by the Clerk in the hands of the Messenger of the Council, or in case of his sickness or absence from the city, a police officer of the city, at least a day before the meeting thereof, when the same is practicable. The officer in whose hands any such notice is placed, shall on the day he receives it, promptly deliver the same to the member to whom it is addressed, or at his residence or place of business.

RULE III. As soon as convenient after each organization of the Council, there shall be appointed by the President the following standing committees, viz:

The following committees to consist of seven members, of which at least two shall be from each ward:

1. The Committee on Streets Generally; and the two members in a ward with the chairman of the committee, shall be a committee for the ward.

2. The Committee for the Relief of the Poor.

The following committees to consist of three members, of which one shall be from each ward.

3. The Committee on Finance.
4. The Committee on Light.
5. The Committee on Water.
6. The Committee on the Fire Department.
7. The Committee on Cemeteries.
8. The Committee on Elections.
9. The Committee on Claims and Salaries.
10. The Committee on Police.
11. The Committee on Public Grounds and Buildings.
12. The Committee on Accounts.
13. The Committee on Health.

The following committees to consist of three members:

14. The Committees on Primary Schools, one committee for each ward.

15. The Committee on the First Market; two members from Jefferson ward and one from Madison ward.

16. The Committee on the Second Market; two members from Monroe ward and one from Madison ward.

The President shall place himself, or he may be placed by the Council, upon any of the said committees.

The Council may by resolution raise select committees, for a special purpose, which if not otherwise directed, shall be appointed by the President.

Each of said committees shall examine all such matters as

may stand referred to it by ordinance, or as may from time to time be referred to it, and report thereon to the Council.

RULE IV. If the Council direct any matter to be the special business of a future meeting, or a meeting be called for a special business, the President shall at such future meeting, so soon as the proceedings are read and signed, announce such special business, and it shall have priority over all other business.

RULE V. No person who is not a member of the Council, shall orally address it, until leave to make such address has been applied for through a member of the Council, and granted by it.

RULE VI. Every petition, communication or address to the Council, shall be in respectful language, and except in cases where it is otherwise allowed, shall be in writing.

RULE VII. Every application for a remission or repayment of a fine or tax shall be verified by the oath or affirmation of the applicant, and without special order shall stand referred, if a tax, to the committee of finance; if a fine or other claim, to the committee of claims. Before the committee reports to the Council on the application, there shall (unless the committee dispense therewith) be reported to it the facts in regard to such tax by the Assessor, and the facts in regard to such fine by the police officer who reported the case to the Mayor.

RULE VIII. Every resolution that is proposed shall be reduced to writing before any question is taken on it. And the name of every member offering a resolution shall be recorded on the journal.

RULE IX. A member shall address himself to the President, and be recognized by him as entitled to speak, before he proceeds. After being so recognized, the member (except when called to order by the President or another member) shall not be interrupted during the time allowed him. No member shall speak more than ten minutes at any one time, unless he be chairman of a committee, in explanation of a report or ordinance, when he shall be allowed, if he desire it, fifteen minutes; nor shall any member speak more than twice upon the same question. Remarks may be made by the presiding member under the same restrictions.

Rule X. All debate shall be regular, decent, and without altercation or personal invective: it must also be pertinent to the question.

Rule XI. The presiding member shall not allow any one to speak longer or more frequently than these rules permit. He shall in this and all other matters preserve order, and decide any question raised concerning it; but any member may appeal from his decision to the Council, which may affirm or reverse such decision.

Rule XII. The previous question may be called at any time, three members concurring.

Rule XIII. No resolution appropriating money, nor any ordinance shall pass on the day the same shall be introduced. And no ordinance shall be amended, suspended or repealed, except by ordinance regularly introduced and passed; and it shall not be amended unless the whole section be re-enacted.

Rule XIV. Every appointment to office by the Council shall be by *viva voce* vote. When a vote being taken, it appears that a majority of the members present do not concur in a vote for the same person, there shall be another vote taken, either then or at such other time as the Council may determine on.

Rule XV. Every member present when a question is put on an ordinance or resolution, shall, unless interested or excused from voting by the Council, vote on one side or the other of such question. And every member present when the roll is called upon the occasion of an appointment to office, shall vote for some person to the office, unless it be an office created by the ordinance concerning the police force of the city; in which case he may decline voting for any person nominated, and the fact of his so declining shall be recorded on the journal.

Rule XVI. After a member has at any meeting been entered as present, he shall not, without leave of the Council, absent himself from such meeting until its adjournment. A member violating this rule shall pay a fine of ten dollars.

Rule XVII. The proceedings at any meeting of the Council shall be read at its next meeting, before any other business. And after the errors appearing therein (if any) are corrected, the same shall be signed by the person acting as President at the time the same are so read.

Rule XVIII. No question decided by the Council shall be again brought forward during the year for which the Council was elected, unless the same be moved within two months after the Council has acted upon it, and on a motion for reconsideration there be in favor of such reconsideration votes equal to or greater than the majority of the members present when the question was before decided. And when the motion is for reconsideration of an ordinance passed on any previous day, such motion shall not be in order, unless made before such ordinance takes effect. This rule shall not prevent an ordinance from being amended, suspended or repealed by an ordinance introduced and passed in the manner allowed by the thirteenth rule.

Rule XIX. All business unfinished at the expiration of the year for which the Council was elected, shall be considered as laid on the table, and may be acted upon thereafter, at the pleasure of the Council.

Rule XX. Any rule herein adopted may, at any particular time, be suspended for a special purpose, by a vote of two-thirds of the members present at the time.

CHAPTER VIII.

OF THE MAYOR'S COURT.

1. The Mayor's court shall be held every day, except Sunday, in the City Hall or in such other place as the Council may designate. The jurisdiction of the court shall extend to all cases arising within the jurisdictional limits of the city, of which a justice of the peace may take cognizance under the laws of the state, and to all cases arising under the charter or ordinances of the city where the penalty does not exceed one hundred dollars; or where there is a claim against the city or a person

therein, if it does not exceed one hundred dollars, exclusive of interest. And the judgment shall be final in all civil cases where the matter in controversy, exclusive of costs, is not more than twenty dollars.

2. The Mayor may appoint a clerk at a compensation not to exceed that of the second officer of police of the city, who shall perform such duties as clerk as the Mayor may require of him.

3. If any person who has been duly summoned as a witness to attend and give evidence before the Mayor or justice of the city, touching any matter or thing pending before him under the charter or any ordinance of the city, shall fail to attend in obedience to the said summons, he or she may be fined at the discretion of the Mayor or other justice of the city, in a sum not exceeding twenty dollars.

CHAPTER IX.

OF THE MESSENGER OF THE COUNCIL.

1. There shall be appointed annually in the month of December, by the Council, a Messenger of the Council, who shall hold his office for one year, and until his successor is appointed.

2. It shall be the duty of the Messenger to be and remain in the Chamberlain's office from nine o'clock A. M., to three o'clock P. M., unless when engaged in the discharge of his duties. He shall attend on the Council when it is in session, and on the committees of the Council when they hold their sessions in the City Hall; and shall perform such services as the Council or said committees may require of him. He shall also act as the Messenger of the Chamberlain, when the Council or the committees do not require his services. He shall have the care, keeping, cleaning and warming of the City Hall, and shall light the lamps in the passages, the Council Chamber, the Chamberlain's office, and any other room in which a committee of the Council shall hold its meeting for the time; and he may with the approval of the chairman of the committee on public

grounds and buildings, have repairs done to the building: provided such repairs shall not in any one case exceed ten dollars; and the expense thereof shall be paid by the Auditor, upon the order of the chairman of said committee. And he shall perform such other services as the Council may prescribe by resolution. But he shall not be required to wait upon the court or any of the offices in the City Hall.

3. The Messenger shall have the power and authority of a policeman within the City Hall and the lot in which it stands, and also the sidewalks adjoining thereto

---

CHAPTER X.

OF THE AUDITOR AND CHAMBERLAIN OF THE CITY.

1. At the first meeting of the Council, after its annual organization, or as soon thereafter as practicable, there shall be appointed by it an Auditor of Accounts and a Chamberlain, who shall also be the clerk of the Council. The term of office of each of them shall commence on the first day of May, and continue one year, and afterwards until a successor shall be qualified.

2. Each of said officers shall give bond, to be approved by the Council, the penalty of which shall be thirty thousand dollars The bond of the Auditor shall be deposited with the Chamberlain, and the bond of the Chamberlain shall be deposited with the Auditor; and they shall be spread upon the journal of the Council.

3. The person appointed to either of said offices shall not act therein, until he shall, in the presence of the Council, take an oath, to be administered by its President, or, in his absence, by the member presiding for the time, that he will faithfully perform the duties of his office to the best of his skill and judgment.

4. If the bond of either of said officers be not approved by the Council, or the oath prescribed be not taken by him before the first of May, the appointment shall be considered as annulled, and the Council shall proceed at its next meeting, or as soon thereafter as may be, to make a new appointment.

5. Said officers, or either of them, may be removed from office by the Council at any regular meeting, or at a meeting called specially for the purpose, and with notice to the members. And if either of said offices shall become vacant, the Council may appoint a person to fill the vacancy, who shall give bond, and qualify as hereinbefore prescribed.

6. The Chamberlain and Auditor shall nominate to the Council three persons for each clerkship, to be filled in their respective offices, and from the number thus nominated respectively, the Council shall elect one to serve as the clerk of the Chamberlain, and one to serve as clerk of the Auditor, but such clerks shall not act as such until they shall have taken an oath that they will faithfully discharge the duties of their office to the best of their skill and judgment. The clerks so appointed may be removed by their principals.

7. The Chamberlain shall in person, or with the assent of the Council, by his clerk, attend the meetings of the Council, and enter correctly its proceedings, and in a book kept for the purpose record all the ordinances. The book of such proceedings, and the book of ordinances, shall be kept by him with an index, referring to the different matters therein, and shall be open at all time to the inspection of any member of the Council. The said Chamberlain shall make copies of or extracts from any thing in said books when and as often as he may be required so to do by the Council, the President, or any chairman of any committee thereof. He shall regularly furnish the chairman of each committee with a copy of the resolution constituting it, and of all resolutions referring matters to his committee; and shall in his office file all papers, and preserve all books and papers which may come to him officially; and whenever the Council is about to make an appointment to an office, shall, if the person then filling such office be in default, inform the Council of the fact.

TITLE 2.

OF THE REVENUE OF THE CITY.

CHAPTER XI.

CONCERNING THE RECEIVING AND PAYING MONEY AT THE TREASURY.

1. All money to be paid into the treasury of the city, if the amount exceed five hundred dollars, shall be paid by the person liable to pay the same, or his agent, into such of the banks of the city of Richmond as the Council may by resolution prescribe, in the following manner: A warrant shall first be obtained from the Auditor, directing the Chamberlain to receive the sum to be paid, specifying on what account the payment is to be made. The Chamberlain shall by his order upon the said warrant, direct the cashier of one of the said banks to receive

the sum therein mentioned for the city of Richmond; and upon receiving the same the proper officer of the bank shall give a certificate on the same warrant, that the sum mentioned has been received. Upon the return of the warrant, order and certificate, the Chamberlain shall give a receipt for the sum so paid, which shall be carried to the Auditor, and his receipt therefor shall be the acquittance of the party making the payment.

2. All moneys to be paid into the treasury of the city, except the bills for gas and water, if the amount does not exceed five hundred dollars, shall be paid by the person liable to pay the same, or his agent, to the Chamberlain, in the following manner: A warrant shall first be obtained from the Auditor, directing the Chamberlain to receive the sum to be paid, specifying on what account the payment is to be made. Upon the payment of the money to the Chamberlain, he shall give a receipt for the same, which shall be carried to the Auditor; and his receipt therefor shall be the acquittance of the party making the payment. Bills for gas and water shall be paid directly to the Chamberlain, who shall receipt therefor, keep an account thereof, and make daily reports of such receipts to the Auditor.

3. All moneys, if over one hundred dollars, received by the Chamberlain under the preceding section, up to Wednesday at two o'clock of each week, shall be deposited by him on that day in one of the said banks of this city, to the credit of the city; and so all moneys, if over one hundred dollars, received by him up to Saturday at two o'clock of each week, shall be deposited in like manner.

4. Any person bound to pay money into the city treasury, who shall pay the same otherwise than according to the first and second sections of this chapter, shall remain liable for such money, and be subject to every fine, forfeiture or penalty to which he would have been subject if he had not paid the same.

5. All money paid into bank, in pursuance of the first and third sections of this ordinance, shall stand on the books of the banks to the credit of the city. But the Chamberlain shall have no authority to draw any of said money, except by his check drawn upon a warrant issued by the Auditor. If any money in bank, to the credit of the city as aforesaid, shall be

paid otherwise than upon his check drawn upon such warrant, the payment shall not be valid against the city.

6. The hours for transacting business in the offices of the Chamberlain and Auditor shall be as follows: from eight in the morning until three in the afternoon, from the first day of April to the first day of November, and from nine in the morning until three in the afternoon, during the rest of the year.

7. The proceedings of each of said officers shall be entered in books kept for the purpose, and the books, vouchers and papers properly arranged and preserved.

8. The committee of accounts shall examine the accounts for the necessary contingent expenses of each of said officers, and report to the Council for payment such as they may approve.

9. When it is necessary for either of said officers to be absent from the city, or from his office on account of sickness, the other shall be informed thereof. During such absence, the duties of the officer so absent shall be performed by the clerk in his office.

10. The said officers and their sureties shall be liable for any default or breach of duty of their clerks respectively, during their absence, in performing the duties of said absent officer.

11. The fiscal year shall commence on the first day of February, and end on the last day of January.

12. Any person having a claim against the city of Richmond, for salary as an officer of the city, or for interest upon bonds of the city, may apply to the Auditor, and he shall allow so much on account thereof as may appear to be due.

13. All the claims authorized by ordinance, to be paid on the order of a committee, shall be drawn on the Auditor, and all other claims against the city shall be presented to the Council, and such of them as shall be allowed, for the amount allowed shall be certified by the clerk of the Council to the Auditor, and these claims shall be entered upon his books.

14. After any claim is allowed under this chapter, a warrant shall be issued by the Auditor for the sum to be paid, which shall be signed by the Auditor and attested by his clerk. Every warrant shall express the particular head of general revenue or expenditure on account of which the money is received or paid.

15. There shall be kept on the books of the Auditor's office an account against the Chamberlain as treasurer; a separate account for each of the subjects on which there are standing committees of the Council; an account with each officer or agent of the city to whom advances may be made by order of any committee; and such other accounts as may be necessary to exhibit plainly the condition of every branch of the revenue and expenditures of the city.

16. On the last day of each quarter of the fiscal year the Auditor shall compare the books of his office with those in the Chamberlain's, and strike the balance on his books, showing the amount of money in the treasury; which balance he shall carry forward to the next quarter.

17. All unsettled accounts on the books of the Auditor shall be balanced on the last day of each fiscal year, and the balances brought forward on the first day of the new fiscal year. For this purpose there shall be a general ledger of accounts, which shall be kept, so as to show all the balances due to or from the city.

18. The Auditor shall, in books kept for the purpose, keep a register of all city property; and also of all bonds or certificates of debt issued by the city.

19. The Chamberlain on his books shall state the accounts of money received and paid, so as to show distinctly the net produce of each branch of the revenue, and the whole amount thereof, and also the amount of disbursements.

20. He shall keep a list of the warrants drawn upon the treasury in every fiscal year, numbered from one upwards.

21. The Chamberlain shall furnish the Auditor, at the expiration of each quarter of the fiscal year, with a list of the receipts, and a list of the payments at the treasury during such quarter, showing the number, date and amount of each warrant, and in whose name the money was received, or the warrant issued, placing in separate columns the amount of each warrant under which money was received or paid in a different year from that in which it was issued. The Auditor may, however, dispense with such lists at the end of any particular quarter, if he

finds that the purpose thereof can be as well attained by examining the Chamberlain's books for such quarter.

22. The Chamberlain shall keep a general ledger of accounts, into which he shall post all the receipts and disbursements at his office, arranging the disbursements under the heads to which they properly belong. There shall be opened on the said ledger a general account of receipts and disbursements, which on the last day of each quarter of the fiscal year he shall compare with the books kept by the Auditor. After they are made to correspond, he shall strike the balance on said account, showing the amount at that time in the treasury; which balance shall be carried forward to the general account for the next quarter.

23. He shall keep accounts on the books of his office with the different banks in which the money of the city is deposited, on which accounts balances shall be struck at the same periods, showing the amount in bank to the credit of the city at the end of each year.

24. The Auditor and Chamberlain shall each annually, at the regular meeting in February, or as soon thereafter as practicable, make a report to the Council. The report of the Auditor shall contain a statement of the receipts and expenses of the preceding fiscal year, and an estimate of the revenue and expenditures for the succeeding year. It shall also contain a list of all accounts remaining open on the books of his office at the close of the preceding year, on charges made or credits given within such year. The report shall be accompanied with such remarks as may serve to explain the amount of receipts and expenses, and with marginal notes explanatory of the balances reported.

25. The report of the Chamberlain shall contain an account of his receipts and disbursements, and of his transactions as treasurer generally during the fiscal year.

CHAPTER XII.

CONCERNING THE ASSESSMENT OF TAXES.

1. At the monthly meeting of the Council in May, or if the Council shall not meet on that day, then as soon thereafter as practicable, an assessor of taxes for the city shall be elected by the Council, whose term of service shall commence on the first day of July, and continue for one year, and until his successor is elected and qualifies. He shall not act in his office until he has given bond with sureties, in the penalty of two thousand dollars, which is approved by the Council. It shall afterwards be preserved in the Auditor's office.

2. The clerk of the court of Hustings for the city of Richmond, and the clerk of the court of Henrico county, shall be paid annually, the former forty dollars, and the latter fifteen dollars, and the clerk of the circuit court of the city of Richmond shall be paid annually ten dollars, upon the certificate of the Assessor that they have respectively delivered him such lists as are mentioned in the seventh and eighth sections of the thirty-fifth chapter of the Code of Virginia, so far as may relate to lands in this city. Any party interested, may procure at his costs, and deliver to the Assessor an abstract from the land office of any grant issued therefrom for lands in this city, or a statement from the clerk of any court of any such judgment, decree or order, as is mentioned in said eighth section, or of proceedings under chapter fifty-six of the Code, accompanied by evidence of the payment required by that chapter to vest title.

3. The Assessor shall, annually, as soon as may be after the first day of February, ascertain, and in a book (called the land-book), enter separately each parcel of real estate in said city, and enter in as many separate columns as may be necessary the name of the owner of the freehold, his place of residence (descibed, where it can be done, with reference to some particular street or part of a ward), the nature of his estate, whether in fee or for life (charging in the case of a lot leased for a term of years on ground rent, the lot with all improvements thereon not to the lessee but to the tenant for life, or fee simple owner, under whom the lessee holds), the number of the lot, the street on which it fronts, and the number of feet that the lot or part of a lot charged fronts thereon; the value of the buildings on the land, and the value of the land, including buildings; and from whom, when and how the owner derived the land; making transfers on his land-book according to the lists, statements and abstracts mentioned in the second section; and making a note and explanation of each alteration made from the preceding book, showing why and upon what authority it was made. He shall also in said book insert a list of all buildings erected in the city during the preceding year, stating as to each building for what use it is intended, whether it is of brick or wood, and the number of stories.

4. In ascertaining the value, the Assessor shall be governed by the value as it appears on the land-book for the next preceding year, except so far as the Council may otherwise direct by ordinance or resolution. He shall add the value of any old building omitted, and of any addition to or improvement on an old building, and of any new building upon land on his book, and shall in respect to any land or building correct any error in the valuation thereof or otherwise, and supply any omission in his land-book, subject always to the following provisions:

5. When a lot becomes the property of different owners in several parcels, the value at which the whole had been assessed shall be divided by the Assessor amongst the several parcels, having regard to the value of each parcel, compared with that of the whole lot, and the tax shall be apportioned accordingly.

6. When real estate is sold for taxes, if it be purchased by an individual, the Assessor shall note in his land-book the quantity of land sold, and to whom, but shall continue the land upon his said book in the name of the former owner, until the purchaser obtains a deed therefor. If it be purchased in for the city, it shall be entered not in the body of the book, but in a separate list at the end of it. When, however, it is redeemed, it shall be replaced in the body of the book, in the name of the former owner or his grantee.

7. The Assessor in making out his land-book shall correct any mistake made in any entry of the land-book of the preceding year. But land which has been correctly charged to one person shall not afterwards be transferred to another without evidence of record, or furnished as provided in section two, that such transfer is proper, except as follows: When the owner dies intestate, the Assessor may ascertain who are the heirs of the intestate, and charge the land to such heirs. Where the owner has devised the land absolutely, the Assessor may charge the land to such devisee. If under the will the land is to be sold, it shall continue charged to the decedent's estate until a transfer thereof.

8. The Assessor (when he takes the list of taxable personal property) shall carry with him the land-book of the preceding year, and the entry of lands charged to any person resident or

having an agent within the city, shall be shown to such person or his agent, who shall be required to state on oath whether the same be correctly entered, whether any part thereof ought to be transferred to any other person; and if so, to whom, and the nature of the evidence to authorize such transfer; also, to state whether any other land in the city ought to be charged to such resident or non-resident, and to describe the same, as well as to give a description of any of the lands charged to such resident or non-resident, which may not be correctly entered. And the Assessor shall make such use of the information so obtained as he can properly make consistently with the other provisions of this ordinance. Any such resident or agent failing to comply with such requisition, shall forfeit twenty dollars.

9. No new building shall be assessed until it be so far finished as to be fit for use. But it shall then be assessed, whether entirely finished or not, at the same value as if it were finished upon the plan on which it is designed.

10. When from natural decay or other cause any building which may have been assessed shall be either wholly destroyed or reduced in value below one hundred dollars, the Assessor shall deduct from the charge against the owner the value at which such building may have been assessed.

11. The Assessor, or other person appointed for the purpose, in assessing the value of manufacturing or other mills or iron works, shall ascertain the value of all machinery and fixtures attached thereto, and include the same in the valuation of such mills or iron works.

12. Each person of full age and sound mind, not a married woman, shall list the personal property in his possession or care, subject to taxation, situate in the city, and the subjects and persons on account of which he is chargeable with taxes and levies. The property of a minor shall be listed by his guardian; if he has no other guardian, by his father, if living and in the city, if not, by his mother, if living; if neither be living in the city, by the person having charge of the property; of a wife, by her husband, if of sound mind, if not, by herself; of a deceased person, idiot or lunatic, by the personal representative or committee; of a person for whom property is held in trust, by the

trustee, if in the city, if not, by the *cestui que trust*, or his or her father or husband; of a corporation whose assets are in the hands of agents, receivers or factors, by such agent, receiver or factor; of every company, firm, body politic or corporate, by the principal accounting officer, partner or agent thereof. All bonds, evidences of debt and claims, wherever the debtors may reside, and all moneys, shall be listed by the owner thereof or by the person required by this ordinance to list the same for taxation, or by the agent of such owner or other person having the control and custody of such bonds, evidences of debt, claims and moneys.

13. The Assessor shall annually, as soon as may be after the first day of February, ascertain, and in a book (called the personal property book) enter—1st. The name of every male inhabitant of the city who has attained the age of twenty-one years; showing the number of those that are white in a column separate from those who are not white. 2d. The name of each person, whether living in or out of the city, who is possessed in the city in his own right, or as personal representative, committee, trustee, guardian or agent, of any personal property, showing in each case in what character he is possessed of the same. 3d. The name of every incorporated company located in the city.

14. The Assessor shall annually, on the first day of February of each year, or as soon as may be thereafter, in said book enter—1st. The name of each person or firm that carries on the business of merchant, trader or shopkeeper, whether by selling or buying; but this shall not include a person or firm that sells only agricultural products or stock of his or their own growth or raising, or buys for his own use or consumption as a manufacturer or mechanic. 2d. The name of every person or firm that is engaged in the business of a manufacturer, whether of flour, iron, engines, tobacco, machinery, or any other kind of manufacture. 3d. The name of each banker, stock-broker, or other broker; of each agent of a company or corporation located out of the city. 4th. The name of each person or firm carrying on business as an auctioneer. 5th. Of all keepers of ordinaries, of houses of private entertainment, of private boarding houses, of cook shops, eating houses, and lager beer or other

drinking saloons. 6th. Of all persons who sell at private sale or rent out houses, or procure employment for labor for profit, whether auctioneers or not. 7th. Of all keepers of livery stables, and the number of stalls in each. 8th. All dealers in horses, or mules, or cattle, sheep or hogs. 9th. All owners of theatres and buildings or rooms kept for shows or public exhibitions.

15. The Assessor shall state plainly in his book the peculiar character in which a person or firm is listed, and where corporations or agents of companies or corporations are listed, he shall state the nature of the business of each. Where a merchant is listed, whether he sells by wholesale or retail, and whether on his own account or on commission, and whether he has a license to sell spirituous liquors; when manufacturers are listed, what is the nature of the business; and when auctioneers or brokers are listed, whether they do a general business as such, or whether confined to a particular subject.

16. Any merchant, manufacturer, auctioneer, banker, broker, hotel keeper or other person upon whom or upon whose employment a license or class tax is imposed, who shall carry on his or her business in the city without having been listed by the Assessor, or without having filed with the Chamberlain an application for a license to engage in such business, shall pay double the amount of tax which may be assessed or imposed upon him or her on account of said business.

17. It shall be the duty of the Assessor of the city to ascertain whenever any person or firm shall commence any business in the city subject to a license or class tax, after his annual return is made, and to obtain from him or them the amount of capital employed in such business and return the same monthly to the Chamberlain, to be by him reported to the chairman of the finance committee. The said committee shall thereupon determine the class in which such persons or firm shall be placed, and the Assessor shall list them upon his book as such persons are listed in his annual return, and hand a copy of the list to the Collector and to the Auditor. The Assessor shall in his return designate such persons or firms as may have violated the preceding section.

18. It shall be the duty of the Collector of the city to report to the Council monthly such persons or firms mentioned in the sixteenth section as he may find carrying on business in the city without having been assessed with a class tax.

19. Whenever the Assessor shall have reason to doubt whether any persons carrying on business in the city which is liable to or is assessed with a class tax, is permanently located in the city, he shall hand to the Collector the account against such person for such tax, as soon as the same is ascertained; and the Collector shall immediately proceed to collect the said tax, making the same discount upon payment thereof as would have been made if the payment had been made in his office.

20. With respect to personal property, the Assessor shall ascertain from each person—1st. The value of all his visible personal property in the city, except family portraits. 2d. The value of all his stocks in corporations or other joint stock companies located out of the city. 3d. The value of his capital employed in a business carried on out of the city, except so much as is vested in real estate. 4th. The greatest amount on any day between the first day of February and the completion of said assessment, of money owned by him, whether the money be in or out of the city, or in his own possession or in the possion of another. 5th. The amount of interest or profit which has been received by such person or has been converted into principal so as to become an interest bearing subject, or otherwise realized, though not received, within the year next preceding the first day of February, arising from bonds or certificates of debt of any country, state, county, municipal or other public corporation created by this or any other state. 6th. The amount of dividends of banks and railroad and canal companies received by him within the same period.

21. He shall ascertain from each person residing in the city the amount of all solvent bonds and securities, other than those mentioned in the preceding section, and of all solvent liquidated and certain demands and claims, however evidenced, or wherever the debtor may live, owing and coming to such person, whether due or not, on the first day of February, deducting from the aggregate amount thereof the amount of all such bonds, securities,

liquidated claims and demands owing to others from such person as principal debtor, and not as guarantor, endorser, or surety; but in neither case shall unsettled book accounts be included. The aggregate of principal and interest shall constitute the amount of a bond or claim due and payable. The present value, after deducting the legal interest, shall constitute the amount of a bond or claim not yet due and payable, and which bears no interest.

22. He shall ascertain from the proper officers of all corporations and incorporated joint stock companies in the city, except banks of circulation and companies incorporated for the purpose of internal improvement, the amount of their capital, not including that invested in real estate, used, employed or invested in the business for which such companies were respectively incorporated. He shall ascertain also all such companies and institutions which have declared dividends of profits not less than six per cent., and shall list for taxation the amount of such dividends declared within one year next preceding the first day of February in each year. The real estate of such companies and institutions shall be assessed and listed as in other cases.

23. He shall ascertain from the agents of all joint stock companies or corporations located out of the city, except of internal improvement companies, banks and insurance companies, the amount of interest, profits and dividends, made by such agency within twelve months preceding the first of February in each year.

24. There shall be excepted out of section twenty, all carts, wagons, drays and hacks, with their harness and the horses and mules used therewith, for which a license has been paid; also the household and kitchen furniture in an ordinary or house of private entertainment; and all the personal property, accounts, moneys, bonds, securities and liquidated claims which any person shall on oath aver constitutes a part of the capital employed by him or his firm in any trade or business which is taxed as a licensed business or subjected to a class tax.

25. The Assessor shall call upon every person in the city required by this ordinance to give in a list of property, moneys, credits or other subjects of taxation, for a list thereof; and may apply to any officer or agent of a company, or to any person in-

terested therein; and shall furnish or cause to be furnished to each person, forms for lists and valuations; and such person shall, within ten days thereafter, make out and deliver to the Assessor, or deposit with the Auditor, statements of all personal estate, moneys, dividends, interest, capital and credits which such person is required by this act to list, and of all subjects and persons on account of which he is chargeable with taxes. The person who receives such form shall annex, in pursuance thereof, valuations of the property required to be listed, and shall take and subscribe an oath, to be appended to such statement, to the following effect, viz:

"I do solemnly swear, that to the best of my knowledge and belief, the annexed statements contain accurate, full and complete lists of all personal estate, moneys, dividends, interest, credits and capital, whether the same are in or out of the city, which I am required to list, and of all subjects and persons on account of which I am chargeable with taxes, and that in my opinion the valuations of property listed are not below the fair cash value thereof. So help me God."

And the Auditor shall furnish to the Assessor the blank list of taxable property, persons and subjects, with the required oath printed on the back; which said oath shall be taken before the Assessor, or some other person authorized to administer oaths, and it shall be signed by the tax payer; and where a person gives in the list for another, he shall make and sign the oath as if he were acting for himself; and the lists so taken shall be filed by the Assessor with the Auditor; and he shall examine the books to ascertain that they are so filed.

26. If any person be absent from his residence at the time the Assessor calls (and there be no person on the premises authorized to act for such person), the Assessor may leave or cause to be left for such person, at his residence or place of business, with some white member of his family over the age of sixteen years; or if there be no such white person on the premises, may otherwise cause to be delivered to such person proper forms, to enable him to make out the statements aforesaid, with the form of the oath aforesaid appended thereto; and it shall be the duty of such person, within ten days thereafter, to make out and deliver to

the Assessor, or deposit with the Auditor as aforesaid, such lists, with the valuations of property annexed, verified by affidavit, as are hereinbefore required.

27. If the Assessor is not satisfied with the valuation of the property made by any such person, he may, upon his own view, or such information as he may obtain or possess, adopt what he deems a fair and proper valuation thereof; and where it is practicable, the Assessor shall read over the list with the valuations annexed, to the person from whom it is obtained, or on whose information it is made out, and it shall be corrected, if necessary. If any person shall consider himself aggrieved by the valuation of the Assessor, such person and the Assessor shall refer the matters in controversy to the committee on finance; and the decision of the committee shall be final.

28. If any person, after being furnished with the proper forms as aforesaid, shall fail, for ten days, to deliver or deposit the lists in the manner prescribed in this ordinance, he shall forfeit not less than ten nor more than fifty dollars. If any person shall refuse to exhibit to the Assessor any property listed, or required by this ordinance to be listed by him, in order that a fair valuation thereof may be assessed, he shall pay a fine of not less than twenty nor more than one hundred dollars. And the Assessor shall set down the highest valuation which such kind of property may bear.

29. It shall be the duty of the Assessor to make off from time to time, as he shall proceed with his assessment, and complete it immediately upon completing said assessment, an alphabetical list of all persons or firms engaged in any trade or business in the city which shall be subjected to a class tax, in which he shall state the trade or business in which such person or firm is engaged, and the other facts in relation to merchants and others, required to be stated in section fifteen of this chapter. This list he shall deliver to the Chamberlain of the city, who shall call a meeting of the committee of finance for the next day, unless that be Sunday.

30. No tax shall be assessed or collected on any land or building belonging to the city, or to the United States, or the state, or county of Henrico, nor upon any articles of property kept

in such buildings by proper authority and used for public purposes; nor upon any used for divine worship; nor upon any belonging to a college or incorporated academy, or the Mechanics' Institute, and used for college or school purposes; nor upon any belonging to an orphan asylum; nor upon any other property which may be exempt from the city taxes by a law of the state, or an ordinance of the Council.

31. In the Assessor's books each ward shall be separate, and the names required by the third, thirteenth and fourteenth sections shall be arranged in alphabetical order. Opposite to the name of each person or firm shall be extended the amount of the assessed taxes on him and on his property, and on everything entered in connection with his name. The Assessor's property shall be entered and taxes charged to him as in the case of any other person.

32. When in consequence of the failure or refusal of any person to give to the Assessor an account of his property, and state the value thereof, or produce the same to the Assessor to be valued by him, as required by this ordinance, the list thereof shall have been obtained too late to be placed upon the Assessor's books of personal property for the year in which it is so obtained, it shall be entered on the books of the next year along with the list of the next year, and there shall be added to the tax omitted, at the rate of twenty per cent. per annum, on the amount thereof for one or more years, as the case may be.

33. The Assessor, after completing his land-book and his book of personal property, shall make two fair copies thereof. At the foot of each copy, he shall write and subscribe the following oath: "I, A. B., Assessor of taxes for the city of Richmond, do swear, that in making out the foregoing book I have, to the best of my skill and judgment, faithfully pursued the ordinance of the city." The said oath shall be taken before a justice, who shall annex thereto and subscribe the following certificate: "Sworn to before me, C. D., a justice of the peace for the city of Richmond, this —— day ——."

34. Of each book the Assessor shall retain the original until he ceases to be in office, and shall then deliver it to his successor; and the Assessor shall, on or before the first day of

June in each year, deliver to the Auditor the two copies. When this has been done by the Assessor, the copies of said book shall be examined by or under the direction of the committee of finance, and they shall cause to be corrected therein any errors which may be found in the same. The copies as corrected shall be certified by the chairman of the committee of finance. The Auditor shall keep one of said copies in his office, and deliver the other to the Collector of the city taxes. The latter copy may, before such certificate, be delivered to the Collector by authority of said committee; but if afterwards they correct errors, a statement of such errors shall be delivered by them to the Collector. When the amount of tax on any person depends on his class, the committee of finance shall direct the Assessor in what class such person shall be placed.

35. After such certificate by the committee as to any book, no alteration shall be made in it by the Assessor affecting the taxes of that year, unless directed by the Council. On affidavit that a person is charged improperly with a tax, the President of the Council may, by an order in writing, suspend the collection thereof, or of so much thereof as he may see fit, for such time as he may deem sufficient to give an opportunity for an application to the Council to correct the alleged error. But no tax shall be remitted by resolution of the Council after a year from the day on which the book containing the assessment of said tax shall have been certified by said committee.

36. No payment shall be made to the Assessor on account of his services for the year for which he was appointed, until such services are certified by the committee. After such certificate, the Auditor may, on the order of the chairman of said committee, pay to the Assessor, on account of his services for said year, one-half of his salary, deducting five dollars per day for each day beyond the first day of June, that he may have failed to deliver the copies of his books to the Auditor, and pay to him seventy-five cents for each entry on his land-book, transferring lands before charged to one person unto another: provided that when more than one parcel of land is conveyed by the same deed, only seventy-five cents shall be paid for all embraced therein. At the end of said year the Auditor may, on a

like order, pay the said Assessor the residue of his salary for said year.

35. In addition to the other duties prescribed by this ordinance, the Assessor shall perform such services in examining the polls or otherwise, as may at any time be required of him by the Council or by a committee.

CHAPTER XIII.

CONCERNING THE LEVYING OF TAXES.

There shall be levied and collected for each fiscal year, upon the persons and subjects embraced in chapter twelve concerning the assessment of city taxes, the taxes following, to wit:

1. On real estate not exempt from taxation, one dollar and twenty cents on every hundred dollars value thereof.

2. On all personal property, eighty cents on every hundred dollars value thereof; and herein shall be included stocks in corporations or other joint stock companies located out of the city, and capital in a business carried on out of the city, and the capital of all incorporated joint stock companies in the city, which have not declared a dividend of not less than six per cent. within the year next preceding the first day of February.

3. On all money and credits, eighty cents on every hundred dollars thereof.

4. On interest on bonds or certificates of debt of any country, state, county, municipal or other public corporation, received or converted into principal, or otherwise realized though not received, eight per centum on the amount thereof.

5. On dividends on bank stock, eight per centum on the amount thereof.

6. On dividends on stock of railroad and canal companies, six per centum on the amount thereof.

7. On dividends of all other corporations or joint stock companies located in the city which have declared a dividend of not less than six per centum within one year next preceding the first day of February, eight per centum on the amount thereof, which shall be paid by the corporation or joint stock company.

8. On the amount of interest, profits and dividends derived from joint stock companies or corporations located out of the city, except internal improvement companies, banks and insurance companies, eight per centum on the amount thereof, to be paid by the agent.

9. On every male person over the age of twenty-one years, three dollars.

10. Merchants, traders, shopkeepers and manufacturers shall be divided into twelve classes, and shall pay a license tax, if in the first class, of one thousand dollars; if in the second class, of seven hundred and fifty dollars; if in the third class, of six hundred dollars; if in the fourth class, of five hundred dollars; if in the fifth class, of four hundred dollars; if in the sixth class, of three hundred dollars; if in the seventh class, of two hundred dollars; if in the eighth class, of one hundred dollars; if in the ninth class, of fifty dollars; if in the tenth class, of twenty-five dollars; if in the eleventh class, of ten dollars; if in the twelfth class, of five dollars.

11. Bankers, stock brokers and other brokers shall be divided into nine classes, and shall pay a license tax, if in the first class, of one thousand dollars; if in the second class, of seven hundred and fifty dollars; if in the third class, of six hundred dollars; if in the fourth class, of five hundred dollars; if in the fifth class, of four hundred dollars; if in the sixth class, of three hundred dollars; if in the seventh class, of two hundred

dollars; if in the eighth class, of one hundred dollars; if in the ninth class, of fifty dollars.

12. Auctioneers shall be divided into nine classes, and shall pay a license tax, if in the first class, of one thousand dollars; if in the second class, of seven hundred and fifty dollars; if in the third class, of six hundred dollars; if in the fourth class, of five hundred dollars; if in the fifth class, of four hundred dollars; if in the sixth class, of three hundred dollars; if in the seventh class, of two hundred dollars; if in the eighth class, of one hundred dollars; if in the ninth class, of fifty dollars.

13. Sellers, by wholesale or retail, of wines or spirituous liquors, or a mixture thereof, shall be divided into six classes, and shall pay a license tax, if in the first class, of two hundred dollars; if in the second class, of one hundred and fifty dollars; if in the third class, of one hundred dollars; if in the fourth class, of fifty dollars; if in the fifth class, of twenty-five dollars; if in the sixth class, of ten dollars: and this shall be in addition to any tax he may pay as merchant, shop keeper or auctioneer; but apothecaries, who only keep wine or spirituous liquors in their stores, and sell the same by retail as medicine, upon the prescription of a physician, shall not be required to pay this tax.

14. Keepers of ordinaries and houses of private entertainment shall be divided into six classes, and shall pay a license tax, if in the first class, of one thousand dollars; if in the second class, of seven hundred and fifty dollars; if in the third class, of five hundred dollars; if in the fourth class, of two hundred and fifty dollars; if in the fifth class, of one hundred dollars; if in the sixth class, of fifty dollars.

15. Keepers of private boarding houses shall be divided into five classes, and shall pay a license tax, if in the first class, of one hundred and fifty dollars; if in the second class, of one hundred dollars; if in the third class, of fifty dollars; if in the fourth class, of twenty-five dollars; if in the fifth class, of ten dollars: but no person shall be considered as keeping a boarding house who does not have more than four boarders at one time.

16. Keepers of cook shops and eating houses shall be divided into five classes, and shall pay a license tax, if in the first class,

of three hundred dollars; if in the second class, of two hundred dollars; if in the third class, of one hundred dollars; if in the fourth class, of fifty dollars; if in the fifth class, of twenty dollars

17. Agents to sell at private sale or rent out houses, or to procure employment or labor, for profit, shall be divided into six classes, and pay a license tax, if in the first class, of four hundred dollars; if in the second class, of three hundred dollars; if in the third class, of two hundred dollars; if in the fourth class, of one hundred dollars; if in the fifth class, of fifty dollars; if in the sixth class, of twenty-five dollars.

18. Dealers in horses, mules, cattle, sheep or hogs, shall be divided into three classes, and shall pay a license tax, if in the first class, of one hundred dollars; if in the second class, of fifty dollars; if in the third class, of twenty-five dollars.

19. Keepers of lager beer or other drinking saloons shall be divided into five classes, and shall pay a license tax, if in the first class, of three hundred dollars; if in the second class, of two hundred dollars; if in the third class, of one hundred dollars; if in the fourth class, of fifty dollars; if in the fifth class, of twenty dollars.

20. Agents and sub-agents of any insurance company or office, whose principal office is located out of the city, shall be divided into seven classes, and shall pay a license tax, if in the first class, of one thousand dollars; if in the second class, of seven hundred and fifty dollars; if in the third class, of five hundred dollars; if in the fourth class, of four hundred dollars; if in the fifth class, of three hundred dollars; if in the sixth class, of two hundred dollars; if in the seventh class, of one hundred dollars.

21. Express companies having a place of business in the city, shall be divided into two classes, and shall pay a license tax, if in the first class, of five hundred dollars; if in the second class, of two hundred and fifty dollars.

22. Telegraph companies shall be divided into two classes, and shall pay a license tax, if in the first class, of two hundred dollars; if in the second class, of one hundred dollars.

23. Owners of theatres and buildings or rooms kept for shows

or public exhibitions, shall be divided into six classes, and shall pay (in addition to the license tax imposed on them by chapter 17) a license tax, if in the first class, of five hundred dollars; if in the second class, of four hundred dollars; if in the third class, of three hundred dollars; if in the fourth class, of two hundred dollars; if in the fifth class, of one hundred dollars; if in the sixth class, of fifty dollars.

24. Keepers of livery stables shall pay a tax of one dollar on each stall.

25. Any person who desires to commence a business which is assessed with a class tax, may apply to the chairman of the committee of finance, and the committee shall determine the class in which he shall be placed; and upon paying into the treasury, in the mode prescribed in chapter 11, the tax assessed upon his class, he shall have the privilege of doing said business as if he had been listed by the Assessor.

26. The aforesaid taxes on licenses shall go into the hands of the Collector of City Taxes, and be collected by him as taxes on property are collected; and the same shall be subject to a deduction for prompt payment, as are taxes on property.

27. The committee of finance shall, with the aid of the Assessor's list, and the Assessor's book, and such other helps as they may think will aid them, place each of the persons and firms employed in the trade or business referred to in sections ten, eleven, twelve, thirteen, fourteen, fifteen, sixteen, seventeen, eighteen, nineteen, twenty, twenty-one, twenty-two and twenty-three of this chapter, in the class to which the committee shall be of opinion such person or firm properly belongs, looking to all the circumstances of the case. And the Assessor, in making out his books, shall be governed by the action of the committee.

28. When the committee of finance shall have classified the persons and firms referred to in the preceding section, the classification so made shall remain in the office of the Auditor for at least one week; and the Auditor shall give notice thereof in three of the daily papers published in the city, and shall also give notice of the time, not less than one week from the date of the notice, when the committee of finance will meet to hear ap-

plications from all persons who shall think that they are put into too high a class. And the said committee shall, after hearing the party and any evidence he may produce, change the class of such person or firm, or permit it to remain as it has been fixed by them, as shall appear to the committee just and equal.

CHAPTER XIV.

CONCERNING THE COLLECTION OF THE ASSESSED TAXES.

1. At the first meeting of the Council after its annual organization, or as soon thereafter as practicable, a Collector of City Taxes shall be appointed by the Council, whose term of service shall commence on the first day of May, and continue for one year, and until his successor is elected and qualifies. He shall give bond in the penalty of thirty thousand dollars, payable to the "City of Richmond," with surety deemed sufficient by the Council, with condition for the faithful discharge by him of the duties of his office. He shall not act in his office until his bond is approved by the Council. It shall afterwards be preserved in the Auditor's office. If the Collector shall fail to qualify and

give bond approved by the Council, before the first of May, the Council shall revoke his appointment, and proceed to appoint a Collector of City Taxes.

2. The Collector may, with the consent of the Council, appoint a deputy or deputies, who may be removed from office by the Collector or by the Council. During the continuance in office of the Collector, a deputy of his may discharge any of the duties of the office of Collector; but the Collector and his sureties shall be liable therefor.

3. The Collector of the City Taxes shall annually give notice, in at least four of the daily newspapers of the city, for fifteen days prior to the fifteenth day of June, that he will attend at his office daily, between the hours of nine o'clock A. M., and six o'clock P. M., from the fifteenth to the thirtieth of June, inclusive, for the purpose of receiving from any person charged with city taxes, the whole or one-half of the amount of tax charged, deducting from the whole amount, or one-half, as the case may be, ten per centum thereon. The Collector shall in like manner give notice for fifteen days prior to the fifteenth of December, that he will attend at his office daily, between the above mentioned hours, from the fifteenth to the thirty-first of December, inclusive, for the purpose of receiving from any person who has already paid one-half only of the city taxes charged to him, the remaining half, deducting from such half ten per centum thereon.

4. The Collector shall daily, from the fifteenth to the thirtieth of June, inclusive, and from the fifteenth to the thirty-first of December, inclusive, pay into the city treasury the amount received by him for city taxes during the said periods, retaining a commission of one and a half per centum thereon. The amount of taxes received by the Collector between the thirtieth of June and the fifteenth of December, and between the thirty-first of December and the last day of February, he shall pay into the city treasury at the end of every week, retaining a commission of one and a half per centum thereon.

5. The Collector shall make out lists of the taxes received by him from the fifteenth to the thirtieth of June, inclusive, and from the fifteenth to ths thirty-first of December, inclusive,

showing the date of receipt, the names of the persons charged with tax, the amount charged and the amount paid the Collector, after deducting the above mentioned ten per centum. And the Collector shall, as soon as practicable after the expiration of the above mentioned periods of payment, prepare an alphabetical arrangement of the the said lists for more convenient reference thereto.

6. The Collector shall proceed to collect all of the taxes assessed on the books of the Assesor, and all taxes of which an account or statement is delivered by the Assessor to the Collector, under any ordinance of the city. He shall commence his collection annually on the fifteenth day of June, or as soon thereafter as practicable.

7. If all taxes with which any person or any estate of a decedent is assessed, be not paid before the first day of September, the Collector may distrain, except where one-half thereof has been paid under the third section.

8. Any goods or chattels in the city belonging to the person or estate assessed with taxes, may be distrained therefor.

9. The goods and chattels of the tenant or other person in possession, claiming under the party or estate assessed with taxes on land, may be distrained, if found on the premises. But when taxes are assessed wholly to one person on a lot, part of which has become the freehold of another by a title recorded before the commencement of the year for which such taxes are assessed, the property belonging to the owner of that part shall not be distrained for more than a due proportion of such taxes.

10. No deed of trust or mortgage upon goods or chattels shall prevent the same from being distrained and sold for taxes assessed against the grantor in such deed, whilst such goods and chattels remain in the grantor's possession; nor shall any such deed prevent the goods and chattels conveyed from being distrained and sold for taxes assessed thereon, no matter in whose possession they may be found.

11. Where the Collector cannot find sufficient goods or chattels to distrain for taxes, any person indebted to, or having in his hands estate of the party assessed with such taxes, may be applied to for payment thereof out of such debt or estate, and a

payment by such person of the said taxes, either in whole or in part, shall entitle him to a charge or credit for so much on account of such debt or estate against the party so assessed. If the person applied to do not pay so much as it may seem to the officer ought to be recovered on account of the debt or estate in his hands, the officer shall, if the sum due for such taxes exceed not one hundred dollars, procure from a justice a summons directing such person to appear before the Mayor's court, at such time as may seem reasonable; and if the sum due exceed one hundred dollars, shall procure from the clerk of the court of Hustings for the city a summons, directing such person to appear before said court on the first day of the next term thereof. And from the time of the service of any such summons, the said taxes shall constitute a lien on the debt so due from such person, or on the said estate in his hands.

12 If such summons be returned executed, and the person so summoned do not appear, judgment shall be entered against him for the sum due for such taxes, and for the fees of the clerk and the officer who may execute the summons.

13. If the person so summoned appear, he shall be interrogated on oath, and such evidence may be heard as shall be adduced, and such judgment shall be rendered as upon the whole case shall seem proper.

14. A tenant from whom payment shall be obtained by distress or otherwise, of taxes due from a person under whom he holds, shall have credit for the same against such person out of the rents he may owe him, except where such tenant is bound to pay such tax by an express contract with such person.

15. Any officer who shall return real estate as delinquent for the non-payment of taxes, when such taxes, or any part thereof, have been received by him, shall forfeit, if the return was made by design, ten times the amount of taxes so actually received, and if the return was by mistake, twice the amount, one-half of which forfeiture shall in each case be to the city, and the other half to the person charged with such taxes. And if the Collector shall return any real estate as delinquent, when he had either found, or by using due diligence might have found sufficient property within the city liable to distress for the taxes for

which such real estate is returned delinquent, he shall forfeit to the city a sum equal to five times the amount of the said taxes.

16. For horses or any live stock distrained or levied upon, the Collector shall provide sufficient sustenance whilst they remain in his possession. Nothing distrained or levied upon shall be removed by him out of the city, unless where it is otherwise specially provided. A distress or levy shall be reasonable.

17. In any case of goods and chattels which the Collector shall distrain or levy upon for taxes, and which he may be directed to sell by an order of the court or justice (unless such order prescribe a different course), he shall fix upon a time and place for the sale thereof, and publish notice of the same at least ten days before the day of sale, at the door of the courthouse of the city, and on a court day. The Collector shall, at the time and place so appointed, sell to the highest bidder for cash, the said goods and chattels, or so much thereof as may be necessary.

18. If such goods and chattels be mules, work oxen or horses, they shall be sold at the courthouse between the hours of ten in the morning and four in the afternoon. The sale shall be on some day of a term of the court, except where the parties shall, at or before the time for advertising the same, in writing, authorize the Collector to dispense with the provisions of this section, in which case the sale shall be according to the preceding section.

19. When there is not time on the day appointed for any such sale, to complete the same, the sale may be adjourned from day to day until it shall be completed.

20. If there be good cause to believe that a person assessed with taxes, not on real estate, intends to remove his property out of the city, or to sell out or close his business therein, the Collector may, unless such taxes be paid on demand, distrain therefor, although the first day of September may not have arrived, and although one-half thereof may have been paid. To enable the Collector to ascertain the amount of taxes charged to any such person, the Assessor, if his books have not been returned, shall, on the application of the Collector, deliver him a statement of such taxes. Whenever taxes are received under this section by the Collector, before the 15th day of June, the Collector

shall, within one week thereafter, pay the same into the city treasury. Annually, on or before the first day of February, the Collector shall render to the Auditor an account of all taxes which shall have been in his hands within the year ending on that day, except such taxes as he may be entitled to credit for on account of real estate purchased for the city under the ordinance concerning the sale of land for taxes, and except the taxes embraced in the lists hereinafter mentioned in the twenty-first and twenty-second sections.

21. The Collector annually shall make out after the last day of December, and deliver before the first day of February, to the Auditor, verified on oath, a list of property on the Assessor's book improperly placed thereon, or not ascertainable, stating in such list the names, alphabetically, of the persons charged with the taxes on such property, and the amount of such taxes; subjoined to which list, the Collector shall make a memorandum of any persons or property which he thinks have been omitted on the books, and of any other errors which he has reason to believe exist therein.

22. The Collector shall annually make out a list of the taxes other than on real estate which remain uncollected, with the names of the persons charged with such taxes placed alphabetically; which list shall be verified by his oath, and delivered by him to the Auditor on or before the first day of February, and a copy thereof shall be posted at the front door of the City Hall during the February term of the Hustings court.

23. The lists mentioned in the two preceding sections shall be examined by the Auditor and laid before the Council. The Auditor shall credit the Collector on account of the taxes mentioned in said lists with such amount as the Council may direct; and of that mentioned in the twenty-first section, he shall, as soon as practicable, deliver a copy to the Assessor, who shall correct his books as may appear proper. After such credit is directed on account of any list, the Collector shall not receive any of the taxes mentioned therein; but the list mentioned in the twenty-second section shall be placed by the Auditor for collection, in the hands of such person and on such commission as the Council may direct.

24. If, after the Collector receives such credit on account of real estate purchased for the city as is mentioned in the twentieth section, and such credit as the Council may direct under the preceding section, any of the taxes which shall have been in his hands remain unpaid, he or his representative shall, on being notified thereof by the Auditor, pay into the city treasury the amount of such taxes, deducting therefrom a commission of one and a half per centum thereon. If there be a failure to make such payment for three days after such notice, the Collector shall have no commission on said amount; and the Chamberlain shall deliver a copy of the Collector's bond to the Attorney for the city, who shall proceed thereon.

CHAPTER XV.

CONCERNING THE SALE OF LAND FOR TAXES.

1. The year for which taxes on real estate are assessed shall be deemed to commence on the first day of January; and there shall from that day be a lien on real estate for the taxes assessed thereon within the year so commencing.

2. The Collector of the city taxes shall annually, after the first day of January, and before the February term of the Hustings court for this city, cause to be published twice in each week, for the four weeks preceding said February term of the court, in two or more newspapers printed in this city, a list of

the real estate in this city on which taxes remain unpaid for the last or any preceding year, mentioning the amount due for taxes on each lot or part of a lot, and the name of the party assessed therewith, and describing such lot or part of a lot as it is entered in the Assessor's books. The Collector shall also post a copy of the said list on one of the doors of the City Hall on the first day of the January term of the said court of Hustings.

3. To the list and copy so published and posted, he shall subjoin a notice that each lot or part of a lot therein mentioned, or so much thereof as shall be sufficient, will be sold at public auction between the hours of twelve in the morning and four in the afternoon, at the City Hall, on the first day of the said February term of the court of Hustings, unless there be previously paid the taxes on the same and twenty per centum on such taxes, for the charges.

4. If the said taxes and such per centum be not previously paid, the Collector shall proceed to make sale accordingly; and the sale may be adjourned from day to day, and proceed between the hours aforesaid, until it shall be completed. If, however, the sale be not completed on the last day of the court, it shall be adjourned to the first day of the next court. It may then proceed, and be adjourned in like manner as at the previous term. Whenever there is an adjournment to the next court, notice thereof shall be given by advertisement in two or more of the city papers twice a week for four weeks.

5. The Collector shall sell separately so much of each lot or part of a lot as shall be sufficient to satisfy the taxes thereon, with such per centum and a commission of ten per centum on such taxes for the Collector.

6. The Collector shall not, directly or indirectly, purchase any real estate sold. If he does, he shall forfeit to the city twenty dollars for every such purchase, and the same shall moreover be void.

7. The Collector shall make out for each purchaser a receipt to the following effect:

Memorandum of Real Estate within the City of Richmond, sold this —— day of ———, eighteen hundred and ———, for the non-payment of Taxes thereon for the year ———.

Name of party charged with the taxes.	Description of land charged.	Amount of taxes due.	Quantity of land sold.	Name of purchaser.	Amount of purchase money.

Received of ——, —— dollars and —— cents, the amount of purchase money for the land mentioned in the above memorandum; and received of him, in addition thereto, a fee for this receipt of twenty-five cents.

Which receipt shall be delivered by the Collector to the purchaser on the purchaser's paying him the said purchase money and fee.

8. The Collector shall make out a list of the sales, with the following caption thereto: "List of real estate within the city of Richmond, sold in the month (or months) of ——, eighteen hundred and ——, for the non-payment of taxes thereon for the year (or years, if for more than one year) eighteen hundred and ——." Underneath shall be the several columns mentioned in the seventh section, with a like caption to each column. And there shall be an additional column, showing the date of each sale, unless the sales were all on one day, in which case the day may be mentioned in the caption.

9. The Collector shall subscribe and take before a justice the following oath: "I, A. B., Collector of the taxes of the city of Richmond, do swear that I used due diligence to find property within this city liable to distress for the taxes mentioned in the foregoing list, but could find none; that I have received no part of the said taxes in any other way than by means of the sales mentioned in the said list; that the said list is, I verily believe, correct and just; and that I am not directly or indirectly interested in the purchase of any of the real estate therein mentioned."

10. The said list, with a certificate of the said oath subjoined or attached thereto, shall be returned to the Auditor on or before the last day of February, or, when the sales are continued to the March court, the last day of March.

11. The owner of any real estate so sold, his heirs or assigns, or any person having a right to charge such real estate for a debt, may redeem the same by paying to the purchaser, his heirs or assigns, within two years from the sale thereof, the amount for which the same was so sold, and such additional taxes thereon as may have been paid by the purchaser, his heirs or assigns, with interest on the said purchase money and taxes at the rate of ten per centum per annum from the times that the same may have been so paid; or the same may be paid within the said two years to the Chamberlain of the city, in any case in which the purchaser, his heirs or assigns, may refuse to receive the same, or may not reside or cannot be found in the city of Richmond.

12. The purchaser of any real estate sold for taxes and not redeemed, shall, after the expiration of two years from the sale, obtain from the Auditor a deed conveying the same, wherein shall be set forth what appears in his office in relation to the sale If the sale be not of the whole lot or part of a lot that is delinquent, the purchaser shall have the part sold surveyed and laid off, at his expense, by the Surveyor of the city, so as not to include the improvements on the same, if it can be avoided. A plat and certificate of every such survey shall be delivered to the Auditor, and referred to in his deed, and annexed by him thereto. For every deed executed under this section the Auditor shall be entitled to one dollar, which the purchaser shall pay him on the delivery of the deed.

13. When the purchaser has assigned the benefit of his purchase, the deed may, with his assent, evidenced by his joining therein, or by a writing annexed thereto, be executed to his assignee. If the purchaser shall have died, his heirs or assigns may move the court of Hustings of this city to order the Auditor to execute a deed to such heirs or assigns.

14. If no such deed or order of court be made under this chapter within one year after the expiration of the said two

years, the former owner, his heirs or assigns, may, after such year, and before such deed or order is made, redeem the land by paying such amount, with such additional taxes and such interest as is mentioned in the eleventh section, together with the costs of the survey or report (and interest thereon), if any shall have been returned to the Chamberlain. The payment under this section may be to the Chamberlain.

15. When the purchaser of any real estate, sold for taxes, his heirs or assigns, shall have obtained a deed therefor under this ordinance, and within sixty days from the date of such deed, shall have caused the same to be recorded in the clerk's office of the court of Hustings for this city, such estate shall stand vested in the grantee in such deed as it was vested in the party assessed with the taxes (on account whereof the sale was made) at the commencement of the year for which the said taxes were assessed, notwithstanding any irregularity in the proceedings under which the said grantee claims title, unless such irregularity appear on the face of the proceedings. And if it be alleged that the taxes, for the non-payment of which the sale was made, were not in arrear, the party making such allegation must establish the truth thereof, by proving that the taxes were paid.

16. Any infant, married woman, insane person, or person imprisoned, whose real estate may have been so sold, or his heirs, may redeem the same by paying to the purchaser, his heirs or assigns, within two years after the removal of the disability, the amount for which the same was so sold, with the necessary charges incurred by the purchaser, his heirs or assigns, in obtaining the title under the sale, and such additional taxes on the estate as may have been paid by the purchaser, his heirs or assigns, and interest on the said items, at the rate of ten per centum per annum from the time the same may have been paid. Upon such payment within two years after the removal of such disability, the purchaser, his heirs or assigns, shall, at the cost of the original owner, his heirs or assigns, convey to him or them, by deed with special warranty, the real estate so sold.

17. When a parcel of real estate is offered for sale as aforesaid, by the Collector, and no person present bids such sum as is required by the fifth section, the Collector shall purchase the

same on behalf of the city for the taxes thereon and the said twenty per centum. A list of the real estate so purchased by the city shall be made out by the Collector, and after being verified by him on oath, shall, on or before the last day of February, or of March, if the sale is made in March, be delivered by him to the Auditor, who shall make out a copy thereof and deliver it to the Assessor, and credit the Collector with the amount for which the said real estate may have been so purchased, but not with any commission thereon. There shall be no right to such credit unless the said list be so delivered on or before the said last day of February, or of March, if the sale is made in March.

18. The previous owner of any real estate so purchased for the city, his heirs or assigns, or any person having a right to charge such real estate for a debt, may, within two years and until a further sale thereof by authority of the Council, redeem the same by paying to the Chamberlain the amount for which such real estate was so purchased, with such additional sums as would have accrued for taxes thereon if the same had not been purchased for the city, and interest at the rate of ten per centum per annum on the former amount from the date of the purchase, and on the additional sums from the fifteenth day of December in the year in which the same would so have accrued. When real estate so purchased is redeemed, the Chamberlain shall certify the fact to the Assessor.

CHAPTER XVI.

CONCERNING THE SALE OR PLEDGE OF SECOND HAND ARTICLES.

SEC.
1. Dealers in second hand articles to obtain license, and pay a tax thereon.
2. License to be obtained from the Council; how.
3. Person obtaining a license, to put up a sign; what book he must keep.
4. When house may be kept open; when he may buy, &c.

1. Hereafter the keeper or keepers of every shop within the limits of the city of Richmond, where any kind of second hand articles, such as watches, jewelry, junk, old metals, or other like commodities, are purchased, sold, bartered, exchanged or pledged,

shall obtain from the city Council a license to do so; and shall pay for said license the sum which shall be fixed by the Council at the time of granting the same; which shall in no case be less than one hundred dollars; and such license shall not be transferred from one person to another, without the consent of the Council.

2. Application for such license shall be made to the Council; and every application shall be accompanied by the recommendation of at least three respectable housekeepers of the city, who shall certify that the applicant is a fit and proper person to be entrusted with such license. After the license is authorized by the Council, the applicant shall pay into the treasury of the city, in the mode prescribed in chapter eleven, the amount fixed by the Council; and the Chamberlain shall thereupon issue to the applicant a license, which shall continue for one year, unless sooner revoked or forfeited; and shall take from the said applicant a bond in the penalty of one thousand dollars, with two sureties, who shall be freeholders, and shall be approved by the Chamberlain, conditioned for the faithful observance of the provisions of this ordinance and all other ordinances hereafter passed in relation thereto.

3. Every person receiving such a license shall put over the principal entrance to his or her shop, a sign designating that he or she is licensed, and containing his or her name; and shall keep a book, in which shall be written, at the time of every purchase, barter or pledge, a description of the article or articles purchased, bartered or pledged to him or her, the name and residence of the person or persons from whom received, and the day when such purchase, exchange or pledge was made; and such book shall be at all times open to the inspection of the Mayor of the city, the Chief of Police, or any person duly authorized to inspect the same, by either of them.

4. Such shop shall not be kept open for the purchase, exchange or pledge of any of the articles referred to herein, nor shall any purchase or exchange be made or pledge taken by the keeper or keepers of any such shop, or by any person for them, except between sunrise and sunset; and said shops shall be open at all times to the inspection of the Mayor of the city, the Chief of Police, or any person duly authorized by either of them to inspect the same.

5. Every person having obtained a license, who shall violate any of the provisions of this chapter, shall forfeit the same, and shall pay a fine of not less than ten nor more than one hundred dollars. And every person keeping such shop and carrying on business therein, without a license, shall pay a fine of not less than twenty nor more than one hundred dollars; and each day in which said business is carried on, shall be a separate offence.

CHAPTER XVII.

CONCERNING LICENCES GRANTED BY THE MAYOR.

SEC.
1. What tax shall be paid upon licenses for theatrical performances, circuses, &c.
2. What tax shall be paid on peddlers, bowling alleys, billiard tables and pistol galleries.

SEC.
3. How license to be obtained from the Mayor; what it shall state.
4. When Mayor may suspend a license.
5. Fines for acting without license.

1. A tax shall be paid to the Chamberlain of seven dollars per week, or at the rate of two hundred dollars per year, until the ensuing first of February, on theatrical performances at a public theatre; of thirty dollars for every circus exhibition, or exhibition of animals, or jugglers; and ten dollars for every other public show, exhibition or performance, for every twenty-four hours, or each time of performance, unless the same be in a room fitted for public exhibitions; in which case, the proprietor or occupier of such room may pay either seventy-five dollars for a year, or the said ten dollars for each twenty-four hours, at his election; and when there are two or more rooms fitted up in the same building, each separate room shall pay a like tax, and a separate license shall be obtained therefor. But no tax shall be required on a performance consisting only of vocal or instrumental music; or from a lecturer on a literary or scientific subject; or from a mechanic or artist exhibiting a work of painting or sculpture, or a work or production of his own invention or art, or a model illustrating such invention or art: and the Mayor may, in his discretion, dispense with the tax in the case of a performance, exhibition or show for a religious or charitable purpose.

2. No person shall act as hawker or peddler, or keep a billiard table, bowling alley or pistol gallery, for the accommodation of others, in the city, without first paying to the Chamberlain the taxes following, to wit: Hawkers and peddlers shall pay a tax at the rate of twenty dollars per year; keepers of billiard saloons, at the rate of fifty dollars per year for the first table in each saloon, and twenty-five dollars per year for each additional table; bowling alleys, at the rate of twenty dollars per year on each alley; and pistol galleries, at the rate of twenty-five dollars per year. Such licenses shall expire on the ensuing first of February.

3. When, in any case mentioned in the two preceding sections, the tax shall have been paid or dispensed with, the Mayor may grant or refuse a license to exercise the privilege for which the tax is so paid or dispensed with. But if the Mayor shall refuse to grant the license, the party applying for it may appeal to the Council, and the Council may direct it to be granted. Such license shall state what amount of tax (if any) is paid; to whom the license is granted; what privilege may be exercised under it; in what house, room or place, and for what time.

4. In any case, the Mayor may defer issuing, or after issuing, may suspend a license for any performance, exhibition or show, until the house or room in which the same is to be, shall have been examined by three freeholders of the city, appointed for the purpose by his warrant, and until he is satisfied by their report, in writing, that such house or room has doors and openings of such number and so arranged as, in the case of fire, to afford facilities for escape, and that the same is sufficiently strong and safe. Every such report shall be filed by the Mayor in the Chamberlain's office.

5. If any person shall do, engage in, or permit anything, for which a tax or license is required by this ordinance, without first paying such tax, and obtaining the Chamberlain's receipt therefor, and without having a license therefor, he shall be fined not less than ten nor more than twenty dollars for every such offence, and if the tax shall not have been paid, shall be liable also for the same; which shall be recoverable forthwith.

TITLE 3.

OF THE CITY DEBT.

CHAPTER XVIII.

CONCERNING THE DEBT OF THE CITY OF RICHMOND.

1. All certificates or bonds for the permanent debt of the city, shall be only in sums of fifty dollars, or some multiple thereof. They shall be registered in the Auditor's office, and be under the seal of the city, and subscribed by the President of the Council and the Chamberlain.

2. The person appearing on the books of the office in which any certificate is registered, as the owner thereof, shall be deemed the owner as it regards the city, so as to make valid all payments by the city of Richmond on account thereof to such person or his personal representative, made before a transfer of the certificate on the books of the said office.

3. But if the person so appearing on the books as owner, shall, *bona fide*, and for valuable consideration, sell, pledge, or otherwise dispose of such certificate to another, and deliver to him the certificate, with a power of attorney authorizing the transfer thereof to him on the books of the proper office, the title of the former in the said certificate (both at law and equity) shall vest in the latter for the whole amount of the certificate, or so much thereof as may be necessary to effect the purpose of

the sale, pledge or other disposition; and it shall so vest, not only as between the parties themselves, but also as against the creditors of and subsequent purchasers from the former, subject to the preceding section.

4. Upon the delivery of the said certificate at the office in which it is registered, a transfer may be made on the books of the said office, either of the whole amount or of any part thereof, by the person appearing on the said books as the owner, or by another having a power of attorney from him, duly authenticated, authorizing such transfer. Upon a transfer the former certificate shall be cancelled, and one or more new certificates shall be issued (according to the provisions of the first section), not exceeding together the amount of that cancelled. But no transfer shall be made on the said books within ten days next preceding the first day of January and the first day of July.

5. The officer in whose office any certificate is registered, shall, when applied to, cancel it and issue new certificates (of the multiple of fifty dollars), not exceeding together the amount of the former.

6. Every cancelled certificate shall remain filed in the Chamberlain's office. Every new certificate shall be registered, signed and countersigned like the former certificate.

7. When any certificate shall be lost by the holder thereof, he may produce to the officer in whose office the said certificate is registered, proof of his having advertised the same once a week for three months in a newspaper, file in the office of the said officer an affidavit setting forth the time, place and circumstance of the loss, and execute a bond to the city, with one or more sureties approved by the said officer, conditioned to indemnify all persons against any loss in consequence of issuing a new certificate in place of the one so lost; and thereupon the said officer may issue a new certificate and register the same.

8. Notes for a temporary debt of the city, shall be signed by the President of the Council and the Chamberlain.

CHAPTER XIX.

CONCERNING A SINKING FUND.

1. From the accruing revenues of the city there shall be appropriated annually a sum exceeding by one per centum the aggregate amount of interest due in each year, upon the present debt of the city, which shall be called "the sinking fund," and which shall be applied to the payment of the interest upon said debt, and the principal of such part as may be due or redeemable in the year. If no part be due or redeemable in the year, the residue of the sinking fund, after the payment of such interest, shall be invested in certificates of debt or bonds of the city, or of the United States, or of one of the states of the United States, until some part of the debt of the city shall become due, when the said certificates of debt or bonds shall be sold and applied to the payment of the principal of the debt of the city.

2. Whenever hereafter there shall be contracted by the city any debt not payable in twelve months, there shall be appropriated in like manner, annually, a sum exceeding by one per centum the aggregate amount of the annual interest agreed to be paid thereon at the time it is contracted; which sum shall be a part of the sinking fund, and shall be applied and invested as provided in the next preceding section.

3. The sums of money hereinbefore directed to be appropriated, shall be the first charge upon the treasury; and it shall be the duty of the Auditor and Chamberlain to ascertain the amount of interest which will fall due on the first day of January and the first day of July in each year, and pay off the same in preference to any other charge or claim upon the treasury; and also to apply the remaining one per centum upon the debt as hereinbefore directed in preference to any other charge or claim. All the provisions of this chapter shall be carried out from year to year, until the city shall no longer owe any debt.

TITLE 4.

OF THE CITY PROPERTY.

CHAPTER XX.

CONCERNING STOCK IN JOINT STOCK COMPANIES.

1. There shall be annually appointed by the Council, at its stated meeting in October, or as soon thereafter as practicable, three proxies in each company wherein stock is owned by the city, whose term of office shall continue until their successors are appointed, unless they be sooner removed.

2. In a meeting of stockholders in a company the vote of the city on its stock may be given by such of the proxies appointed to such company as may be present, or by a majority of those present. If it be apprehended that any proxy will not be in attendance, the Council, or if it be not sitting, and the meeting of stockholders is sitting, or to sit within two days, three members of the Council (of whom the President shall be one) may, without removing such proxy, make a temporary appointment in his stead, to be in force during his absence.

3. The proxies of the city in any company shall, from time to time, make report to the Council of matters affecting the interest of the city in such company, and lay before it copies of the report of the president and directors of such company, the proceedings of the stockholders thereof, and other documents relating to the company's works.

4. When a meeting of stockholders in a company in which the city owns stock is held out of this city, each proxy of the city attending such meeting, shall be paid four dollars per day for every day of such attendance, and at the rate of four dollars for every twenty miles of necessary travel in going to and returning from such meeting.

CHAPTER XXI.

CONCERNING THE GROUNDS AND BUILDINGS OF THE CITY.

1. The committee on public grounds and buildings shall be charged with, and have the care and management of all the grounds and other real property of the city, both within and without the city, except as hereinafter mentioned, so far as relates to the improvement and repairs thereof. No improvements or repairs shall be made or done to or upon any of the said property by the committee, at a cost exceeding one hundred dollars per month, in any one year, without authority from the Council.

2. The said committee shall report to the Council annually, or oftener, as they deem it proper, the state and condition of all the lands and buildings belonging to the city, and all such improvements and repairs as they may deem proper to have made or done to or upon any portion of the said property, or to the streets or other highways adjacent thereto, and at the same time render an account of all moneys received and expended by them; which said report shall be accompanied by an estimate of the costs of such improvements or repairs, to be made by the superintendent of public grounds, as well as of all money expended by them or under their order in the improvement or repairs of the same.

3. The Engineer of the city shall be the superintendent of

all the grounds and buildings within and without the city, belonging to the city, except as hereinafter mentioned. He shall once in every three months, or oftener, if he deem it necessary, report to the said committee the state and condition of the said property, the repairs done or necessary to be done upon or to the same, and the cost thereof, and make such suggestions as he may deem proper for the improvement of the said property, or any part thereof. Under the control and direction of the said committee, he shall, as far as practicable, keep all said property in good order, and prevent injury to any part or portion thereof, and for that purpose he is hereby given and vested with the powers and authority of a police officer of the city, and shall report promptly to the Mayor all violations of any ordinance of the city or of the law of the state, committed in, to or upon said property. It shall moreover be his duty to purchase all fuel necessary for the use of the city, and have the same properly stored.

4. The said Superintendent may, under the direction of the committee, make and sign any contract for the execution of work ordered by them under this ordinance, or under authority from the Council; and whatever work is so ordered, when executed, shall be paid for by a draft upon the Auditor, stating the amount to be paid and for what; which draft shall be signed by the chairman of the committee, after examining and approving the same.

5. If the Council shall at any time authorize any buildings or other real estate owned by the city, to be rented out, the Superintendent shall, under the control and direction of the committee, rent out the same, and shall report to the Auditor of the city all such contracts, stating the property rented, and to whom, what rent is to be received, when it commenced and when it is to terminate.

6. This chapter shall not apply to the almshouse and the grounds attached to it, the water works, the gas works, or the burying grounds.

CHAPTER XXII.

CONCERNING ST. JOHN'S BURYING GROUND.

Whereas the lots on Richmond Hill, on which the old church stands, and which are known in the plan of the city of Richmond, by the numbers ninety-seven and ninety-eight, were for a long period of time, used as a place of burial for the citizens generally; and in 1799 the Council purchased from John Adams, lot number one hundred and eleven, and from Richard Adams, Jr., executor of Thomas B. Adams, lot number one hundred and twelve, and obtained deeds conveying the same to the city, which deeds were admitted to record in the county court of Henrico, on the 8th of April, 1800; and thereupon the Council by an arrangement with the vestry of the said church, caused the said four lots, comprising one entire square, to be enclosed by a brick wall; and the square has thenceforth been used as a place for the interment of the dead of every religious denomination, until the Council obtained other cemeteries; and whereas, at the time of said arrangement it was understood that the corporate authorities of the city should incur all the necessary expense attending the erection of gates and steps, and keeping the enclosure in good repair; and should at all times have power to establish such requisitions as they might think proper as to the ground within said enclosure; therefore,

1. At the regular meeting of the Council in the month of December of each year, or as soon thereafter as practicable, there shall be appointed by the Council three persons, who may be members, of the Council or citizens, to act as a committee of the square in which the old church is situated. Any vacancy in said committee may, at any time, be filled by the Council.

2. The committee shall cause to be kept in good order the whole of said enclosure, with the gates and steps for passing through it, and everything that is within the enclosure and out-

side the church. For these purposes the Auditor shall pay, upon the order of the chairman of the committee, a sum not exceeding two hundred dollars in any year. Nothing in this section shall be construed to authorize the committee to prevent or interfere with the use of the church by the congregation thereof.

3. No body shall be buried in said square except by consent of the committee. Nor shall any body be buried in any place in the city other than at a burying ground owned by the city, except in the burying ground of the Society of Friends, on Cary, between Nineteenth and Twentieth streets, or that of the Hebrew congregation. Any person who shall bury or cause to be buried a dead body in a place in the city not allowed by this section, shall pay to the city a fine of five dollars for every day that said body shall remain in such place.

CHAPTER XXIII.

CONCERNING THE CITY CEMETERIES.

1. The committee on cemeteries shall have the control and management of the Shockoe Hill and Oakwood cemeteries. So far as the same is not already done, or the ground is not already appropriated, the committee shall have authority to lay off the grounds into sections, half sections and quarter sections, and to fix the price of each section, half or quarter section, and to

divide the grounds so as to appropriate a part for the burial of colored persons. But the burial of colored persons in Shockoe Hill cemetery shall not be authorized in any part thereof which is now reserved for the burial of white people. The committee shall also have a general control over the manner and arrangement of the interments in said cemeteries; of the preservation, improvement and embellishment of the grounds, and over the keepers and other persons employed about them; and they shall from time to time visit and inspect them.

2. The committee shall annually, in the month of July, appoint a keeper for each of said cemeteries, who shall take charge of the same and keep it in order. The keepers shall act under the directions of the committee; and the committee shall take care that they each perform their duties; and if they neglect the same, the committee may remove them, and appoint others in their places, and shall report to the Council the cause of the removal. If at any time either of said offices is vacant, the committee may fill the vacancy; and the keeper so appointed shall hold his office until the next July, unless sooner removed. The said keepers shall receive, as compensation for their services, such fees for burials in the cemeteries as are prescribed in this chapter; and in addition thereto, the keeper of the Shockoe Hill cemetery shall receive annually, in quarterly payments, the sum of three hundred dollars; and the keeper of the Oakwood cemetery shall receive annually, in the same way, the sum of two hundred dollars, and shall live, free of rent, in the house upon the premises; but he shall not cut any wood or tree thereon without the consent of the Council: provided, that these annual allowances shall be withheld by the Auditor until the quarterly returns required by the tenth section of this chapter shall have been made.

3. Any white resident of the city of Richmond or county of Henrico one year, may select in the said cemeteries any section, half section or quarter section, to which no other person has acquired title, and obtain from the keeper a certificate of his location. But no location of any person in his own right, or on his own account, shall be of more than a section or less than a quarter section, unless some military company or some society

shall, with the consent of the committee, purchase one or more sections; and they shall be required to conform to the ordinances.

4. Upon such certificate being presented to the Chamberlain, and upon payment being made to him of such price as may be fixed by the committee for the section, half section or quarter section, as the case may be, the Chamberlain shall issue and deliver to the person making the location and payment, a certificate describing the number of the range and the number of the section; and if the location be of less than a whole section, the number of each half or quarter section, and setting forth that the person is entitled to the section, half section or quarter section so paid for.

5. The person to whom the Chamberlain issues such certificate shall thenceforth be entitled to the section, half section or quarter section so paid for, as a burying place for himself or for any white person, who is a member of his family, or one of his descendants or friends. But there shall be no enclosure erected in the cemetery of greater height than four feet. And when a section, half section or quarter section shall remain without any interment therein for twenty years, and the purchaser shall have died or removed from the city, and no relative of his is known to the committee to reside in the city, they shall give notice thereof once a week for four weeks in a newspaper published in the city; and if no relative of the purchaser appear within thirty days from the last day of said publication, then the said section, or half section, or quarter section, as the case may be, shall revert to the city. And whether there be such reverter or not, the Council may, at any and all times, regulate the interments in said cemetery, or any part thereof, as may seem to it proper.

6. A citizen of this city, or a citizen of Henrico, or any stranger or person visiting the city or county, may be buried in that part of the cemetery appropriated for promiscuous interments, and called the "public portion," on payment of two dollars and fifty cents to the Chamberlain, whose receipt therefor shall be produced to the keeper of the cemetery before the interment is made.

7. Notwithstanding the provisions hereinbefore contained, a person convicted of an offence, for which an infamous punish-

ment is denounced, shall not be interred within the enclosure of the cemetery, unless a majority of the committee assent thereto.

8. The keepers, when informed that a grave is required for the body of any person, if such person is to be buried in a section which has been purchased, shall have the grave dug in the section, in the spot designated by the friend of the deceased who applies to him, and in other cases the grave shall be dug in a proper place; and in either case he shall have the body properly interred therein. For which he may charge, except for a pauper, a price, as follows: For a grave for a person over fourteen years of age, if the coffin be in a box, three and a half dollars; if not in a box, two dollars, and for all other persons two dollars, whether in a box or not.

9. Every grave which the keeper has dug, whether for the body of a white or colored person, shall be at least six feet deep, unless the committee shall authorize a less depth in the "public portion;" and in no case shall it be of less depth than five feet. And no interment shall be made in said "public portion," which shall disturb the remains of a dead body, or which shall displace or injure any monument, stone or slab erected over a grave.

10. Each keeper shall have a book, wherein, upon the interment of a white person, he shall, so far as it can be ascertained, enter the name, age, sex, profession or calling of the person interred; the disease of which he died; and the number or other designation of his grave; and upon the interment of a person of color, the name, age, sex and disease. From this book he shall, in such form as the committee may direct, make an abstract, and report it quarterly to the Council. After the book is fully written up, the original shall be deposited in the Auditor's office for preservation, the keeper preserving a copy thereof in his office.

11. Under the direction of the committee, the keepers shall plant trees and other plants in and through the grounds, and shall improve and keep in order the walks and grounds.

12. The keepers or owners of all other cemeteries or burial places in the city, or whose office is in the city, shall perform the duties in relation to their respective cemeteries, which is required of the keepers of the cemeteries hereinbefore mentioned, by the tenth section of this chapter, except as to depositing the

original book in the Auditor's office. And for failing to comply with this section, such keeper or owners of a cemetery shall be fined not less than ten nor more than one hundred dollars for such failure.

CHAPTER XXIV.

CONCERNING THE GAS WORKS.

1. At the first meeting of the Council after its annual organization, or as soon thereafter as practicable, the Council shall elect a Superintendent of the gas works, who shall go into office on the first day of May, and continue therein for one year, and until his successor is appointed and qualifies, unless sooner removed. And the committee on light, as soon as practicable after

its appointment, shall appoint an Inspector of gas, and report his name to the Council.

2. The committee shall meet in the afternoon, on the first Thursday in every month, and also meet at such other times as they may see fit. They shall have the superintendence and general government of the gas works. And the Superintendent of the gas works and the Inspector of gas shall, so far as may be consistent with the duties prescribed by this chapter, act according to the directions of the said committee.

3. Each of the officers before mentioned, to wit, the Superintendent and Inspector, shall, before acting in his office, give bond with sureties in the following penalty, to wit, the Superintendent in five thousand dollars, and the Inspector in two thousand dollars. There shall also be signed by each of them, at the time of his receiving his official books and papers, a writing specifying, so far as can be conveniently done, what are received by him; and the said writing shall be recorded among the committee's proceedings. When an officer's term of office expires, his official books and papers shall be delivered by him to his successor, or in such other manner as the committee may direct.

4. Each of said officers shall use for an office such room as the Council may prescribe. The whole time of each shall be devoted to the performance of his official duties. Each of them shall attend in his office certain hours every day, except Sunday, the fourth day of July, and Christmas day, unless such attendance be prevented by sickness, or by absence from the city with leave of the committee; and each of them shall, on any of the said excepted days, or at night, perform any service for which there is a necessity, without its being deemed extra service.

5. The hours for each of said officers to attend in his office, as required by the preceding section, shall be as follows: 1. The hours for the Superintendent so to attend, shall be from nine to eleven o'clock, A. M., unless his presence be then required at some portion of the works; and he shall be present at all regular meetings of the committee. 2. The hours for the Inspector so to attend shall, except on the days in which he is engaged in taking the state of the metres, be from seven to nine, A. M., between the first day of April and the first day of October, and

from eight to ten A. M., during the rest of the year; and shall also be, on the days for so turning off the gas, from the time he has finished so turning it off until two hours after sunset; and shall likewise be until sunset of every other day, unless he be at the time engaged elsewhere in the duties of his office.

6. The Superintendent, subject to the control of the committee, shall have a general charge of all the buildings, fixtures and pipes erected or laid down for the gas works, and of the lands on which the said buildings are erected. He shall have the works kept in proper operation, and the gas furnished as pure as practicable, with promptness and regularity, at the city lamps and buildings, and to all persons entitled to its use under the provisions hereinafter contained.

7. Under the direction of the committee, the Superintendent shall have street mains laid down, lamp posts erected, and the public lamps set and kept clean and in good order. He shall preserve a map of the location of the main pipes, showing the course, distance and size of each of them. When there is any extension of the main pipes, the place of such extension and size of the pipe used in making it shall, as soon as possible, be marked by him on the map. He shall enter in a book, to be kept in his office, the quantity, description and cost of the materials used in making such extension, or in erecting any fixtures authorized by the committee, and report the same to the committee at its next regular meeting after such extension is made.

8. The Superintendent, subject to the committee's control, may employ such men as he may deem suitable to perform the necessary work under his supervision, over which, and the subordinate officers in the department, he shall exercise a controlling influence.

9. He shall, at each monthly meeting, lay before the committee a list of articles and materials which will probably be required during the month, together with the cost thereof, and the probable amount necessary to pay the hands employed, and report what, if any, materials are no longer serviceable. He shall have an account kept of the names of the men employed, their kind of work, and the days of the week or month they work. This account shall be so made out as to show what is chargeable

to current expenses, and what to construction in its several branches. At the end of every month he shall enter the substance thereof on roll books, showing opposite each person's name his rate per day and the sum payable to him for the month. The aggregate of what is payable to the men for each period of a month, shall be paid out of the city treasury on the draft of the chairman of the committee in favor of the Superintendent, who shall within three days thereafter go to his office at the gas works, between the hours of four and seven, P. M., and pay to each of the men his part thereof. To each pay roll the Superintendent shall subjoin a synopsis, showing the amount chargeable to each branch of construction or current expenses; and the said pay roll and synopsis shall be laid before the committee at their next meeting.

10. Subject to such restrictions as may be imposed by the committee, the Superintendent may purchase materials, tools and other articles proper for carrying on the operations of the works. What may be so purchased, shall be taken care of by him and used as required. All bills for the same shall be laid before the committee by the Superintendent at the next regular meeting after they shall have been presented. And what the committee may allow for such purchases, or for any necessary current expenses of the works, shall be paid out of the city treasury by the draft of the chairman of the committee, attested by the Superintendent. Such draft, and every order under the preceding section, shall always state whether it is for construction or for current expenses; if the amount be partly for one and partly for the other, the portion of each shall be stated.

11. In a book kept for the purpose, the Superintendent shall, at six A. M., and six P. M., of each day, have entered the state of the station metre, the height of gasometers, the gas made, and the gas used. In the said book entries shall be made in separate columns, to show the gas made per day, gas made per night, gas used per night, coal used per day, rosin used per day, the bushels of lime used per day, and the number of retorts in use. From said book the Superintendent shall, at the end of every month, make therefrom, in a book kept by him, called the retort house journal, concise entries showing on each day of

the month the state of the station metre, the gas made, gas used, coal used, rosin used, and the number of retorts in use, and showing the contents of the gas-holders, the bushels of lime used each day, and whatever else the Superintendent may deem proper to secure a faithful record of the operations of the works; and the same shall be submitted monthly to the committee.

12. As soon as practicable after the last day of every January, the Superintendent shall return to the committee an inventory of materials, tools and other articles, stating the quantity, description and cost of those on hand, and make a report showing what were on hand at the time of his previous return, what have been obtained since, what have been used since, and what remain on hand; showing also how much coal, coke, rosin and lime was used during the year ending the last day of January, and how much gas was made during the year, and what was the largest quantity of gas made, and the largest quantity of gas used in any one twenty-four hours; showing farther, the length and size of the street mains laid during the year, and the length and size of the same laid since the commencement of the works; and showing likewise the number of public lamps, number of private consumers, a list of the officers and number of hands, with their duties and pay during the said year, and any other matters which the committee may direct.

13. The clerk in the Auditor's office shall attend all meetings of the committee, and act as clerk, and make and keep a true record of its proceedings.

14. A book shall be kept in the Auditor's office, with a caption importing that the owners of property, whose names are undersigned, request that the gas may be introduced into the premises mentioned opposite their respective names, upon the terms prescribed by the ordinances of the city. When the owner of any property within the range of the pipes applies for the introduction of gas into his premises, he shall write his name in said book under said caption, and write opposite thereto the date and number of his application, the number of burners that he will probably require, and the location of his premises.

15. As soon as practicable after every such application, there shall be furnished by the Auditor to the Superintendent a copy

thereof; and there shall be furnished to the Inspector by the applicant a plan of the tubing and fittings, with the size and length of each piece of tubing, and the position of each burner plainly marked thereon. Such plan shall be furnished, and the tubings and fittings for conveying gas within the applicant's premises, after it has passed the metre, may be put up by some competent person employed by the applicant. But the tubing, and the screws used in putting up, must be such as the Superintendent allows, and must be consistent with the following section:

16. The relative sizes and lengths of tubing, and proportions of metres introduced for consumers, shall be according to the following tables:

Size of Tubing.	Greatest length allowed.	Greatest number of Burners.	Size of Metres.	Greatest number of Burners.
$\frac{1}{4}$ inch.	6 feet.	1 burner.	2 lights.	4 burners
$\frac{3}{8}$ "	20 "	3 "	3 "	5 "
$\frac{1}{2}$ "	30 "	6 "	5 "	10 "
$\frac{5}{8}$ "	40 "	12 "	10 "	20 "
$\frac{3}{4}$ "	50 "	20 "	20 "	40 "
1 "	70 "	35 "	30 "	60 "
$1\frac{1}{4}$ "	100 "	60 "	45 "	100 "
$1\frac{1}{2}$ "	150 "	100 "	100 "	250 "
2 "	200 "	200 "		

17. All tubings, fittings and fixtures must, after they are put up, be examined and approved by the Inspector, before gas is supplied. He shall make such examination as soon as practicable after he is notified for the purpose, and always within three days after such notification. On such examination, he must compare the work done with the plan, and must, before the gas is supplied, see that the work does in all respects correspond with the plan already furnished, or see that there is furnished another plan corresponding with the work; and must subject the whole of the tubing, fittings and fixtures to trial, with an air pump, under a pressure of a column of mercury ten inches high, and see that they are tight under this pressure, and put up in a workmanlike manner, as well as in their proper places. When in

respect to the work done the Inspector has ascertained all that is here required, he shall introduce gas into the premises, unless the Superintendent order otherwise.

18. The plans shall be legibly marked with the name of the applicant, the location of his premises, and the date of his receiving the gas, and then delivered to the Auditor, who shall number them in the order the applications stand upon his book, and file them in his office. He may allow them to be copied in his presence; but they shall not be removed from his office unless by the committee's orders, or unless it shall be necessary for their safety.

19. The Superintendent shall have laid down street mains and pipes, erect lamp posts, and have the public lamps set and kept clean and in good order. The Inspector shall have made and put on all metre connections, place proper metres on the premises of the respective consumers, and perform properly all duties pertaining to these portions of the business. Especially shall he endeavor to render the metres easy of access, to avoid any injury or inconvenience to the building or its occupants, and to avoid exposing the metres to extremes of heat or cold. For digging the trenches and doing other work requiring no mechanical skill, there may be employed such laborers as the Superintendent may think necessary.

20. The service pipe laid down in a street, from the main to the edge of the street, shall be provided or paid for by the person for whom the work is done. For all the service pipe, turns, cocks and other fittings, from the edge of the street to the metre, the applicant shall pay such prices as the committee shall by resolution determine will afford a fair remuneration for the articles furnished and the labor done.

21. The Inspector shall keep a book called the service-pipe book, wherein he shall keep an account of all the pipes and materials used, from the mains to or about the public lamps, and to or about the premises of private consumers, distinguishing between what is chargeable under the preceding section and what is not, so that the Superintendent, in his annual inventory, may state correctly the amount used, and so that what any person is chargeable with may be collected from him. At the end of

every month, the Inspector shall make out and deliver to the Auditor a report of the name of each person so chargeable, the location of his premises, and the several items for which he is chargeable, with the sum due for each item, and the aggregate amount. Of all his reports, the Inspector shall, in a book used for this purpose, keep copies. And when a report of the Inspector is received by the Auditor, the latter shall endorse thereon the date of his receiving it, and sign his name to such endorsement.

22. When the tenant of premises using gas is about to remove, he shall give the Inspector at least three days' notice thereof, that the gas may be stopped; or he will be chargeable for any gas that may pass through the metre before gas is stopped off. And any person leaving a house without paying for the gas consumed by him therein up to that time, shall not have the use of gas in the house to which he may remove until he has paid the amount so due from him. A consumer, discovering any defect in a metre or service pipe—any escape of gas or deficiency of light—shall give immediate notice thereof at the Inspector's office, that the defect may be remedied; and it shall accordingly be remedied by the Inspector as soon as possible after receiving such notice.

23. The Inspector shall keep a register, showing the date of proving, date of lighting, number of the metre, state of the metre at lighting, number of lights, number of burners and number of additional burners introduced afterwards. He shall also keep a book to be called the metre book, showing the name and location of each consumer, the number of the application and number of the metre. He shall take the register of all weekly metres once a week, of all monthly metres once a month, and inspect and register every other metre once a quarter, and oftener, if necessary, to ascertain whether the metre is or is not in good working condition. If it be not, and the defect can be remedied without removing it, he shall remedy it before leaving the premises; if this cannot be done, he shall report the defect to the Superintendent, who shall have the metre repaired, or a good one put in its place.

24. As soon as practicable after the first day of each month,

the Superintendent shall return to the Auditor an account of the gas used in the street lamps and in the city buildings for which no charge is made; and the Inspector shall return to the Auditor the metre book, with the state of the metres of such persons as are required to pay monthly, and with the state of the metres of all other persons in one of the wards, to wit: Jefferson ward, if the month be February, May, August or November; Madison ward, if the month be March, June, September or December; and Monroe ward, if the month be January, April, July or October. The book shall show the quantity of gas consumed by each person during the quarter or month, as the case may be, for which payment is to be made. Said quantity to be ascertained from the state of the register. When the Inspector has required a metre to be covered to protect it from the frost, or to be filled with alcohol to prevent it from freezing, if such covering or such alcohol be furnished not by the consumer but by the Inspector, the cost thereof shall be charged on said book to the consumer. In the performance of his duties, the committee may employ a suitable man to assist him, at such compensation as the committee on light may fix; and when, from sickness or other unavoidable cause, the Inspector may be unable to perform the duties required of him herein, he shall report the same to the Superintendent, who shall furnish the necessary aid.

25. With the exception of what is used in the street lamps, or in a building or upon land belonging to the city, gas shall never be furnished without charge therefor. It may be furnished at the rate of three dollars per thousand feet to any such association or benevolent institution as the Council may, by resolution, declare entitled to receive it at that rate in consideration of the public benefits conferred by such association or institution. But the supply of gas to every other person shall be upon the condition of his paying therefor at the rate of four dollars for every thousand feet; to be ascertained as prescribed by the preceding section. The committee or the Superintendent, in any case wherein he or they deem such precaution proper to secure the city against loss, may require the deposit of a sum in advance, or other security, to insure payment of what will become due for gas. Payment for gas shall be quarterly, by all per-

sons, except those who, by the Superintendent, may be required to pay monthly or oftener.

26. From the metre book so returned to the Auditor, he shall promptly note in a book, to be kept by him, called the bill book, the name and location of each consumer, the number of the metre, its state as so entered, its state at the previous settlement, and the amount chargeable to said consumer. The Auditor shall also enter in his bill book the name of each person reported to him under the twenty-first section, the sum to be paid by him, and for what.

27. For the respective sums payable by the several persons so reported by the Inspector, or appearing by the metre book to be so chargeable, the Auditor shall promptly make out bills, showing what amount is due without any abatement, and also, what will be due after allowing the deduction provided for in the next section, and have the same presented, by the Inspector, to the persons who are to pay them (or at their place of business or residence), and shall note within three days after sending said bills the day of the delivery of each.

28. From the amount of the bill for gas of a consumer paying quarterly or oftener, there shall, be a deduction of five per cent., provided that the residue of the bill be paid to the Chamberlain at his office, within five days next after its presentment, and before three o'clock, P. M. If a bill for gas, or anything else which is furnished from the works in connection with the supply of gas, shall remain unpaid for ten days next after that on which it is presented, the Auditor shall notify the Superintendent, who shall cause the gas to be stopped from the premises in respect to which the default exists, and not allow it to be used on those premises again until such bill is paid.

29. The Superintendent shall make such sales of coke and other articles as the committee may authorize. Upon any such sale, the price required by the committee shall be paid to the Superintendent, who shall give to the purchaser a receipt for the sum paid, bearing date the day of the payment, and stating the name of the purchaser, the article sold, and its quantity.

30. The Superintendent shall, on the first day of every month, pay to the Chamberlain the moneys received by him, under the

previous section; and shall report to the committee at each regular meeting an account of the coke or other articles sold in the previous month, and the quantity. And if the Superintendent shall fail to pay over the money so received by him, or to make the report hereby required, in the first case, the Auditor, and in the other, the committee, shall report such failure to the Council. And in all cases where the Superintendent fails to make a report required of him, his salary shall not be paid until it is made.

31. During the first five days of every month, the following returns shall be made to the Auditor by the Superintendent and Inspector, severally, of the respective sums payable since their previous several returns on the following accounts; that is to say, there shall be a return, by the Superintendent, of the money received by him for coke and other articles sold, a return, by the Inspector, of the persons from whom money has become payable for the consumption of gas, and of the persons from whom money has become payable for other articles chargeable under the twentieth and twenty-first sections.

32. The Auditor shall keep a ledger, wherein, for every month, he shall enter from his bill book the name and location of each consumer (whose bill is made out in, or for that month), the date to which his bill comes, the state of his metre, the feet of gas chargeable, amount of discount, amount paid, and when paid. If any bill remains unpaid for fifteen days after its presentment, the Auditor shall make out another bill for the amount due, with the addition of ten per centum thereon, and shall deliver the same to the Collector of the city taxes, taking his receipt therefor, who shall collect the same as if it were due for city taxes; and shall, after deducting five per centum for his compensation, pay the balance to the Chamberlain within thirty days after the bill is put into his hands; and the official bond of said Collector shall extend to secure the faithful collection and payment of the said money. But any bill may at any time be paid to the Chamberlain with the addition of five per centum: provided, however, that if the amount of any such bill be due from a tenant, or one who was tenant of the premises when it became due, the owner of the premises or a tenant under him other than the

person from whom such gas bill is due, may pay the same to the Chamberlain without the addition of any per centage thereon. It shall be the duty of the Auditor to demand from the Collector monthly settlements of such bills as are placed in his hands; and for failure to make such settlement the Collector shall forfeit the per centage which he is hereby authorized to deduct.

33. Annually, as soon as practicable after the last day of January, the Auditor shall make out accounts to ascertain the following results, to wit: 1st. The amount expended for the construction of the gas works from their commencement to the beginning of the preceding fiscal year. 2d. The amount expended for construction during said year. 3d. The amount paid to the Chamberlain for income during said year. 4th. The amount disbursed during said year for current expenses. 5th. The net balance of the year's income remaining after paying current expenses, and after paying the interest on all moneys expended for the construction and extension of the works. 6th. An account charging the gas works with all expenditures on account of them, including interest, and crediting them with all receipts, including a charge for gas used in the street lamps and in the city buildings which is not paid for, and the money received for coke and other articles sold, and the price of said coke or other articles applied to the use of the city; so made out as to show for what the charge is made or credit given. The committee shall examine said accounts, and return the same to the Council with the Superintendent's inventory, a report from him of the condition of the works, and any plans of the committee for extending the works, or adding to the buildings or machinery. The plans for such extensions or additions, and the contracts therefor, must always be submitted to and approved by the Council, before said plans are executed, and before said contracts shall be binding on the city.

34. The Chamberlain shall keep on his books accounts of the money expended about and received from the gas works, so as to ascertain the results contemplated from the accounts required by the preceding section, and as soon as practicable after the accounts so required are returned, shall examine the said accounts, and compare the same with those on his books, and if he find any variance in the results, shall inform the Council thereof.

35. At the end of every week the Inspector shall make to the Superintendent of Streets a report designating the location, and quantity and kind of paving needed in the streets, in which street mains and service pipes have been laid; and the Superintendent of Streets shall have it replaced as soon as possible. These reports shall be entered and signed as required by the twenty-first section.

36. It shall be the duty of the Superintendent, the Inspector, and such other men engaged about the works as the Superintendent shall from time to time designate, to attend at places, when from fire or other cause, there is danger of a loss of gas by burning or waste, with a stop-cock key, and pliers, to shut off the gas, remove metres, or do anything else proper for the safety of property belonging to the city connected with the gas works.

37. If any person shall deface or injure any house, wall, lamp, metre, or other fixture connected with or pertaining to the gas works, or shall tie to a lamp post, or any fixture connected therewith, any horse or other animal, or any boat, batteau or other vessel, or shall, without authority from the Superintendent, or other authorized agent of the committee, climb a lamp post, or light a lamp, or open a communication into, or remove any of the pipes, or shall put up any pipe or burner, in addition to what may have been put up by authority and approved, or introduce the gas into such additional pipe or burner, or leave the end of a pipe or other opening without being secured with a blind cap, secured so as to prevent a leak, or in any manner consume or waste the gas, without paying for the same, every person so offending shall pay the whole cost of restoring the property injured (if any), the amount to be assessed by the Superintendent or Inspector, and also pay a fine of not less than two nor more than twenty dollars for each offence. The whole of the amount received to be paid to the Chamberlain. If, however, any person shall accidentally injure a street lamp, or other property of the city gas works, and shall voluntarily pay to the Chamberlain, before he has been summoned to appear before a magistrate, the amount of the damage done, he shall be exempt from any further penalty under this section.

38. After gas has been introduced into any premises, no gas fitter or other person than the Inspector, shall disconnect or in-

terfere with any metre without a written permit from the Superintendent. Nor shall any person disconnect any of the tubings or fittings, or open the same for extension, alteration or repair, without obtaining from the Inspector or one of the other officers a written permit, whereof there shall be forms in a permit book, on the margin of which there shall be a copy or sufficient memorandum of every permit that is given. Such permit may be had whenever the office is open. When such permit is given, or when there is a leak in, or injury to the metre or pipes within the premises, the Inspector may stop the flow of gas at the cock outside said premises. After gas has, for any purpose, been stopped by the Inspector or authorized agent of the committee, it shall not be let on until it is authorized by said Inspector or such agent. Any person violating this section in any respect, shall pay a fine of not less than five nor more than twenty dollars.

39. Every person occupying any lot or tenement into which gas is conveyed under this chapter, shall permit the Superintendent or Inspector, or any authorized agent of the committee, to enter such lot or tenement, at seasonable hours, to examine the service pipe, metre, and other gas apparatus, or take up, repair or remove the same, or to see if this ordinance has been violated. Any person refusing so to do shall, for each refusal, pay a fine of five dollars.

40. The committee, or the Superintendent, subject to their approval, may at any time have the communication of any service pipe cut off, if they deem it necessary to protect the works against abuse or fraud. And they, or the Superintendent, with their assent, may make from time to time such further rules and regulations, not inconsistent with this ordinance, as may be found necessary or deemed advisable to ensure the proper management of the works, and the faithful performance, by the officers and workmen, of their duties.

41. Every officer of the gas works shall report to the Superintendent every violation that shall come to his knowledge of this or any subsequent ordinance relating to the gas works, and the Superintendent shall prosecute all who may be guilty of any such violation, reporting the same to the committee at its next monthly meeting, and shall diligently enforce this ordinance.

CHAPTER XXV.

CONCERNING THE MARKETS.

1. Of the markets in this city, that formerly known as the Old Market, shall, with the vegetable market attached thereto, be called the First Market, and that formerly known as the New or Shockoe Hill Market, shall, with the vegetable market attached thereto, be called the Second Market.

2. Annually, in November, or as soon thereafter as practicable, there shall be appointed by the Council a clerk for each of said markets; each of which clerks shall, before acting in his office, give bond with sureties in the penalty of two thousand dollars.

3. Over each market a general supervision shall be exercised by its committee, and whenever a market is held, the clerk

thereof shall attend it. No market shall be held on Sunday. On all other days the market shall be held as follows: From the first day of May until the first day of September following, on Monday, Tuesday, Wednesday, Thursday, Friday and Saturday, from daylight until ten o'clock A. M., and on Saturday from five to nine o'clock P. M.; from the first day of September until the first day of May following, on Monday, Tuesday, Wednesday, Thursday and Friday, from daylight until twelve o'clock M., and on Saturday from daylight until sunset. If after the time prescribed for holding any market, a person be found thereat with anything for sale, he shall forfeit such thing to the city, and shall pay a fine of not less than two nor more than twenty dollars.

4. As soon as practicable after the market is closed on any day, and always before it is next held, the Clerk shall have his market house, with the streets and alleys adjoining, watered, swept and cleaned. The whole market premises, including such ground as may be used with or pertain to the market, shall be kept by him clean and neat. And twice a year he shall have his meat market house whitewashed inside.

5. Meat, fish and vegetable stalls, benches and stands at the several markets, shall be assessed annually on the last Monday in December, by the committees on the markets respectively. But no person shall occupy a meat stall or bench until he obtains a license from the Council, first having satisfied the Council as to his character and capacity. And such license may be revoked, at the pleasure of the Council, for a violation of any of the criminal laws of the state, or of the ordinances of the city, or for any other cause which the Council may deem sufficient: provided that whenever the current price of meat shall exceed twenty cents a pound in the markets, such meats may be sold by any person or persons at any place or places in the city, without obtaining a license therefor. And such sales without a license may be continued for six months, though the current price of meats in the markets may be reduced to less than twenty cents per pound.

6. The rent of a bench, stall or stand at a market shall be paid to the Clerk of the market in advance for such time, not

exceeding three months, as the committee may direct. Not more than one stall, bench or stand shall be rented to or occupied by the same person at the same time: and a renting shall always be for a year at a time, except in cases provided for in the following section.

7. If the rent of a stall, bench or stand be in arrear more than ten days, or if by reason of death or other cause, there be a failure for ten days to supply the same with wholesome meat or vegetables, as it has been rented for the one or the other, the committee may declare such stall or bench to be vacant. In every such case, and in every case in which the license of a renter of a stall or bench is revoked, the Clerk of the market, after posting at the front of the market house notice, for at least twenty-four hours, shall rent the stall, bench or stand for the balance of the year to the highest bidder. If from such renting there cannot be satisfied all that the previous occupant became bound for, the Clerk, on behalf of the city, shall proceed, by warrant or otherwise, against the party liable for the residue, to recover the same as soon as may be after said residue becomes payable.

8. At or near the end of a year for which a stall, bench or stand of the meat or vegetable market is rented, if there be more than one applicant for it, or if the committee see cause so to direct, the Clerk of the market, after posting notice as aforesaid, shall rent such stall, bench or stand at auction for the highest premium that may be bid in cash beyond and in addition to the rent assessed by the committee. The aggregate of said rent and premium shall thenceforth be the rent per annum for said stall, bench or stand, until the same is again rented at auction. And no renter of a stall, bench or stand shall be permitted to rerent the same; but if any such person shall not desire to use it, it shall be surrendered to the city, and shall be rented out by the Clerk of the market, as prescribed in the seventh section of this chapter.

9. If any of the following things be sold by any person not a butcher, at a market, there shall at the time of such sale be paid by such person to the Clerk of the market, as follows: For each slaughtered beef, twenty-five cents; for each slaughtered veal,

mutton, hog or shoat, ten cents; for each sturgeon, ten cents; and for each pig, five cents. Any person violating this section shall for every offence pay a fine of not less than one nor more than twenty dollars.

10. If any person shall before daylight of any day take possession of any place or stand upon any sidewalk around or about either market, and exhibit for sale thereat any article not of his own raising, growth or produce, he shall for every such offence forfeit to the city such articles so exhibited, and shall moreover be fined not exceeding twenty dollars. And if any person shall sell or offer for sale any fish, fowl, eggs, butter, fruit or vegetables, not of his own product, raising or growth, without first paying a tax therefor—if a huckster, of twenty cents per day, and if any other person, of ten cents per day—to the Clerk of the market, he shall for every such offence be fined not exceeding twenty dollars; and in all cases arising under this section, the burthen of proof shall be upon the seller to show that the articles so exhibited, sold or offered for sale, were caught, taken, raised or produced by him.

11. No fish shall be sold or offered for sale in either of the market houses, or anywhere within the police jurisdiction of the market houses, except under the sheds called the fish markets, or at such other place as may be designated by the committee on markets. Any person violating this section shall pay a fine of not less than ten nor more than twenty dollars.

12. After market hours a person may sell or purchase about the streets, other than about a market house or its precincts. But no person shall offer for sale at a market any slaughtered beef, pork, mutton or other meat, butter, eggs, fish, fowls, vegetables or any other articles, which shall have been purchased at a market or elsewhere in the city, or while on their way to market, within six miles thereof, except butter, eggs, fowls, fruit or vegetables, which shall have been made, raised or produced more than fifteen miles from the city. Nor shall any person engaged in selling at a market any slaughtered beef, pork, mutton or other meat, butter, eggs, fish, fowls, fruit, vegetables or any other articles, purchase by himself or by the agency of another, either for himself or any other person, on the same day that he is the

seller thereof, any slaughtered beef, pork, mutton or other meat, butter, eggs, fish, fowls, fruit, vegetables or any other articles. Any person violating this section shall forfeit what is so purchased, and shall for such violation pay a fine of not less than ten nor more than fifty dollars; and in addition to such fine, shall be prohibited from offering for sale, either on his own account or as agent for another, at either market, any of said articles, until he shall receive permission so to do from the Council. And if any person shall sell or offer for sale anything whatever at any market in the city, after he shall have been so prohibited and before he shall have received permission to do so from the Council, the thing so sold or offered for sale shall be forfeited to the city, and the party so offending shall moreover be fined not less than ten nor more than fifty dollars for each article so sold or offered for sale.

13. Every butcher shall keep over his stall a sign with his name thereon, painted in letters which can be easily read. He shall be in person neat and cleanly, shall keep clean the benches, and all parts of his stall and the pavement thereof, and shall whitewash the interior twice a year. No butcher shall extend any of the blocks, benches, or other fixtures of his stall beyond the distance of nine feet out from the side wall. No person shall occupy a stand more than eight feet along the line of the curbstone. And no butcher at a meat market nor any seller at a fish or vegetable market shall leave about the market house after market hours, any loose barrel, box, bench or plank.

14. No butcher shall erect or have at a market house any box in which to lock up meats, unless such box be elevated on legs at least two feet above the floor or pavement of the market house, and be constructed according to a plan furnished by the committee of such market. And every butcher having at a market house a box shall have it thoroughly cleansed at least once a week. No article shall be kept therein for a longer period than one week, unless it be smoked or salt meat. If at any time any article therein become offensive, or if brine or anything else be found dripping from any such box on the floor or pavement of the market house, the article thus offensive or producing such dripping, shall, by order of the Clerk, be imme-

diately removed from the market house. A person violating this or the preceding section in any respect, shall, for every such violation, pay a fine of not less than one dollar nor more than five dollars; and every day that any such violation continues, shall be deemed a distinct offence.

15. Every butcher shall each day bring to the market house the hides with the ears of every animal brought by him that day to the market for sale, and shall keep the same exposed to public view for at least two hours. No butcher shall bring any dog within or to the market during market hours. Nor shall he bring to the market after the first of May and before the first of November following, any beef tallow, except such as may be necessarily attached to the hind quarters of beef. Nor shall he leave in a market house or any adjacent street, alley or ground, the head or a foot or other part of an animal. Nor shall any person deposit any filth, offensive matter, dirt or rubbish in or about either market house or any such street, alley or ground. Any person violating this section in any respect shall, for each offence, pay a fine of not less than two nor more than ten dollars.

16. If any person shall, at either market or within two hundred yards thereof, keep tied later than an hour after sunrise any live calf, sheep, lamb, hog or shoat, he shall, for every such offence, pay a fine of five dollars, unless such animal arrive at the market at a later hour, in which case it may remain about the market house for a time not exceeding one hour, and during that time may be offered for sale.

17. Any butcher or other person who shall sell or offer for sale, at a market, any sturgeon not previously skinned, or any unsound meat, fish, flesh, fowl, eggs, or other unsound article, or any meat which is distempered or blown, raised or stuffed, or which is dressed or garnished falsely, or in a way calculated to deceive, shall pay a fine of not less than five nor more than twenty dollars, and forfeit what is so sold or offered for sale.

18. The Clerk of each market shall examine all meats, fish and fowls offered at such market for sale, and take possession of such as by the preceding section are prohibited from being so offered, and unless on an appeal by the person offering the same to the committee of the market, the decision of the Clerk be re-

versed, the said Clerk shall cause what he so takes possession of to be buried in a suitable place.

19. No person selling fruits or vegetables at market, by measure, shall sell the same in any other than dry measure; and the said measure shall be of the same size at bottom and top. No person shall buy or sell at market any beef, pork, mutton, veal, shoat, lamb or butter, in any other manner than by weight. And no article sold or offered for sale at a market shall be weighed with steelyards. Every butcher shall keep, in a conspicuous part of his stall, his patent platform balances and weights, or his scales and weights; the scales well balanced and in good order and the weights correct. Any person violating this section shall pay a fine of not less than one dollar nor more than five dollars. No person shall sell on commission for the owner articles brought to the market for sale; or buy articles at the market house for sale again in the city or elsewhere; and for the violation of this provision the articles shall be forfeited to the city; and there shall be a fine of not less than two nor more than twenty dollars.

20. The Clerk of each market shall, from time to time, examine the scales, balances, weights and measures used by persons at such market, to see whether they are sealed according to law and conform to the preceding section; and also examine butter and other articles sold or offered for sale by weight, to see that they are not deficient. Persons having at market illegal scales, balances, weights or measures, shall forfeit the same to the city. Articles offered for sale by weight, and found deficient, shall likewise be forfeited to the city; or if sold, the value thereof shall be forfeited. In every case in which the Clerk of a market shall have good cause to believe that anything is forfeited under this section or under any other section of this chapter, he shall seize the same, and summon the person in possession thereof at the time of the seizure, to appear before the Mayor, or some other justice, at some time within twelve hours, to show cause why the said thing should not be adjudged forfeited. Any person convicted under this section shall be excluded from the market either as principal or agent.

21. No person shall sell from any stand, cart or wagon, on

Sixth, Marshall or Broad street, adjacent to the Second Market, until all the benches within the vegetable market and the square on the eastern side thereof are fully occupied, and then only at such places as the Clerk of said market may, under the instructions of the committee, direct. A person violating this section shall, for every such violation, pay a fine of one dollar.

22. The Clerk of a market may order any butcher or other person having at his market a cart, wagon, dray or other vehicle, or a horse or beast of burden, to remove the same; and if such butcher or other person fail to obey the order, he may be fined one dollar for every fifteen minutes such failure may continue.

23. If a person at a market use obscene, profane or threatening language, or shall fight thereat, he shall be fined not less than five dollars nor more than ten dollars for each offence.

24. The Clerk of a market shall prosecute all offenders against this ordinance. To enable him the better to execute his office and preserve order about the market, he shall have the powers of a police officer within two hundred yards around the market in every direction.

25. There shall be appointed by the Clerk of each market, a deputy to be approved by the committee of said market; which deputy shall in case of the Clerk's sickness, or temporary absence, perform the duties of Clerk, and for this purpose shall have the like powers. The deputy's pay shall be at the rate of two dollars per day, for such time as he may actually perform the duties of Clerk. The same shall be paid out of the Clerk's salary, unless upon the recommendation of the committee the Council shall otherwise direct.

26. The Clerk of each market shall, on the first day of every January, April, July and October, render to the Auditor an account, verified on oath, of all moneys which he may within the preceding three months have received by virtue of his office, stating when and from whom the same was received, and pay to the Chamberlain the amount thereof. If he fail for twenty days to render such account or to make such payment, the Auditor shall report such default to the Council at its first meeting afterwards, and shall suspend the payment of his salary until the report is made. It shall be the duty of the said Clerks to keep regu-

lar accounts of their daily receipts, and submit the same to the inspection of the committees on the markets whenever required by any member of either committee. It shall not be lawful for the Clerk of either market to buy articles of any kind offered for sale therein, or within two hundred yards thereof, for any person or persons other than for his own use or family consumption. For any violation of this section, the Clerk so offending shall be fined not less than fifty nor more than one hundred dollars.

CHAPTER XXVI.

CONCERNING THE WATER WORKS.

1. At the first meeting of the Council after its annual organization, or as soon thereafter as practicable, the Council shall elect a Superintendent of the water works, who shall enter on his office on the first day of May, and continue therein for one year and until his successor is elected and qualifies, unless sooner removed. Before acting in his office he shall give a bond

with sureties in the penalty of five thousand dollars, which shall be approved by the Council. When his term of office expires his official books and papers shall be delivered by him to his successor, or disposed of in such other manner as the committee on water may direct.

2. The committee on water, as soon as practicable after its appointment, shall appoint an Assistant Superintendent of the water works, a Superintendent of the pump house and an Assistant Superintendent of the pump house, who may be removed at any time by the committee. Upon every appointment to either of these offices the committee shall report to the Council the name of the person so appointed.

3. The committee shall have the superintendence and general government of the water works. The Superintendent of the water works and the officers mentioned in the preceding section, shall, except as otherwise prescribed by this chapter, act according to the directions of said committee. The clerk in the Auditor's office shall attend all meetings of the committee, and act as its clerk, and make and keep a true record of its proceedings.

4. The Superintendent, subject to the control of the committee, shall have a general charge of the reservoirs, pump house, and all the buildings, fire plugs, fixtures and pipes erected or laid down for the water works, and of the lands on which the said reservoirs, pump house and buildings are. He shall carefully inspect all parts of the works and have the same kept in good order and in proper operation, and the water furnished as pure and clear as practicable, with promptness and regularity, at the city buildings, and to all persons entitled to its use under the provisions hereinafter contained.

5. The Superintendent of the pump house and his assistant shall remain in or at the pump house, and it shall be their special duty to take good care of the buildings and machinery. But they shall be at all times subject to the control of the Superintendent of the water works.

6. Subject to the control of the committee, the Superintendent may employ in and about the works such men as he may deem suitable and necessary. He shall keep an account of their names, the kind of work done by them, and the days of the week or month they work. He shall quarterly present to the

committee a statement of the materials, tools, and other articles necessary for carrying on the works for the following quarter, and an estimate of their cost. And subject to such restrictions as may be imposed by the committee, the Superintendent may purchase such materials, tools and other articles. What may be so purchased shall be taken care of by him and used as required. All bills for the same shall within three months be laid by the Superintendent before the committee. What the committee may allow for such purchases, or for any necessary current expenses of the works, shall be paid by a draft drawn on the Auditor, signed by the chairman of the committee, and attested by the Superintendent.

7. The Superintendent shall preserve a map of the location of the main pipes, showing the course, distance and size of each of them, and when there is any extension of the main pipes, shall, as soon as possible, mark on the map the place of such extension and the size of the pipe used in making it. He shall enter in a book, to be kept in his office, and shall report to the Auditor the quantity, description and cost of the materials used, and the cost of the labor employed in making such extensions; and the Auditor in books to be kept in his office, shall keep accounts thereof.

8. In a book, kept in his office, the Superintendent shall make an entry of all branch pipes, hydrants and other fixtures from the main in the streets. The entry shall state the quantity, description and cost of the materials used in laying down, and fixing the pipes and fixtures; and it shall designate the point of junction of each branch pipe with the main pipe, and the course and distance of the pipe to the premises supplied thereby, so as, in after time, to avoid difficulty in ascertaining the position of any part of the pipe.

9. A book shall be kept in the Superintendent's office, with a caption importing that the owners of property whose names are undersigned, request that water may be introduced upon the premises mentioned opposite their respective names, upon the terms prescribed by the ordinances of the city. When the owner of any property within the range of the pipes applies for the introduction of water into his premises, he or his agent shall

write his name in said book, under said caption, and write opposite thereto the date and number of his application, the location of his premises, and the purpose for which the water is to be used. The city water shall not be introduced into the premises of any applicant until there is written what is here required.

10. After there is written what is so required, water from the main pipe in the public street or alley, shall without delay be conducted by the Superintendent to the applicant's premises, by means of suitable service pipe and fixtures, with a separate attachment for his particular house or tenement. No hydrant or cock shall be allowed to be on a sidewalk, or in an exposed situation, from which water may be taken without detection; and there shall be placed on the service pipe, near the curbstone, a stop-cock (with an iron cover marked "city water works"), so that the supply of water may be stopped at any time when it is proper to do so. The said applicant may have the water introduced into his premises, from the service pipe laid down by the Superintendent as above directed, by means of suitable service pipe, hydrant and fixtures: provided such work be conducted by practical and competent plumbers, and the materials used in the construction thereof be of the best quality, and of such weight and description as the committee may prescribe in the particular case, or may prescribe for such work in the part of the city where the same is located: and provided, that on the completion of the work, and before the water is turned into it, notice thereof shall be given to the Superintendent or his agent, and the work be by him inspected and approved.

11. The supply of water to any person shall be on condition of his paying a water rent at certain rates; which shall be fifty per centum upon the rates prescribed in the next section.

12. *If for the purpose of building*—For each table used for brick making, twenty-five dollars per annum. When in a building bricks are laid or stone work or plastering done, five cents for each thousand bricks; two cents for each cubic yard of stone work, and twenty cents for each hundred yards of plastering. But if the water be conveyed by hose, barrels or buckets, and not along the gutters, the charge shall be two and a half cents for each thousand bricks; for each cubic yard of stone

work, one cent; and ten cents for each hundred yards of plastering. A license shall be obtained from the Superintendent for each building for which the city water is wanted for any of these purposes.

If for a public building—At the following rate per annum, to wit: For the capitol, seventy-five dollars; state armory, fifty dollars; medical college, fifty dollars; state courthouse, twenty-five dollars; a theatre, twenty dollars; a church, ten dollars; a public hall, ten dollars, in addition to other charges on same building; Henrico county courthouse, sixty dollars.

For schools—At the following rate per annum, to wit: For a boarding school, ten dollars, and three per centum on the actual or estimated rent of the premises used for the purpose. For a private school, six dollars.

For depots, manufactories, workshops and warehouses—At the following rate per annum, to wit: For a railroad depot, seventy dollars, for every locomotive in which the city water is used making six trips in the week, and in the same proportion for every such locomotive making fewer than six trips in a week. This shall pay for all the uses of water at such depot, except for stationary steam engines, water closets and baths. For each stationary steam engine, four dollars for each estimated horse power. But no steam engine shall be supplied except where the water is taken in the building where the engine is used, for the usual purposes for which water is used in such building. For a rolling mill, or a foundry and machine shop, or a barrel factory, or stemmery, ten dollars, if not more than fifteen persons be employed therein; for each additional person, twenty cents. For each spike machine, thirty dollars. For each manufacturing mill, thirty dollars. For a tobacco manufactory, sixty cents for each hand employed therein; but no charge to be less than ten dollars. For a tobacco warehouse, or a currier shop, twenty-five dollars. For a rectifying establishment, thirty dollars. For a dyeing establishment, fifteen dollars, exclusive of use of steam boiler. For a lager beer, porter, soda or bottling establishment, thirty dollars. For a blacksmith's shop, or a printing office, or a barber's shop, ten dollars. For a carpenter's shop, seven dollars.

Bakeries, restoratives, taverns, stables, billiard saloons, &c. At the following rate per annum, to wit: For a bakery, fifteen dollars, if the tenement be used exclusively as such; if besides being used as a bakery, the bakery be also occupied as a dwelling for a family, then only eight dollors for the bakery. For a house of private entertainment, twelve dollars, and one per centum on the rent of the buildings used for such purpose. For an ordinary, or house of public entertainment, or restorative, twenty dollars, and three per centum on the actual or estimated rent of the premises used for such purpose. For each bar, whether kept in a hotel or elsewhere, ten dollars, in addition to other charges on the same premises. For a livery stable, fifty cents for each stall, whether used or not. For a packet boat office, ten dollars. For a private stable, one dollar for one horse or mule, and all over one, fifty cents for each horse, and one dollar for a private carriage. For a stable where hacks or carriages are kept for hire, one dollar for each horse and three dollars for each carriage or hack, and one dollar for each buggy or wagon. For each mule or wagon lot, twenty-five dollars. For each stable where wagons, drays or carts are kept for hire, one dollar for each horse or mule; and no stable shall be charged less than five dollars. For a billiard saloon, ten dollars.

Stores and offices—At the following rate per annum, to wit: If a tenement be used exclusively as a grocery store, hat store or shoe store, ten dollars for such tenement; if besides being used as a store, the house be also occupied as a dwelling for a family, then only five dollars for the store. If a tenement be used exclusively as a dry goods store or book store, seven dollars for such tenement; if besides being used as a store, the house be also occupied as a dwelling for a family, then only five dollars for the store. For each apothecary store, ten dollars, unless soda water be there manufactured, in which case the same shall be paid as for a soda water manufactory. For each confectionery store, ten dollars; if besides being used as a store, the house be also occupied as a dwelling, then only five dollars for the store; and when candy is made, ten dollars additional. For each auction store, or other store not mentioned above, ten dollars. For each office not otherwise provided for, three dollars.

Dwelling houses, when valued at one thousand dollars or less, five dollars; for each additional family occupying the same house, five dollars each; when valued at more than one thousand dollars and not over two thousand dollars, six dollars; when the house is occupied by more than one family, five dollars each; when valued at two thousand dollars and not over five thousand dollars, eight dollars; when the house is occupied by more than one family, six dollars each; when valued at five thousand dollars and not over eight thousand dollars, ten dollars; when occupied by more than one family, seven dollars each; when valued at eight thousand dollars and not over twelve thousand dollars, twelve dollars; when the house is occupied by more than one family, eight dollars each; when valued over twelve thousand dollars and under fifteen thousand dollars, fifteen dollars; when occupied by more than one family, nine dollars each; when valued over fifteen thousand dollars, twenty dollars.

Baths, water closets, fountains and hose—At the following rate per annum, to wit: For each public bath tub, six dollars. For each private bath tub, three dollars. In the case of a water closet in a public house, for each seat, six dollars. In the case of water closets in a private boarding house, or in a private house, three dollars if there is but one seat, and two dollars each if there be more than one. But no bath or water closet shall be supplied except when the water is taken in the building where such bath or water closet is, for the usual purposes for which water is used in such a building. For a fountain in a yard, fifty dollars, to be used at the discretion of the committee; and for a fountain in a store, five dollars. In such cases as the Superintendent, under the regulations of the committee, may allow the use of small hose, one-eighth nozzle, ten dollars if such use be for sprinkling the carriage way of streets, and three dollars if it be for sprinkling a sidewalk, yard or garden. There shall be a fine of ten dollars on any person who shall for any such purpose use the hose between eight o'clock in the morning and five o'clock in the afternoon, or who shall at any time use hose for washing a carriage or other vehicle with the city water.

13. In any case not hereinbefore provided for, the water rent shall be at such rate as may be fixed by the Superintendent, sub-

ject to the committee's control. And in cases that are hereinbefore provided for, it shall be lawful for the Council, at any time hereafter, to add to or increase the rates for water to be thereafter supplied.

14. Water rents shall be payable half yearly in advance: in Monroe ward, on the first day of January and the first day of July; in Madison ward, on the first day of March and the first day of September; and in Jefferson ward, on the first day of May and the first day of November. Except that when the supply of water is commenced in a ward between the days above fixed for payment of rents in that ward, the person supplied shall, at the time of such commencement, pay at the rate before mentioned up to the next day fixed for payment of water rent in that ward. And rents for water used in brick or stone work, or plastering, shall be payable on the first ensuing day fixed for payment of water rents in the ward in which such water is used.

15. When, upon such application as is before mentioned, a hydrant is erected on any premises, and water commenced to be supplied at such hydrant, rent for such water shall continue to be payable for at least one year, whether the party desires the supply for that length of time or not. In other cases, a person supplied with water may discontinue the use thereof by giving to the Superintendent notice, in writing, for one month prior to the expiration of the time for which he has paid; otherwise, he shall be chargeable for the six months next following such expiration. Though said month's notice be not given, yet, when there are two houses or tenements, and payment for water supplied at the hydrant of each has been made for not less than a year, a water taker, removing from the one to the other, shall give notice of such removal to the Superintendent, who shall, thereupon, stop the supply of water at the one, and furnish it at the other; and payment shall be made accordingly. And if any person who is taking water at a house removes therefrom, he shall give notice thereof on or before the day of his removal; and if he shall fail to do it, he shall pay a fine of not less than five nor more than ten dollars.

16. Fifteen days before the water rents shall be payable, as provided in section fourteen, the Superintendent shall furnish

the Auditor with a correct list of all persons to whom water is supplied, and the sum payable by each for water rent. The Auditor shall keep an account thereof in his office, and shall have bills made out for the same, showing the amount due, and the amount which will be due after deducting five per centum therefrom; and he shall place said bills in the hands of the Superintendent, who shall have every bill presented to the person who is to pay it (or at his residence or place of business), stating, at the foot of the bill, the day of its presentment; and shall, within ten days after receiving any bill from the Auditor, return to him a memorandum, stating the day it was presented.

17. From the amount of the bill for water, there shall be a deduction of five per centum, provided that the residue of the bill be paid to the Chamberlain, at his office, within five days next after its presentment, and before three o'clock P. M. If a bill for water shall remain unpaid for ten days after that on which it is presented, the Auditor shall notify the Superintendent, who shall cause the water to be stopped from the premises in respect to which the default exists (if the same can be done without stopping the water from the premises of others who have paid); and he shall not allow it to be used on those premises again until said bill is paid. If any bill remains unpaid for fifteen days the Auditor shall make out a bill for the amount due, with the addition of ten per centum thereon, and deliver the same to the Collector of the city taxes, taking his receipt therefor, who is hereby authorized and required to collect the same as if it was due for city taxes, and after deducting five per centum for his compensation, pay the balance to the Chamberlain within thirty days after the bill is put into his hands; and the official bond of the said Collector shall extend to secure the faithful discharge of his duties under this ordinance. But any bill may at any time be paid to the Chamberlain with the addition of five per centum: provided, however, that if the amount of said bill is due from a tenant, or one who was a tenant of the premises when it became due, the owner of the premises or a tenant under him, other than the person from whom the water rent referred to in said bill is due, may pay the same to the Chamberlain without the addition of any per centage thereon.

It shall be the duty of the Auditor to demand from the Collector monthly settlements of such bills as are placed in his hands, and for failure to make such settlement the Collector shall forfeit the per centage which he is authorized by this section to deduct.

18. If any person, other than the Superintendent or his agents, shall introduce into any lot or tenement, water from the city pipes, or introduce any ferule or other fixture into any of said pipes, or construct or lay down, or have constructed or laid down any pipes or other works, for the purpose of introducing water into a lot or tenement, or break up any street, lane, alley or road for the purpose of constructing or laying down any such pipes or works, every person so offending shall pay a fine of not less than ten nor more than fifty dollars; and every twenty-four hours during which such work or fixture shall continue, shall be a distinct offence. But after water has been introduced into a lot or tenement, as provided in section ten of this ordinance, the fine shall not be incurred by the owner or occupier of such lot or tenement, when he, by permission in writing of the Superintendent, or (if he refuse) by permission of the committee, causes to be attached to the said pipes, fixtures for water closets, boilers, baths, wash basins, or other things for which water is required, provided such fixtures be constructed by practical and competent plumbers, and the materials used in their construction be of the best quality, and sufficiently strong to withstand double the required pressure, and provided that on the completion of the work, notice thereof be forthwith given to the Superintendent or his agent, and the work be by him inspected and approved.

19. No plumber shall make any addition to, or alteration of, any fixtures connected with the water works, without having first received a written permit from the Superintendent or the committee to do so; nor shall any attachment be made for any purpose whatsoever from any pipe, except it be the pipe supplying the premises for which such work is to be done; and all pipes put in by plumbers shall have separate stop cocks to each branch thereof, so that no difficulty may occur in shutting off the water when it is necessary to do so, under a penalty of ten dollars for each violation.

20. Every person occupying any lot or tenement into which

water is conveyed, under this ordinance, shall permit the Superintendent or his agent, or any authorized agent of this city, to enter such lot or tenement, at seasonable hours, to inspect the works therein, or to see if this ordinance has been violated. Any person refusing so to do, shall, for each refusal, pay a fine of five dollars.

21. If any person shall deface or injure any house, wall, cock, wheel, fire plug or other fixture connected with or pertaining to the water works, or shall bathe in the reservoir, basin or canal thereof, or deposit any offensive matter, or any stick, mud or rubbish in said reservoir, basin or canal, or shall, without lawful authority, climb over or get through the fence or enclosure of the reservoir, or place any building material, rubbish or other matter on the stop-cock of a street main or service pipe, or obstruct access to any fixture connected with the water works, or remove or injure any pipe, fire plug, hydrant or cock, or open any of them so as to waste the water, or if any person shall use the city water for a purpose for which he has neither paid nor obtained a license to use it, every such person shall, for each offence, pay a fine of not less than five nor more than twenty dollars.

22. When the occupier of a lot or a tenement, on which has been erected or placed a hydrant, cock or other fixture to supply water, shall permit the water to run from the hydrant, cock or fixture, without proper care to prevent waste, or shall permit the water to be used, taken or received by any person, other than said occupier, or a member or visitor of his family, there shall, in each case, be a fine on the said occupier of not less than five nor more than twenty dollars, and in the latter case there shall be a like fine, also, on the person so using, taking or receiving the water; and in every such case the Superintendent shall stop the water from said lot or tenement, and not turn it on again until a satisfactory assurance is given him that the like case will not happen again. So, likewise, if any hydrant, cock or other fixture be found leaking, and the owner or occupier of the premises shall refuse or fail to have the necessary repairs made, the Superintendent shall stop the water from said lot or tenement, and there shall be a fine of ten dollars on any person who

shall turn on the water before such repairs are made. If any person not acting under the authority of the Superintendent or the committee, shall turn the city water on any premises whatsoever; or if any person shall take, receive or use the city water before first having paid the charges for the same, he shall pay a fine of ten dollars for each offence.

23. Notwithstanding the preceding provisions, the committee may grant to any poor person, without charge therefor, license to use the water from a hydrant on another lot or tenement, with the permission of the occupier thereof. The Superintendent shall keep a separate list of all licenses granted under this section.

24. Nothing in this chapter shall prevent the occupier of a lot or tenement, supplied with city water, from having, when his hydrant or pipe is out of order, the use of water from a hydrant on another lot or tenement, with the permission of the occupier thereof; nor prevent any person from taking city water to extinguish fire; nor prevent city water from being used by a fire company in examining, or practicing, or cleaning and putting in good condition their engines and hose.

25. The Superintendent shall diligently enforce all ordinances relating to the water works, and prosecute all who may violate any of their provisions; and it shall be the especial duty of the police to report violations of this chapter which come within their knowledge.

TITLE 5.

HEALTH.

CHAPTER XXVII.

CONCERNING HEALTH AND THE CITY HOSPITAL.

1. The committee on health shall exercise a general supervision over the hospital, and recommend to the Council such improvements in or about the premises as they may deem advisable.

2. The Council shall annually, at the first monthly meeting in May, or as soon thereafter as practicable, elect a hospital physician, who, in addition to the duties prescribed in this chapter, shall be the superintendent of quarantine.

3. The committee may employ a person as housekeeper of the hospital, who shall reside therein and keep it and the furniture thereof in good order, and when necessary act as nurse; and who shall perform such other duties as the committee may require. The committee may also, at and for such times as they may see occasion, employ other nurses and attendants, and a superintendent of the hospital, who shall respectively perform such duties and under such regulations as the committee may prescribe. The committee may pay the superintendent, physician and housekeeper, nurses and attendants, for their respective services, such compensation as said committee may deem reasonable, not exceeding, for the superintendent, two dollars for each day that he

is employed; and not exceeding, for the physician, three dollars for each day that he attends at the hospital, except on such days as he may visit in the hospital more than three patients, and then not exceeding four dollars per day if there be four patients, and not exceeding five dollars per day if there be five or more. But before the superintendent shall have authority to act as such, he shall enter into bond with security to be approved by the committee, in the penalty of five thousand dollars, with condition for the faithful discharge of his duties; which bond, with the approval of the committee endorsed thereon, shall be filed with the Auditor.

4. The committee may authorize such vehicles and horses to be purchased and kept for the removal of persons to the hospital, and such other things to be obtained for the comfort or cure of persons in the hospital, or for use and consumption therein, as they may deem proper. The compensation mentioned in the preceding section and the expenses incurred under this section shall be paid by the Auditor, upon the drafts of the chairman of said committee: provided what is so paid shall not exceed what may be appropriated by the Council for such compensation and expenses.

5. There shall be received into the said hospital all persons infected with any infectious disease dangerous to the public health. Negroes shall be in separate apartments from white persons, and females in separate apartments from males.

6. The physician to the hospital shall be the health officer of the city. He shall have all the powers and perform all the duties devolved upon health officers by the laws of the state It shall be his special duty to remove to the hospital all persons in the city infected with any infectious disease dangerous to the public health of the city, unless such person be sick at his own residence, or cannot be removed without danger of life.

7. All expenses incurred for the removal of any person infected with a dangerous disease, and for maintaining, nursing and curing him, or incurred in entering any lot, house or vessel suspected of having persons or things infected with a dangerous infectious disease therein, and removing them to the hospital, shall be paid to the Superintendent of the hospital (who shall

account therefor quarterly to the Chamberlain), by such infected person, or by the owner of such lot, house or vessel, as the case may be; or if such person or owner be a married woman, by her husband; or if an infant, by his parent or guardian. An account of all such expenses not paid to the Superintendent shall, by him, be filed with the Chamberlain, who shall, unless the amount thereof be paid, or the committee on finance otherwise direct, cause the same to be recovered from the person liable therefor, by suit or warrant, as the case may be.

8. Every physician practising in the city of Richmond, who shall be in attendance upon a patient affected with small-pox or varioloid, shall report the name and location of the patient to the board of health, in writing, within twenty-four hours after he is satisfied of the existence of the disease; and he shall also report the recovery or death of every such patient under his charge: and for his failure to comply with either of these requirements, the physician so offending shall be fined ten dollars for every twenty-four hours he so fails to report such patient.

CHAPTER XXVIII.

CONCERNING THE BOARD OF HEALTH.

1. Annually, in the month of May, there shall be appointed by the Council three physicians, one from each ward, who shall constitute a board of health. They shall, at the first regular meeting after their appointment, choose a president, who shall continue in office until his successor is appointed. The board shall have the services, when required, of the clerk to the Chamberlain, and keep a journal of their proceedings; which may be at all times examined by the Council.

2. The members of the board shall inspect their wards care-

fully twice a month, from April to September, and once a month for the balance of the year, visiting all localities suspected of being unhealthy or exposed to disease. They shall suggest to the Council such measures as they think fit to preserve the health of the city, and especially to prevent the introduction and spread of contagious and infectious diseases, and to prevent or regulate the pursuit of callings prejudicial to the public health or comfort. They shall also consider and report upon all such matters as may be referred to them by the Council, and make monthly reports of their proceedings.

3. The members of the board are hereby invested with police authority in the performance of their duties. They may require deleterious matter wherever found to be removed by the occupant of the premises (or by the owner, if the premises are unoccupied), and conveyed beyond the limits of the city; and they may require yards and premises and the street gutters in front of any premises, when they think it important to the health of the neighborhood, to be cleansed and limed by the occupant or owner of such premises. They shall report to the Mayor all offences against the health regulations of the city, and all persons who fail, after five days' notice, to remove deleterious matter, or to cleanse and lime their premises and the gutters in front as aforesaid; and thereupon such persons shall be fined, in the discretion of the Mayor, not less than five nor more than twenty dollars, unless he is satisfied of their inability to comply with the orders of the board of health.

4. No person shall deposit or cause to be deposited in any street or public or private alley, any filth, garbage, ashes, rubbish or other such thing, under penalty of being fined not less than five nor more than twenty dollars for every such deposit; and each day such deposit remains shall be a distinct offence.

5. Whenever, in the opinion of the board, it shall become necessary, the board may require the services of the city hands and carts, under their direction, in cleansing particular localities, and may order lime from the city gas works or elsewhere to be distributed in such localities.

6. When a city scavenger shall have been appointed, the occupant of any house or lot shall cause all garbage and decayed,

refuse or offensive matter to be put in boxes or barrels, and in the most convenient place on such lot for removal, under penalty of a fine of not less than one nor more than ten dollars.

7. The members of the board of health shall receive annually for their services one hundred dollars each.

CHAPTER XXIX.

CONCERNING SINKS, CESSPOOLS AND PRIVIES.

1. There shall be elected by the Council, annually, in the month of May, not more than two persons in each ward of the city, who shall hold their offices for one year and until their successors are elected, unless sooner removed, whose duty it shall be, upon the application of any resident of the city, to cleanse and purify his sink, cesspool or privy.

2. Each of said officers shall have an office in the ward for which he is elected, and shall keep a slate or book at his office, and at the station house in his ward, upon which notice may be given that his services are needed; and when the said notice is given, he shall perform the required service without delay, at rates to be agreed upon between himself and his employer; or in case of disagreement, at rates to be fixed by one of the officers of police living in the ward in which the work has been done. If before the work is commenced the parties cannot agree upon the price to be paid for it, the person whose sink, cesspool or privy is to be cleansed, may dismiss the officer, and give notice to and employ any other of the said officers in the city.

3. Each of said officers shall, upon the order of the board of health, perform his duty in cleansing any sink, privy or cesspool upon premises occupied by those who are unable to pay therefor,

and his rate of compensation shall be fixed by one of the officers of police living in the ward where the work is done, and paid in the mode now provided for paying expenses incurred by the board of health.

4. Each of said officers shall provide suitable close carts adapted to the purpose of removing the night soil and other filth; and their work shall be done between ten o'clock P. M. and daylight in the winter, and eleven o'clock P. M. and daylight in the summer. And the night soil and other filth removed by them shall be deposited at the places designated by the board of health, and shall be there deodorized or otherwise so disposed of that the same shall not be offensive. And if said officers removing said night soil or other filth shall spill any of it in the streets or alleys of the city, or shall fail to deposit it at the places indicated by the board of health, and deodorize or otherwise dispose of the same as herein directed, they or he shall pay a fine of not less than two nor more than twenty dollars for each offence.

5. Each officer shall keep a register of the time he performs his duty at any place, and report the same monthly to the board of health.

6. Hereafter no sink or cesspool shall be sunk unless the same be at least ten feet deep, and be lined at the sides and on the bottom with brick or stone; and the owner or occupant of premises to which any sink or cesspool belongs shall not permit the contents thereof to rise within two feet of the surface of the earth: and any person offending in either of the foregoing particulars shall be fined not less than five nor more than twenty dollars; and each day the offence continues after notice thereof and an order that the same shall be remedied or abated, shall be counted and treated as a separate offence.

7. The officers elected under this ordinance shall each give bond in the sum of one thousand dollars, with sureties to be approved by the Council, with condition for the faithful performance of his duties.

8. No person shall remove from any premises in the city the night soil contained in the sinks, privies or cesspools of such premises, except the officers appointed under section one of this

chapter. Nor shall the owner or occupier of any such premises employ any person to remove said night soil except the officers appointed as aforesaid. Every person violating this section shall be fined not less than five nor more than fifty dollars.

CHAPTER XXX.

CONCERNING DEAD ANIMALS.

1. Hereafter if any person not authorized so to do by contract with the city of Richmond shall remove from the city any dead horse, mule, cow or other cattle, or the carcass thereof, he shall be fined for the removal of every such animal or carcass not less than five nor more than thirty dollars.

2. It shall be the duty of the owner of every such dead animal as is mentioned in the preceding section, and of the owner or occupier of the lot and premises wherein such dead animal or the carcass thereof may be, to give notice of the death of such animal, or of its being on his lot or premises, to the person contracting with the city for the removal of such animals from the corporate limits thereof. And if the owner of such animal, or the owner or occupier of the lot whereon the body of any such animal may be, shall fail to give such notice to such contractor for six hours after he shall know or be informed of the death of such animal, or that it is on his lot, he shall be fined not less than five nor more than ten dollars.

3. The contractor for the removal of dead animals from the city, shall fix at least one place in each ward of the city, where the notice required in the preceding section may be given, and shall publish the same in three of the daily papers of the city every day for two weeks, and shall keep a sign at the said places to indicate the same; and he shall have some person or a book

or slate at each of said places, to whom the notice may be delivered, or in which it may be written.

4. If the said contractor shall fail to remove any dead animal or carcass within six hours after notice thereof has been left at the place designated by him, or has been given to him in person, he shall be fined not less than five nor more than twenty dollars: provided, that the hours of the night shall not be computed in either this or the preceding section.

5. It shall be the duty of every policeman who shall know of a dead animal or carcass lying in a street or alley or lot in the city, to give notice thereof to said contractor in the mode prescribed in the preceding section; and for the failure to remove such dead animal within six hours from the time when the notice is so given, the said contractor shall be liable as hereinbefore provided.

6. If the said contractor shall fail to comply with his contract in removing dead animals a proper distance from the city, so that the same shall become offensive to the people in any part of the city or of the suburbs, he shall be fined not less than ten nor more than thirty dollars for each offence; and shall moreover be liable to an action on his bond for a breach of the condition thereof.

CHAPTER XXXI.

CONCERNING QUARANTINE.

SEC.
1. Quarantine ground established.
2. Who and what shall perform quarantine.
3. Who shall be Superintendent of quarantine.
4. Quarantine to be governed by the statute.
5. What Superintendent shall provide.
6. Vessels subject to quarantine; what they shall do.
7. What the Mayor may order.
8. Superintendent to board vessels subject to quarantine, &c. What he shall enquire and report. How long vessel shall remain in quarantine; may go to sea.

SEC.
9. What Superintendent may direct and do as to vessels, &c., subject to quarantine.
10. Vessels performing quarantine, how designated.
11. Lighters, when only to be employed to load or unload vessels at quarantine.
12. How passengers under quarantine shall be supported.
13. Vessel released from quarantine, master shall deliver his permit to the Mayor.
14. No person to go on board, or have communication with vessel in quarantine; if he does, may be kept there.

1. There shall be established, by and with the concurrence of the county court of Henrico, a quarantine ground for the city

of Richmond, between a line drawn across James river, from a point at high water mark on the Henrico side, and a point at high water mark on the Chesterfield side of said river, so as to touch the lower end of Hancock's island; and a line drawn from the Henrico side, at a point at high water mark, opposite Warwick, to a point at high water mark on the Chesterfield side; which points shall be designated and marked by the superintendent of quarantine.

2. Quarantine shall be performed on the said ground by vessels, persons and merchandize coming, or brought from any port or place whence the Council, by resolution, published in one or more of the newspapers published in the city of Richmond, shall declare it probable that any plague or other infectious disease may be brought, during such time, and in such manner as shall be directed by the Council, by resolution published as aforesaid; and until they are discharged from such quarantine no such person or merchandize shall be brought on shore, or go, or be put on board any other vessel, but in such case and in such manner as shall be permitted by the orders of the Council; and the vessels and persons receiving goods out of such vessels shall be subject to the orders concerning quarantine, and for preventing infection, which shall be made by the Council.

3. The hospital physician shall be the superintendent of quarantine, who, during the time of actual quarantine performed on said grounds, shall receive five dollars *per diem* for his services; and he shall have such assistants as the Council may appoint.

4. The quarantine herein provided, and all persons, vessels and goods subject thereto, shall, in all things, be governed and regulated by the twelfth, thirteenth, fourteenth, fifteenth, sixteenth, seventeenth, eighteenth, nineteenth and twentieth sections of chapter eighty-six of the Code of Virginia, and any acts amending the same, and such regulations consistent therewith as the Council may ordain.

5. The superintendent of quarantine shall, under the direction and approval of the Council, provide, by contract, sufficient buildings and shelters for the safe keeping of the goods or merchandize which it may be necessary to land from on board of any vessel performing quarantine in obedience to this ordinance,

18

as well as for the accommodation of the persons superintending or performing quarantine.

6. All vessels subject to quarantine shall, immediately on their arrival, anchor within quarantine anchorage ground, and there remain with all persons arriving in them, subject to the examinations and regulations imposed by law.

7. The Mayor, whenever in his judgment the public health shall require it, may order any vessel at the wharves of the city, or in their vicinity, into quarantine or other place of safety; and may require all persons, articles and things introduced into the city from such vessel, to be seized, returned on board, or removed to the quarantine ground. In case the master, owner or consignee of the vessel cannot be found, or shall neglect or refuse to obey the order of removal, the Mayor shall have power to cause such removal at the expense of such master, owner or consignee; and such vessel or persons shall not return to the city without the written permission of the Mayor. Such vessel, when removed to the quarantine ground, shall, in all respects, be subject to the regulations of quarantine.

8. It shall be the duty of the superintendent of quarantine to board every vessel subject to quarantine, or to visitation (if, in the opinion of the superintendent, such visit be necessary), immediately on her arrival; to inquire as to the health of all persons on board, and the condition of the vessel and cargo, by inspection of the bill of health, manifest, log-book or otherwise; to examine, on oath, as many and such persons on board of vessels suspected of coming from a sickly port, or having, or having had during the voyage, sickness on board, as he may judge expedient, and to report the facts and his conclusions to the Mayor. Vessels subject to quarantine shall, under the authority and direction of the superintendent, remain at quarantine at least thirty days after their arrival, and at least twenty days after their cargoes shall have been discharged, and shall perform such further quarantine as the superintendent shall prescribe, unless sooner discharged by his written permission. But nothing in this ordinance contained shall prevent any vessel arriving at quarantine from again going to sea, or returning to the port of departure before breaking bulk.

9. The superintendent shall have power to direct the location, within the quarantine anchorage ground, of any vessels subject to quarantine regulations; to cause any vessel under quarantine, when he shall judge it necessary for the purification of the vessel or her cargo, to discharge the cargo at the quarantine ground, or some other suitable place out of the city; to cause any such vessel, her cargo, bedding, and the clothing of persons on board, to be ventilated, cleansed and purified, in such manner and during such time as he may direct; and if he shall judge it necessary to prevent infection or contagion, to destroy any portion of such cargo, bedding or clothing which he may deem incapable of purification; to prohibit and prevent all persons arriving in vessels subject to quarantine from leaving quarantine until fifteen days after the sailing of their vessels from their ports of departure, and fifteen days after the last case of pestilential or infectious disease that shall have occurred on board shall have terminated, and ten days after their arrival at quarantine, unless sooner discharged by his written permission; to permit the cargo of any vessel under quarantine, or any portion thereof, when he shall judge the same free from infection, to be conveyed to the city of Richmond, or to such place as may be designated by the Mayor, after having reported in writing to the Mayor the condition of said cargo and his intention to grant such permission; but such permission shall be inoperative without the written approval of the Mayor; to permit the cargo of any vessel under quarantine, or any part thereof, if in his opinion it will not be dangerous to the public health, to be shipped for exportation by sea: but the vessel receiving the same shall not approach nearer than the lower edge of Rocketts bar, without the written permission of the Mayor.

10. Every vessel performing quarantine shall be designated by colors fixed in a conspicuous part of her main shrouds.

11. No lighters shall be employed to load or unload vessels at quarantine, without permission of the superintendent, and subject to such restrictions as he shall impose.

12. All passengers under quarantine who shall be unable to maintain themselves, shall be provided for by the master of the vessel in which they shall have arrived; and if the master shall

omit to provide for them, they shall be maintained on shore, at the expense of such vessel; and such vessel shall not be permitted to leave quarantine until such expense shall have been repaid.

13. The master of any vessel released from quarantine and arriving at the city of Richmond, shall, immediately after such arrival, deliver the permit of the superintendent to the Mayor, or to such person as he shall direct; but such vessel shall not approach nearer than the lower edge of Rocketts bar, without the written permission of the Mayor.

14. No person, without the permission of the superintendent, shall enter within the enclosure of the quarantine ground, or go on board of, or have any communication or intercourse or dealing with, any vessel under quarantine. Any person going on board a vessel under quarantine, without license from the superintendent, may be compelled to remain there, in the same manner as he might have been if he had been one of the crew of the vessel.*

*NOTE. By the Statute Code, ch. 16, § 14, p. 398, any person violating quarantine regulations shall forfeit not less than five nor more than five hundred dollars.

TITLE 6.

POLICE.

CHAPTER XXXII.

CONCERNING THE POLICE FORCE OF THE CITY.

1. The Mayor of the city for the time being is and he is hereby declared to be the head of the police of the city, and subject to such provisions and regulations as the Council may prescribe by ordinance—the said police shall be subject to his authority.

2. The police force of the city shall consist of one officer, who shall be styled "The Chief of Police," six or more "officers of police," who shall be designated as first, second, third, fourth, fifth, sixth, &c., officers of police, and they shall rank in the order of their numbers, beginning at the first, who shall be first in rank; and one hundred policemen, from whom there shall be appointed ten sergeants: and the Mayor may, when from peculiar circumstances he shall believe it to be necessary, increase the policemen to any extent the public necessities may require: provided, he shall report any such increase to the next meeting of the Council. The said officers of police and sergeants shall, in criminal cases, have the same powers, perform the same duties, receive the same fees, and be subject to the same penalties as are prescribed by law for constables; and two of said officers of police shall reside in each ward of the city.

3. The city shall be divided into three police districts by the limits of the wards of the city; but these districts may be altered from time to time by the Chief of Police, under the control of the Mayor. The present watchhouses at the First and Second Markets shall continue to be so, and that at the First Market shall be designated as the first, and that at the Second Market shall be designated as the second watchhouse; and there shall be a place designated as "Police Headquarters." Under like control the Chief of Police shall divide the districts into beats, and may alter their limits.

4. Subject to the orders and authority of the Mayor, the Chief of Police shall be the chief executive officer of police, and shall have control of it and of its officers and members and of all persons at any time employed in it; and he may at any time, with the approval of the Mayor, make rules and regulations for the government of the police, not inconsistent with the ordinances of the city; he shall report to the Mayor every day all that he is bound to notice in discharge of his duty, the members

of police he may have suspended, and the men unfit for duty, and make to him a report upon the reports of the officers of police; he shall have the general charge of the peace and good order of the city, and see to the observance of the ordinances of the city and acts of assembly relating to it, and in any emergency he may direct the whole police force, or any part thereof, to any place in the city he may deem proper.

5. The Chief of Police shall daily assign two officers of police and two sergeants to duty in each district; and he shall distribute the policemen in such proportions as may seem proper, among said districts, after deducting a proper number, including two sergeants, to remain at the two watchhouses for sudden emergencies; and he shall make such regulations for a proper system of relief (other than dividing the police into two portions, one for day and one for night), that at all times during the day-watches one-fourth of the police force shall be on duty, and at all times during the night-watches three-fourths of the police force shall be on duty. One of the sergeants not assigned to districts shall remain at each of the watchhouses, in command of the same and of the policemen left there, and shall receive and take charge of all persons arrested by the police and delivered to him at his watchhouse.

6. If the Chief of Police is, for any cause, unable to attend to the duty of assigning the officers of police and policemen to their districts, the first police officer or the one highest in grade present shall perform the duty. And if an officer of police is unable to attend to his duties or is absent, the Chief of Police may appoint one of the sergeants to perform the duties.

7. The Chief of Police shall fix the periods of the day at which each of the two officers of police assigned to a district, shall enter on duty; and the officer of police on duty shall, during his hours of service, have the general charge of the district and of its police arrangements; and each officer of police shall keep a muster roll of the police of his district assigned to him, and call it at the hours of relief, and shall deliver it to the Chief of Police; he shall report in writing to the Chief of Police any delinquency on the part of any policemen that shall come to his knowledge, and any excuses made by any policeman

for absence from duty, or the unfitness of any member for his office; and any charge that may be made against a member. And with the assistance of his sergeant he shall keep a book in which he shall enter all arrests, disposal of prisoners, nuisances reported, ordinances enforced, complaints and applications of citizens, and other police matters, and he shall deliver daily with his muster roll a copy of such entries during his hours of service of the preceding day.

8. When necessary, the policemen shall, by means of rattles or otherwise, summon to their assistance other policemen from adjacent districts. When a person is apprehended by policemen in a district other than that in which there is a watchhouse, they shall proceed with him to the next district in the direction of a watchhouse, and by means of rattles or otherwise, summon the policemen of that district, and transfer him to such policemen, who shall, in like manner, convey and transfer him, till delivered at the watchhouse.

9. Each officer of police shall report to the Chief of Police every nuisance or obstruction that he may find in any drain, gutter or other part of a street or alley, or that he has reason to believe or is informed is in any house, or upon any land in the city; and shall execute the orders of the Mayor in regard to any such nuisances or obstructions. Each of them shall, when in his opinion repairs are required, without delay report the same, if they be required to a street or public alley, to the Superintendent of Streets; and if to a pipe, hydrant, or other fixtures of the water works, or any fixture of the gas works, in a street or public alley, to the respective Superintendents of such works. Each of them shall report to the Chief of Police every violation of any ordinance of the city that he has reason to believe, or is informed has been committed; and make such other reports, and give such other notices and information as may be prescribed by any ordinance, or be useful in the enforcement thereof.

10. The whole of the police shall endeavor to prevent the commission of offences in the city, and to preserve the good order and peace thereof, and secure its inhabitants from personal violence, and their property from loss and injury. They shall

earnestly endeavor, when any offence is committed in the city, to detect and arrest the offender, and strive to enforce all ordinances prescribing any fine or punishment for, and all acts of assembly relating to, offences in the city or the police thereof. Although an officer or policeman be applied to when it is not his time for regular duty, he shall, upon application, whether in the day or night, do all that the emergency requires.

11. It shall be the duty of the Chief of Police, at least twice in each week, to explore in person all of the streets and alleys of the city, and to give information and prosecute for the violation of the laws of the state and ordinances of the city concerning any matter of police regulation, and by all legal means to endeavor to enforce the same; and he shall attend at the Police Headquarters at sunrise, where and when each of the officers of police shall report to him the condition of his district during the previous twenty-four hours, and especially shall report all offences therein committed either against the laws of the state or the ordinances of the city, and the names, if known, of the persons committing the same; and whether said offenders were arrested; and the names of all persons who he may deem to be material witnesses against such offenders. He shall also report to said Chief of Police all misconduct or neglect of duty by any policeman under his command.

12. The Mayor, annually in May, or as soon thereafter as practicable, shall nominate to the Council persons from among whom the Council may appoint the Chief of Police and the police officers hereinbefore provided for. Any police officer appointed by the Council may be suspended from his office until the next meeting of the Council, by the Mayor, and may be removed at any time by the Council. A vacancy occurring during the year in any office to which there was an appointment on such nomination, may be filled in like manner. The number of persons nominated by the Mayor to any meeting of the Council, for any office of police, shall be at least three times as great as the number of offices then proposed by him to be filled; and an appointment to an office may be from amongst any nominated for it, or nominated for any other police office to be filled. If the Council shall by resolution decline to appoint to an office

from amongst the persons nominated, the Mayor shall make a further nomination to it of at least three other persons.

13. The Mayor shall appoint the policemen and sergeants, and they may be discharged by the Mayor or Council, or by the Chief of Police, when he sees cause for prompt action, subject to the approval of the Mayor. The policemen, as well as the officers of police, shall reside within the city: and no person shall be appointed a policeman who cannot read and write.

14. The Mayor shall exercise a general superintendence and control over the entire police, pursuant to the ordinances of the city, and shall, from time to time, make report to the Council of the state of the police, with such suggestions for its improvement as he may see fit; and no police officer or policeman shall be absent from the city without his leave.

15. The Attorney of the city shall, when required by the Mayor, prepare forms in respect to any matter connected with the police of the city, of which the Mayor may have blanks printed, at the expense of the city, for the use of the police.

16. The salaries and compensation of the police officers and privates shall be such as the Council may by resolution from time to time prescribe; but said salaries and compensation shall be fixed in advance for a certain period, not exceeding three months, and during such period shall not be diminished. The salaries and compensation shall be payable monthly; and any policeman prevented by sickness from doing service, shall receive the same pay upon his producing the certificate of a practicing physician that he was sick.

17. No officer appointed to any office under this ordinance shall receive from the city, for services in such or any other office, any other compensation than is herein mentioned. And every policeman shall upon oath account for and pay over daily to the officer under whose command he is at the time, all costs that he may receive, and all sums he may be entitled to as informer, with all money to which the city may be entitled; and the officers of police shall in like manner, with their daily reports to the Chief of Police, account for and pay over to him all such moneys and all the moneys received by him to which the city is entitled. And the Chief of Police shall in the first four days of

every month, in like manner, account for and pay into the treasury of the city all such moneys. And no member of the police shall receive a gratuity from any person whatever. But he may receive any reward which may be advertised for the apprehension of criminals, or which may be offered by the executive of the state or by the municipal authorities of the city.

18. The Chief of Police, with the concurrence of the Mayor, shall fix on the uniform, badges and number which shall be worn by the officers of police, the sergeants and policemen, which shall always be worn by them when they appear in public, whether they are on duty or not; and the badges and number shall be furnished at the expense of the city. And every person applying at the watchhouses, shall be entitled to have the name of any person wearing the particular number that the applicant may name. And every policeman shall be armed ordinarily with a baton not less than twenty-two inches long and one and three-quarters inch thick, at the expense of the city; and in cases of emergency, with revolvers and other suitable weapons; and the Chief of Police shall procure a suitable quantity of such weapons with which he may arm the police, furnishing them also with badges; and each person shall give his receipt for such weapons and badges as he may receive, which shall remain the property of the city. And the Mayor shall have authority, if he thinks proper, to provide a suitable number of muskets for each watch-house wherewith to arm the police in cases of great emergency.

19. If any person except a policeman shall publicly wear any such uniform, badge or number, as may be worn by a policeman, he shall forfeit and pay for such offence, not less than one nor more than twenty dollars.

20. It shall not be lawful for any officer or policeman to be employed to attend at any theatre or other place of public amusement or entertainment.

21. If any member of the police shall be found to frequent any of the public houses or bar rooms where spirituous or fermented liquors are vended, except in his official capacity, and if it shall be ascertained that any of them are in the habit of using intoxicating liquors to excess, it shall be sufficient cause for the immediate dismissal of such offending member.

22. The policeman on duty at night in a district shall light the street lamps, and extinguish them at such times as he may be directed by the proper agent of the committee on light.

23. If any person shall resist any police officer or policeman in the discharge of his duty, he shall pay a fine of not less than ten nor more than twenty dollars. And if any white person shall fail or refuse to aid or assist a police officer or policeman, when called upon so to do by such officer or policeman when in the discharge of his duty, he shall be fined not less than five nor more than twenty dollars.

24. There shall be a police contingent fund of twenty-five hundred dollars, to be designated the secret service fund. The Mayor may, from time to time, draw on the said fund for such sums as he may think necessary in detecting and arresting offenders, and rendering the police efficient; and shall keep a book specifying the sums drawn, and for what purpose used; which book, on request, he shall exhibit to the chairman of the committee on police.

25. To the committee on police, without any special order for that purpose, shall stand referred all matters and statements required by this ordinance to be made to the Council, or any other matter specially reported by the Mayor concerning the police.

CHAPTER XXXIII.

CONCERNING THE FIRE DEPARTMENT OF THE CITY.

SEC.

1. Of the supervision and control of the committee.
2. Of what officers, men and engines the Fire Department shall consist; how appointed; term of service; oath of office; who shall constitute the Board of Control; how Fire Department kept up.
3. Engines, &c., provided by the Council. No other fire company to be organized in the city or keep engine, &c.; penalty for so doing.
4. Meetings of the Board of Control; to keep a journal; who clerk; their powers and duties.
5. Who to command Fire Brigade, or company; officer in command to control and inspect engines, &c.; order repairs; what his powers during inspections and fires; shall report to the Council in May; what.
6. What and when commanders shall report to principal engineer; what he shall inspect and what prevent.
7. By whom person absent from duty when there is a fire to be reported; reports to be returned monthly; fines to be imposed; absence of principal engineer to be reported to the Council.

1. All the powers and duties hereinafter vested in or imposed upon the Fire Department, or any officer or member thereof, shall be exercised and performed under the supervision and control of the committee on the Fire Department; and all engine houses, engines, apparatus and other property connected with the Fire Department of the city, shall, in like manner, be under the supervision and control of the said committee.

2. The Fire Department of the city of Richmond shall consist of a Chief Engineer, four commanders, four foremen, two enginemen, two helpers, two hostlers and seventy-two firemen. The Chief Engineer and the commanders shall be appointed by the Council biennially, in the month of May. The commanders shall be numbered by the Council, and shall rank according to their numbers, the highest in rank being number one. They and the Chief Engineer shall hold office until their successors qualify, and before acting, shall take the following oaths: The Chief Engineer shall make oath that he will discharge the duties of his office to the best of his abilities; and each commander shall take the same oath, and also that he will obey the lawful orders of his superior officers. The Chief Engineer and commanders shall constitute a "Board of Control," and shall immediately after their qualification, appoint four foremen, two enginemen, two helpers and two hostlers, who shall hold their positions until their successors are appointed. The commanders, under such regulations as the Board of Control may prescribe, shall enlist seventy-two firemen for general service in the Fire Department, for the term of two years, who shall sign articles of enlistment in the form prescribed by the Board of Control.

Before acting, the foremen, enginemen, helpers, hostlers and firemen shall take the oaths prescribed for commanders; and certificates of all oaths under this chapter, taken before any person qualified to administer oaths, shall be deposited among the records of the Board of Control. The Fire Department shall be kept up to its full force by enlistment and appointments made as aforesaid, whenever vacancies occur.

3. All engine houses, horses, engines, hose and apparatus, and all hooks and ladders and all other instruments for the extinguishment of fires, for the use of the Fire Department, shall be provided by the Council. And it shall not be lawful for any persons to organize a company or association within the city for the purpose of acting as a fire company, or to keep within the limits of the city any fire engine or reel, with a view to act as such company or association. And every person appearing in any street of the city as a member of such company or association for the purpose of acting as a fire company, or bringing into any street of the city such fire engine or reel, shall, for every such offence, pay a fine not exceeding twenty dollars.

4. The Board of Control shall meet once a month, at which meeting the officer present highest in rank shall preside. Three members shall constitute a quorum; and all questions shall be determined by a majority of voices. They shall keep a journal, and submit it when required to the Council; and the clerk in the Chamberlain's office shall be the clerk of the Board of Control. They shall assign a commander, a foreman and a proper complement of men to each company, and station the companies in the several wards as they think best. They shall supply each company with the necessary engine, hose and apparatus; keep them in repair; prescribe a uniform, and make all needful rules and regulations for the Fire Department, consistent with the laws of the state and ordinances of the city, and perform all other duties imposed on them by ordinance. The system of fire alarms may be prescribed by the Board of Control.

5. The Chief Engineer, or in his absence, the officer highest in rank, shall command the Fire Department. Each commander, or in his absence, his foreman, shall command his own company. The officer in command of the department shall have the control

of the engine houses, engines, apparatus and all other property of the Fire Department. He shall inspect the same once in every week, order indispensable repairs, and report them to the Board of Control, and see that everything is kept in a condition for efficient service. He shall have semi-annual inspections of the apparatus and the whole department. During fires and inspections he shall control all fire plugs, maintain order among the firemen and bystanders, preserve property, command both city and fire police, note and report to the Mayor all violations of law, or of the city ordinances, and do all things proper for the efficient operation of the department He shall report annually to the Council in the month of May the names and ages of the firemen, the number and localities of the fires which have occurred during the year, the causes thereof, if they can be ascertained, the names of the owners of the property destroyed or injured, the amount of such destruction or injury, the amount of insurance, the name of the insurance companies, and such other matters touching its operations and organization as he shall think proper.

6. Each commander shall, under such regulations as the Board of Control may prescribe, report monthly to the Chief Engineer the names and residences of his firemen, the condition of his engine house, engine, hose and apparatus, specifying such repairs as he thinks necessary or desirable. He shall inspect the engine house, engine and apparatus at least once in every day, and cause the same to be kept clean and in good condition. He shall report to the Mayor all persons loitering in or about the engine house. He shall report to the Chief Engineer all misconduct among his men, and shall prevent minors and colored persons from running with the engine, taking hold of any part of the apparatus, or meddling with the same in any way. He shall report all such persons to the Mayor, and if he knowingly permit such meddling he shall be fined by the Mayor five dollars for every offence.

7. The commander of each company, or if he be absent, the foreman, or if he be absent, the policeman of the company, shall report to the Chief Engineer, immediately after a fire, every officer or fireman who shall not be on duty in a reasonable time after an alarm of fire is first given. The Chief Engineer shall

return monthly to the Board of Control a list of such reports, and the Board of Control shall impose the following fines, unless sufficient excuses are rendered: Two dollars on each commander, one dollar and a half on each foreman, three dollars on each engineman, two dollars on each helper or hostler, and one dollar on each fireman. They shall certify the same quarterly to the Auditor, and he shall deduct such fines from the pay of the officers and men. If the Chief Engineer be absent from fires or inspections, without excuse, the Board of Control shall report him to the Council.

8. The Chief Engineer and commanders may be suspended by the committee until the next meeting of the Council, and may be removed by the Council, and the other members of the department may be discharged by the committee or by the Board of Control at any time.

9. If any officer or other member of the department be insubordinate, disorderly or negligent, he may be fined by the Board of Control, not exceeding ten dollars; which fine shall be certified and deducted from his pay as above prescribed.

10. If any person interfere with a fireman in the discharge of his duty, or loiter about the engine houses, or if any minor or other person meddle with the engines, hose or apparatus, as hereinbefore mentioned, he shall be fined by the Mayor not less than five nor more than twenty dollars.

11. The Chief Engineer shall cause each commander to detail annually one or more men for police duty, and shall assign one to the command of the squad. They shall constitute the fire police; and it shall be their special duty to maintain order during fires; to keep the ground clear by ropes across the streets or otherwise, to protect property from fire and pillage; to arrest and commit to the station houses all persons who persist in interfering with the firemen after due admonition to desist therefrom; to report to the officer in command all violations of law or of the ordinances of the city, and to execute his orders. Each policeman while on duty shall wear a badge on his breast.

12. The police of the city in the neighborhood of a fire shall assist the fire police, and during fires obey the orders of the officer in command of the Fire Department. They shall carry

the names and residences of the officers of the department in their district, and shall call them on an alarm of fire at night.

13. The enginemen, helpers and hostlers attached to the steam fire engines shall not engage in any other occupation, except by the special permission of the Board of Control.

14. The officer in command of the department in time of riot or insurrection shall, on the requisition of the Mayor, assemble his department and assist the police of the city in restoring order or quelling insurrection.

15. All accounts for work done shall be examined by the Board of Control and certified to the committee on the Fire Department, who shall examine, and if they allow them, certify the same to the Auditor; or if they think proper they may report such accounts to the Council, with a recommendation either that they be allowed or rejected.

16. The fire engines shall have no names but the letter of the company; and each company shall be designated by some letter of the alphabet, and by no other name.

17. The word "firemen," wherever used in this chapter, shall apply equally to the members of the hook and ladder company, and the phrase "engine house" shall apply to the house in which their apparatus is kept.

18. Hereafter no person under twenty-one years of age, and who does not list for state or city taxes, shall be eligible to membership in the department; and hereafter no person shall be elected a member thereof unless he is a citizen of Richmond; nor shall any member be allowed to remove his residence beyond the corporate limits of the city.

19. Upon occasion of any alarm of fire, whenever any fire engine or hose or ladder carriage or apparatus belonging thereto shall be passing along any of the streets of the city, it shall be the duty of the drivers of all vehicles to give the way nearest the middle of the street for the unobstructed passage thereof; and any driver of any vehicle failing so to do, shall be fined not less than ten nor more than twenty-five dollars.

20. The Chief Engineer or the officer in command of the Fire Department, whenever it is reported to him or comes to his knowledge, that any building is in danger of being fired, either

from carelessness of the owner or occupant, defective chimney or other cause, shall, if he thinks there is good reason so to do, give notice to said owners or occupants in writing, to correct the same within twelve hours thereafter; and if it is not done within the time specified, he shall report the case to the Mayor.

CHAPTER XXXIV.

CONCERNING STREETS.

SEC.

1. Engineer, Superintendent of streets and Overseer of city hands appointed by the Council; when.
2. Committee on streets generally, when to convene; what a quorum; who may call a meeting.
3. They may purchase materials and hire hands; who to manage hands; how money paid.
4. They shall recommend repairs and improvements of streets and culverts; when two-thirds vote of Council necessary for repairs.
5. Ward committee to view streets, &c., and direct repairs in their ward.
6. Their orders for the execution of work to be in writing, and recorded.
7. What officer to make a contract for work; contract to be filed with Auditor.
8. Who to superintend work; his duty.
9. How work authorized by committee paid for.
10. Grade of streets; how made; how altered; how certified.
11. How corners and lines of streets designated.
12. When owners of lots shall connect with culverts; what he shall pay; how collected.
13. Culverts; who to grant leave to enter them.
14. How leave to enter a culvert obtained.
15. On what terms culvert may be entered.
16. Penalty for injuring or obstructing a culvert.
17. Sidewalks; width thereof.
18. Cellar doors; how constructed. How leave obtained to use sidewalk.
19. Owner of house to pay a tax for.
20. Vault under street; who may allow it, and how constructed.
21. Vaults and cellars to be properly made and kept in order; penalty for failure.
22. What sidewalks to be paved whole width.
23. What to be paved four feet width.
24. When owner of lot paving sidewalk may be paid; how much, and how paid.
25. Flagstones; at what crossings to be laid down.
26. Flagstones to be laid down where private alleys and stables; width.
27. Who to pay for them; how collected.
28. When work to be done in a street, &c.; how permission had to deposit materials therein, or obstructed.
29. In building what part and how long street may be used to deposit materials.
30. What signs may be put up; how much of sidewalk merchant may occupy, and how; when auction in street allowed; when not.
31. Who to keep open paved gutter.
32. What dirt, &c., from lot may be put in street; how long to remain.
33. Filth, &c., or nuisance not to be put or remain in street; penalty therefor; what not nuisance; when railroad car not.
34. Post for awnings may be erected on sidewalk; of what description.
35. Horse racks may be erected in front of each tenement; of what description.
36. Who to give information of nuisance.
37. Engines, &c., not to exceed rate of four miles an hour; when to ring bell.
38. Horses to wagon, &c., to walk; horse racing and fast driving in street prohibited.
39. Horse not to be tied or driven on sidewalk.
40. Driver not to lock wheels or crack whip; to hold reins in hand.
41. How vehicles to pass each other; where not to stop.
42. Officers may order vehicles to be removed.
43. When offender may be arrested without warrant.

1. At the first meeting of the Council after its annual organization, or as soon thereafter as practicable, the Council shall appoint an Engineer of the city, a Superintendent of streets, and an Overseer of city hands, who shall go into office on the first day of May and continue therein for one year and until a successor is appointed and qualifies, unless sooner removed.

2. The Committee on streets generally shall convene as soon as may be after their appointment, and as often thereafter as they deem proper. There shall be present a majority of them to constitute a meeting, and of that majority there shall be at least one from each ward. The chairman, or any three of the committee, may at any time call a meeting of the committee.

3. The committee on streets generally shall cause to be hired for the city such number of hands as they may be authorized to hire by resolution of the Council. They may cause to be purchased such materials, horses, mules, carts and tools as they may deem proper for the work in which said hands may be employed, and take such measures as they may deem necessary to have such hands furnished with proper food, clothing and lodging, and to have proper stableage and provender for the said horses and mules and a suitable shelter for the carts, gear and tools. To these ends bonds with security, payable to the city, in such penalty and with such conditions as they may deem fit, may be required and taken from any person with whom they may contract, and such bond shall be filed with the Auditor. The hands and other things, when so purchased and hired, shall be under the immediate management of the Overseer of the city hands, who shall not be the person with whom any contract shall

be made under this section. Any sum or sums of money payable for any such purpose or hiring, or upon any contract made by the committee on streets generally, under and by virtue of this section, shall be paid upon a draft on the Auditor, stating the amount to be paid and for what given, signed by the chairman of the committee of streets generally, and attested by the clerk.

4. The committee on streets generally shall, by report in writing, attested by their clerk, recommend from time to time to the City Council to order such repairs and improvements to the streets, and the construction and repairs of such culverts or sewers of the city as the said committee may think should be ordered by the Council. No order for any such repairs, improvements or construction, not so recommended by the committee on streets generally, attested as aforesaid, shall be passed by the Council, unless by a vote of two-thirds of the members present.

5. The committee on streets for each ward, or a majority of them, shall, as soon after their appointment as practicable, view the streets and public alleys in or bounding their several wards, and note such repairs and improvements in the same as they, or a majority of them, may deem necessary. The said ward committee, or a majority of them, may order such repairs and improvements in the streets and public alleys of their respective wards as they, or a majority of them, shall think proper, and may direct the Superintendent of streets to cause the same to be made under their direction: provided that the sum paid for such repairs and improvements, for each ward, shall not exceed the rate of one hundred dollars per month in any one year; and provided, also, that there shall not be paid in any one month, for such repairs and improvements, a sum exceeding one hundred dollars, with the addition thereto of such sum as might have been expended, under this section, in the previous months of the same year, but which was not expended.

6. Every order by the committee on streets of a ward, for the execution of work, shall be in writing, and signed by them, or a majority of them, and it shall be recorded by the Superintendent of streets, and the record thereof read by him to the committee on streets generally at their next meeting.

7. Contracts for any culvert, bridge or masonry, shall be made and signed by the Engineer, upon being authorized by the committee on streets generally. And contracts for grading or filling up streets; for paving or repairing streets or sidewalks; for putting down curbstone or stone crossings, and the like, shall be made and signed by the Superintendent of streets, upon being authorized by the committee on streets generally, or the committee on streets for the ward, when these last have authority to act. Every such contract shall contain such provisions for security of the city as the committee authorizing it may direct; and no payment shall be made on any such contract until it is filed with the Auditor.

8. Work contracted for shall be superintended by the officer who makes the contract for it. Whether contracted for or not, the officer having to superintend it shall take care that it conforms to the established grade and is in all respects properly executed. He shall especially take care that every drain, gutter or culvert, the making of which is under his superintendence, be so made that no obstruction shall exist in any part thereof to the passage of water, or any other thing intended to flow therein, nor any nuisance arise from the manner of its construction.

9. So much as is payable for work done on any contract authorized by the committee on streets generally, shall be paid upon a draft on the Auditor, stating the amount to be paid, and for what; which draft shall be on the back of an estimate made by the Engineer or Superintendent of streets, as the case may be, and shall be signed by the chairman of said committee, after examining and approving said estimate. So much of the work done by order of the committee on streets for any ward, shall be paid upon a draft on the Auditor, signed by the chairman or a majority of the committee for a ward; which draft shall be upon the back of an estimate made by the Superintendent of streets or Engineer, as the case may be, stating the amount, and for what. Whatever else is payable for anything the committee on streets generally are authorized to have done, shall be paid on a draft signed by the chairman of said committee and attested by the clerk: provided, however, that there shall not be paid by the Auditor, under this section, more than forty thousand dollars during any

fiscal year, unless at the end of any fiscal year there shall appear to be a surplus from the revenue of the said year, after setting apart the sinking fund required by the charter, and paying whatever else is required within such year for other purposes than the redemption of the principal of the certificates of permanent debt; in which case the Council, by resolution, may, for the year next after that in which there is such surplus, make an addition to the said forty thousand dollars of such sum as it deems expedient, not exceeding the amount of such surplus.

10. The Engineer shall report to the committee on streets generally, and the said committee to the Council, such grade or grades of the streets and public alleys of the city as have been, or in his opinion, or in the opinion of said committee, ought to be established, with such profiles thereof as may be deemed proper by himself, or as he may be directed by said committee to make. The Council may act on the grade of such part of a street or alley as is reported by said committee, and may establish for such part whatever grade it may deem proper. No grade so established shall afterwards be altered, unless directed by the Council, after a previous report from the committee on streets generally in respect to its expediency. Any person intending hereafter to build or erect any house or other structure upon the line of any street or public alley, shall first obtain from the Engineer of the city, or in his absence or inability to act, from the Superintendent of streets, a certificate in writing of the line and adopted grade of such street at the place where such house or structure is to be erected; and it shall be the duty of the Engineer or Superintendent of streets to file in the Auditor's office a duplicate of the said certificate. If any person shall hereafter build or erect, or attempt to build or erect, any house or other structure upon the line of any such street or alley, without having first obtained such certificate, he shall be fined not less than twenty nor more than one hundred dollars.

11. To designate the corners, widths, lines and the established grades of streets, there shall be put or erected stones or posts at such place or places as the committee on streets generally may direct for that purpose.

12. The owners of houses on lots which, according to the

plan of the city, adjoin a street along which a culvert has been or shall be built by the city, shall form a connection from their lots, respectively, with said culvert or some other culvert built by the city; and such connection may be directly with the city culvert or through the culvert of some other person having a direct connection with a city culvert. And every such owner of a house shall pay to the Chamberlain one dollar and twenty-five cents for every foot that his house fronts on a street. Where culverts have been built as aforesaid, or as soon as a culvert so built along a street is completed, the Superintendent of streets shall return to the Auditor a statement of the amount due from each owner of a house under this section, and the Auditor shall make out a bill therefor, and place the same in the hands of the Collector of city taxes, who shall proceed to collect the same, and shall account therefor as in the case of water and gas bills, deducting therefrom a commission of five per centum. And his official bond shall embrace the same. In any case to which this section applies, the owner of the house shall proceed as is provided in the fourteenth and fifteenth sections; and if he fails for three months to make the connection as required in this section, he shall be fined not less than ten nor more than twenty dollars for every ten days he may fail to do so.

13. In cases to which the preceding section applies the Superintendent of streets shall, and in other cases he, or if he refuse, the committee on streets generally, may, by writing, grant permission to any person to make from his lot a connection directly with any culvert or sewer which has been or shall be constructed at the expense of the city, or a connection indirectly therewith, through or by means of any culvert of a party having direct connection with a culvert or sewer constructed at the expense of the city.

14. Persons applying for leave to enter a culvert shall file with the said Superintendent or committee on streets generally, a statement in writing, setting forth on which and between what streets they wish to connect with a culvert or sewer, and on which and between what streets their respective houses front, and the number of feet that the house of each applicant fronts on said street. If the permission be granted, the said statement,

with such permission, shall be filed with the Auditor. Such permission shall be of no effect until the applicant shall pay to the Chamberlain one dollar and twenty-five cents for every foot that his house fronts, as aforesaid, unless the distance from the point of connection with his house to the point of connection with the culvert or sewer of the city be as much as one side of a square; and if the said distance be that much, then one dollar, unless the said distance be as much as two sides of a square; and if the said distance shall be that much, then seventy-five cents. Any person who, without obtaining such permission and making such payment shall make, or have any such connection as is mentioned in the next preceding section, shall pay a fine of not less than ten nor more than fifty dollars; and every ten days that such connection shall continue without such permission shall be a distinct offence.

15. When a person obtains such permission, and makes such payment, he shall make his connection of brick, stone or iron, in a substantial, safe and workmanlike manner, and so make it as to do no injury to the water or gas pipes of the city. His connection with a culvert or sewer of the city shall be made at such point and in such manner as the Superintendent of streets may direct; and the person making it shall forthwith, after it is made, cover the culvert or sewer with earth, as it was before the connection, and in ten days after the connection, shall have such pavement or curbstone as was injured or removed (to make such connection) so repaired or restored as to be in as good order as it was before. Any person failing to comply with this section in any respect, shall pay a fine of not less than five nor more than twenty dollars; and every ten days that such failure shall continue shall be a distinct offence.

16. If a person shall, either in a street or upon a lot, put any stone, brick or other solid thing, into any culvert or sewer, or shall in any way whatever injure, impair or obstruct any culvert or sewer, or a fixture thereof, he shall pay a fine of not less than five nor more than twenty dollars.

17. Except where it is or may be otherwise specially provided, upon each side of every street, which is thirty feet wide or more, there shall be a sidewalk of the following width, to wit: five

feet, if the street be less than forty feet wide; seven feet, if it be forty and less than fifty feet wide; twelve feet, if it be sixty and less than one hundred feet; and eighteen feet, if it be one hundred feet wide or more: provided, that where a curbstone or a sidewalk has already been laid down, the same may remain until altered by a resolution of the Council.

18. Doors to a cellar shall not extend on a sidewalk more than five feet; and whenever a cellar door is made or repaired (whether the cellar be old or new) the construction thereof shall be such that the door or doors, when closed, shall be level with the sidewalk. On a street less than fifty feet wide there shall not be used any part of the sidewalk as an entrance to a cellar, unless by resolution of the Council, and then the doors shall be so made and kept in such manner as the resolution may prescribe. And in all cases in which any person shall desire to occupy any portion of a street or public alley for the purpose of getting into a cellar or basement, or into a house, he shall apply to the Council by petition in writing, and file therewith a plan showing accurately how much of the walkway he proposes to occupy; and the petition and plan shall be referred to the Engineer of the city, who shall examine the premises and report fully to the Council everything which in his opinion should influence the judgment of the Council in their action upon the application. And this report with the petition shall be submitted to the committee on streets generally, who shall also examine the premises, and report to the Council their opinion whether the application should be granted or refused.

19. Any person owning a house in the use of which any part of a street or public alley is occupied by the permission of the Council for a vault, entrance to a basement or cellar, or to the house, or for any other permanent purpose, shall pay annually therefor to the city a rent of five cents for each superficial foot. And the Superintendent of streets shall measure the same and make return thereof to the Assessor of city taxes, showing the name of the owner of the house; and the Assessor shall charge the same to the owner as a part of the taxes on said house.

20. The committee on streets for the ward in which a vault is desired under a sidewalk may, by writing, grant permission to a

person to have the same made; and the person obtaining the permission shall file the same with the Superintendent of streets within ten days. Such person shall have it made with a substantial brick or stone arch, which shall extend from the front wall of the house before which the vault is, no nearer than two feet six inches to where the inner edge of the curbstone is or will be when laid down. The openings to the vault shall not be more than eighteen inches in diameter, and shall be near the said line, unless, in the opinion of the Superintendent of streets, that is impracticable. It shall be level with the sidewalk, as it then is, but may afterwards be removed, if necessary, when the grade of the street is established or changed. It shall be secured with a cast iron covering, fixed in a solid frame of stone or iron, so laid that the upper part of the frame shall be as nearly level with the pavement as it can be, consistently with the turning the water from the opening; and it shall be secured with such bolt or weight as the Superintendent of streets may direct; and the person obtaining permission to make a vault shall have the same completed, under the direction of the Superintendent of streets, within thirty days, unless further time is allowed by the committee for the ward.

21. If any cellar or vault heretofore made conform neither with this ordinance nor with the ordinances in force at the time of the passage hereof, or if hereafter, when a cellar or vault is made or repaired, the same be not such as is required by this ordinance, the owner of the house to which the cellar or vault is attached shall pay a fine of not less than ten nor more than twenty dollars; and every day that the cellar or vault shall not be as hereby required shall be a distinct offence. And if the occupier of a house to which a vault is attached suffer the same to be open or unfastened at any time other than when it is opened for putting something therein, or shall then suffer it to be open or unfastened longer than is absolutely necessary for that purpose, or if the owner or occupier of a house to which a vault or cellar is attached, shall fail, in any respect, to keep in safe and proper order the opening to such vault, or the doors to such cellar (whether made heretofore or hereafter), he shall pay a like fine. The suffering a vault to be opened or unfastened as

aforesaid, or the failure to keep in safe and proper order such opening or doors, shall be deemed a distinct offence each day or night thereof.

22. A sidewalk on any street whereof the carriage-way has been or shall be paved in whole or in part, may be paved in whole or in part (though a sidewalk on such street shall have been paved in whole or in part by the owner or otherwise), or if the whole or any part thereof require repaving, it may be repaved in whole or in part, with good paving brick, by order of the committee on streets for the ward in which such sidewalk is. But the expense of the paving done under this section, in each ward, shall not, in any one fiscal year, exceed one thousand dollars.

23. The committee on streets for any ward may order any sidewalk in such ward, where the carriage-way is not all paved, to be paved to the extent of four feet of the width of the sidewalk; and when such four feet shall have been paved, may, at any time, order the same to be repaved or repaired; and upon such order, the Superintendent of streets shall cause the work to be done, and the Auditor shall pay therefor: provided, that the sum paid under this section for each ward shall not, in any one fiscal year, exceed five hundred dollars.

24. When the proprietor of a lot adjoining a sidewalk shall hereafter, at his own cost, pave such sidewalk or put down curbstone thereupon, in the manner approved by the committee on streets generally, a draft may, at such time as hereinafter mentioned, be drawn in favor of such proprietor, by the chairman of said committee; and the Auditor, on such draft, shall pay him such sum as may appear by an estimate of the Superintendent of streets, thereto annexed, to be at the date of said draft, the fair value to the city of said curbstone and of said pavement. The draft on account of the pavement shall not be drawn until the curbstone is put down, or the sidewalk paved on so much of the length of the street on which the sidewalk is, as is between the two nearest intersecting streets; and the committee on streets for the ward shall authorize the same to be drawn. What is paid under this section and the twenty-second and twenty-third sections of this chapter, in any fiscal year, for pavement in any one ward, shall not, altogether, exceed the

amount allowed by the said twenty-second and twenty-third sections.

25. At the intersections of streets of which the sidewalks are paved with brick, the Superintendent of streets shall, under the directions of the committee on streets for the ward, cause to be paved with granite flagstone, well imbedded in sand, suitable crossings to connect with the brick pavement. Any person desiring to cross any sidewalk to enter any private alley, on his or her premises, shall first obtain permission so to do from the committee on streets of the ward in which said property lies, and shall pave the sidewalk with granite flagstone, and shall cause the curbing to be placed upon a level with the top of the gutter. No person shall be allowed to place a bridge or any other obstruction in or over any paved gutter.

26. Upon every street of thirty feet wide or more, where alleys are opened, or carriage houses or stables erected in such manner as to make it necessary to cross the sidewalk with horses or vehicles, there shall be placed at such alley, or in front of the entrance to such lot, stable or carriage house, by the owner or occupier of the property, suitable flagstone crossings of the width of the brick pavement on said street.

27. When such use is made of the sidewalk, and the owner or occupier of the lot or premises neglects to have such flagstone crossings so placed, the committee on streets for the ward in which such lot or premises is, may, in writing, direct the Superintendent of streets to cause the work to be executed; and unless the cost thereof be paid by the owner or occupier of the lot or premises, the Superintendent of streets shall, annually, between the first day of February and the first day of June of each year, report in writing the respective amounts wherewith the owners are respectively chargeable, to the Assessor for the city, who shall, on the property in respect to which the owner is chargeable, assess (in addition to the other taxes thereon), for the year in which he receives such report, the amount with which such owner is reported chargeable.

28. When a person, by reason of an office under or contract with the city, has to do work in a street or public alley, or on any property of the city, there may be put by him such things,

for such time and in so much of said street or alley, or of a street or alley convenient to said property, as may be authorized by a resolution of the Council or of the committee on streets generally, or by the committee on streets for the ward wherein that part of the street or alley is; but no such resolution of the committee on streets generally shall avail to give such authority any further than may be consistent with a resolution of the Council; and no such resolution of the committee on streets for a ward shall avail to give such authority any further than may be consistent with a resolution of the Council or of the committee on streets generally. And whenever any person shall be engaged in digging a ditch or sinking a pit in any street or public alley, he shall place barriers sufficient to prevent a person or animal from falling in such ditch or pit; and at night, unless the street or alley immediately adjacent thereto be lighted with gas lamps, shall place a light near such ditch or pit. If he fail so to place such barriers and light, he shall pay a fine of not less than five nor more than twenty dollars; and every night on which the failure continues shall be a distinct offence. And when a person, by reason of an office under or contract with the city, has to do paving or other work directed or authorized by the Council, upon any public street, lane or alley in the city, he may erect, set up or place a rope, chain or bars across any of said streets, lanes or alleys which he is about to mend or repair, or in which he is about to execute such other work as may require this protection, to such an extent and for such a length of time as may be authorized by the committee on streets generally. And if any person or persons shall throw down or remove such rope, chain or bars, or ride on, drive upon or otherwise injure the said work, or interrupt the workmen during its progress, every such person shall, for every such offence, pay a fine of not less than ten nor more than fifty dollars.

29. Any person engaged or about to be engaged in building, repairing, excavating, or making any improvements on a house or lot on which materials are to be used, or from which they are to be removed, may deposit materials in that part of the street or public alley opposite and next to his premises, on so much of the carriage-way as does not exceed one-half the width thereof,

so that the use of the gutter be not obstructed. But where two persons are building or making other improvements hereby authorized, opposite each other on the same street, each shall occupy but one-fourth of the street. And no such deposit of materials shall be made in a street so as to obstruct improvements which the city is making in said street. The committee on streets for the ward in which such premises are may, on being satisfied of the necessity thereof, grant a special permit in writing, authorizing such materials to be deposited in a part of said street or alley opposite another's premises, on so much of the carriage-way as aforesaid, or may authorize the deposit to commence earlier or continue longer than is hereinafter provided. But except by such permission, the deposit shall not be made in any case of small repairs more than one day, nor in other cases more than three days before the work is commenced; and the remains shall be cleanly removed, in case of small repairs, by the end of the first day, and in other cases by the end of the third day next after that on which the work is finished. And a person engaged in repairing a roof, wall or chimney of a house on a street or public alley, shall place barriers sufficient to warn a foot passenger against passing such roof, wall or chimney. If he fail to place the same he shall pay a fine of ten dollars; and every day on which the failure continues shall be a distinct offence. In no case shall a sidewalk or paved gutter be obstructed under this section, unless it be actually necessary for placing such barriers, or for the execution of the work.

30. Any person employed in business in the city may put up a sign made of tin, which does not extend over the sidewalk more than three feet from his place of business, and is not less than ten feet above the sidewalk; and may in front of his place of business and next thereto occupy with his goods one-third of the sidewalk. But he shall not suspend his goods or other articles so that they shall extend from the front of his house more than one foot towards the street. And any person putting up a sign or occupying the sidewalk, or suspending his goods otherwise than is herein authorized, shall pay a fine of not less than one nor more than ten dollars for each offence; and the sign shall be removed by the police. And when a merchant or other per-

son, after doing business on a street or public alley, declines such business and sells by auction his stock of goods; or when the property of a decedent, who at the time of his death was a resident of the city of Richmond or county of Henrico, is sold by his representative; or when property is sold under a deed of trust thereon, made by a person who at the time of executing said deed was such a resident; or when property is levied on in said city or county, and sold therein by an officer under a warrant of distress, execution or other legal process; or when property is sold under the judgment or decree of a court or magistrate, there may, on the day of sale, be occupied with such goods or property half of the sidewalk and a third of the carriage-way next to the house or other place of such sale. And when at the dock or a wharf an auctioneer sells a cargo, half of the sidewalk and a third of the carriage-way next thereto may be occupied with such cargo for three days and no more, unless the sale be necessarily postponed because of the weather; in which case the sale shall be within three days after the cause for such postponement shall cease; and the occupation shall be no longer than half an hour after sunset of the day on which the sale is made. If an auctioneer, or any person in his employment, sell or offer for sale at auction any personal property which shall be in any part (either of the sidewalk or carriage-way) of a street or public alley when he is not authorized by this section, he shall, for every article there offered for sale by him, pay a fine of ten dollars.

31. Every person occupying a house or lot shall, as far as such lot extends, cause the paved gutter or drain in a street or any public alley opposite thereto to be constantly kept open and free from obstruction; and if he fail so to do may be fined not less than one dollar nor more than ten dollars; and for each day after the first that such obstruction remains shall be fined not less than two nor more than twenty dollars.

32. Any person may carry from his lot or put in a street or public alley, on any part of the carriage-way nearest to the gutter or drain, ashes, dirt or rubbish: provided the same be free from offensive matter, and be removed by him from said street or alley within twenty-four hours; or if one of the com-

mittee on streets for the ward in which the said lot is shall, in writing, allow a longer time for the removal, then within such time as may be so allowed.

33. If any filth, rubbish, ashes, dirt or other things be carried from a lot or other place and put in a street or public alley, or if any nuisance or obstruction be put or caused to be put or remain therein, in any case in which it is not authorized by the ordinances of the city, the person who so puts or causes it to be so put, or is in fault in respect to its remaining, shall, for any such offence, be fined not less than one nor more than ten dollars; and for each day after the first that the same is upon the street or alley, shall be fined not less than two nor more than twenty dollars. In construing this chapter, no article taken from or to be shipped on board of, or to be used in or about a vessel in the dock, and deposited in the street not more than thirty feet from the northern margin of the dock, shall be deemed a nuisance or obstruction: provided the same be removed within twenty-four hours from and after sunrise of the day next succeeding that on which it was deposited. Nor shall any machine, car or other vehicle of a railroad company placed upon its railroad or rail-track in a street, be deemed such a nuisance or obstruction, unless the said machine, car or other vehicle, remain in the street upon a railroad or track longer than is necessary to deliver its contents, or longer than is necessary to enable the company's train to be made up, not exceeding in either case three hours, or unless it stops upon the crossing of a street. But no filth or offensive matter shall be delivered from a car in a street.

34. Posts for awnings constructed of either iron or wood, may be placed on the curbstone or near the inner edge thereof, so as not to interfere with the free passage of the streets. The diameter of said posts shall not exceed, if of iron, three inches, and if of wood, six inches. The covering shall be of canvas, and shall be so framed and placed as not to reach at its lowest points nearer than within eight feet of the sidewalk. When wood is used the same shall be neatly dressed, and the entire structure in all cases put up and finished in a neat and workmanlike manner. Any person putting up an awning which shall not conform

to the provisions of this section, shall pay a fine of not less than ten nor more than one hundred dollars; and the awning and posts shall be removed by the order of the Mayor.

35. There may be erected in front of each tenement one frame with two posts not more than six feet apart, with a cross bar, to which horses may be tied. The said posts may be either of wood or iron, well imbedded in the ground, and shall not be less than four nor more than five feet high above the sidewalk; and if of wood, shall not be less than four inches in diameter at the level of the footway. The said posts shall be placed next to the inner edge of the curbstone, or where the curbstone would be if there be none there, and shall be so arranged with cross bar or otherwise as shall not allow the horse or other animal hitched thereat to go upon or stand on the footway.

36. Every person occupying a house or lot on a street or public alley upon which, on that half of the street or alley next to and opposite his house or lot, any filth, rubbish, ashes, dirt, stones or other thing, or any nuisance or obstruction is put or suffered to remain in any case not authorized by this ordinance, shall forthwith remove the same, or give information thereof to the Superintendent of streets, the Overseer of the city hands, or to one of the officers or sergeants of police. And if twelve hours elapse without such removal or information, he may be fined not exceeding ten dollars; and each day that elapses without such removal or information shall be a distinct offence.

37. If any engine, car or other vehicle be drawn or propelled upon a railroad or rail-track in a street, at a greater rate than four miles an hour, the person who does it or causes it to be done, or assists in doing it or causing it to be done, shall pay a fine of ten dollars. Every locomotive engine put or placed upon any railroad or rail-track in this city shall have attached thereto a bell of thirty pounds weight at least, and such bell shall be rung whenever the said engine is about to pass the crossing of any two streets, and shall continue ringing until such engine shall have passed such crossing; and if any such engine shall pass across any street in this city without first ringing and continuing to ring said bell, in manner aforesaid, the owner of said engine, as well as the person then having the control, conduct

and management thereof, shall each be fined not less than five nor more than twenty dollars. And if any person shall blow, sound or use, or cause to be blown, sounded or used, by means of or with steam, any whistle or other thing upon any public street or alley, he shall be fined not less then five nor more than twenty dollars.

38. If any owner or driver of a wagon, dray or cart, whether licensed or not, shall permit the horses, mules or other animals by which the same is drawn, to go in a street or public alley faster than a walk, or to be fed therein; or if any person run a horse race, or cause the same to be run, or shall ride or drive a horse or other animal at a greater speed than six miles an hour, in any public street or alley, he shall be fined not less than two nor more than twenty dollars.

39. No person shall tie or fasten a horse or other animal to any tree or to any box or case around such tree in any street of the city, or upon any sidewalk, or lead or ride a horse or mule, or drive a wagon, dray, cart or other vehicle upon a sidewalk, unless across such part thereof as is or shall be at the time paved with stone or flagging. Any person violating this section shall, for each offence, be fined not less than two nor more than ten dollars.

40. If any owner or driver of a wagon, whether licensed or not, shall in a street or public alley which is paved, drive such wagon with a wheel locked, or if any owner or driver of any wagon, hack, dray or cart, whether licensed or not, shall wantonly crack his whip, to the annoyance of others, or suffer his vehicle, when not receiving or discharging a load, to pass or stand upon a street or public alley without holding the reins in his hands, every such offender shall, for each offence, pay a fine of not less than two nor more than twenty dollars.

41. Any driver of a vehicle meeting any other vehicle in a street or public alley, shall seasonably drive to the right hand, so that each may pass the other without interference. And when in a street or public alley a vehicle is overtaken by any other vehicle, the driver of the former shall bear to the left, until the latter shall have passed. In no instance shall a driver of a carriage, wagon, dray or cart, stop the same in the middle

of a street or public alley, or opposite to an intersecting street or alley, or upon any granite crossing; but he shall always stop the same as near to the sidewalk as he can without being on it or in the gutter A driver violating this section in any respect shall, for each offence, pay a fine of not less than one nor more than ten dollars.

42. Any officer of the police of the city may order any vehicle standing in the street to be removed, as may seem to him most convenient for persons passing by. If a driver shall fail to obey such order, the owner of the vehicle shall pay a fine of five dollars.

43. For any offence against the thirty-eighth, thirty-ninth, fortieth, forty-first or forty-second sections of this ordinance, committed in the presence of any police officer of the city, he may arrest the offender and take him forthwith before the Mayor, or some other justice of the peace. Such officer may pay twenty-five cents for the safekeeping of the vehicle or animal during the absence of the driver or owner, and what is so paid shall be included in the costs, if any, recovered against the offender.

44. If any person engaged in any military exercise shall fire or discharge, in any street or public alley of this city, any cannon, gun, pistol or any other firearms, except on the fourth of July, the twenty-second of February and the nineteenth day of October, or at military burial, or some extraordinary occasion allowed by the Mayor (and by him notified through the newspapers, or by posting handbills or otherwise), or if any person shall, in any street or public alley in said city, play at bandy or throw snowballs, stones or other missiles, or discharge arrows from a bow or crossbow, or blow a horn, he shall be fined not less than one nor more than ten dollars.

45. If any person shall place, or in any manner use, upon the sidewalk of any public street or alley, the carriage-way whereof is paved, any wheelbarrow, hand-carriage, hand-cart, or sled, or shall skate or slide thereon, he shall pay a fine of not less than one nor more than ten dollars. But nothing in this section contained shall prevent any person from passing, with such hand-carriage or cart, across the sidewalk of a street from or to a house or lot, from such street or alley, nor prevent the use on a sidewalk of a hand-carriage to ride or carry infant children.

46. The Engineer shall make a survey and plan of the city, showing distinctly each lot, and the size and number thereof, according to the original plan, each public street and alley, and the width thereof, with such explanations as may be directed by the Council. And in laying down the lines of lots, streets and alleys, he shall have reference to the actual lines thereof, in all cases in which they have been built upon or laid out, as at present, for the last twenty years. And he shall also lay down on said plan the original lines of said lots, streets and alleys, where the same can be ascertained. The said survey and plan shall be returned by the Engineer to the Council; and if approved by the Council, it shall be enrolled among their proceedings, and afterwards recorded in the Clerk's office of the Hustings Court. But said survey and plan shall not be finally approved by the Council until the same shall have been returned, as herein directed, for twelve months, and examined and approved as directed by the charter of the city.

47. The Engineer shall make surveys, plans and estimates of culverts, or other work of any kind whatever to be done in the city, whenever required by the committee on streets generally or by the Council. He shall also be the architect and draftsman of the city, and in respect to buildings and other improvements, make such plans, specifications and estimates as the Council may require, and do, in relation thereto, whatever else it may direct. He shall also comply with all directions or orders given to him by the committee on streets generally or by any other standing committee of the Council, connected with or in relation to any public work or property of the city under their charge requiring, in the opinion of such committee, the skill of an engineer, architect or draftsman.

48. The Superintendent of streets shall attend the meetings of the committee on streets generally, and shall act as their clerk, and keep a record of their proceedings. He shall make such surveys, plans and estimates as he may be required to make by the committee on streets for a ward, and shall also do the same at any time, whenever required by the Council or by the committee on streets generally, and shall perform any other duty connected with his office, whenever required by the committee

on streets generally or for a ward, or by any standing committee of the Council.

4. The Superintendent of streets shall explore the streets and public alleys throughout the city as often as practicable, and report to the Council all encroachments upon any of them. He shall also report promptly to the Mayor of the city any obstruction in or upon any street or public alley coming under his observation. Subject to the control and under the direction of the Superintendent, the Overseer of the city hands shall have holes filled up, crossings, drains and gutters kept clean, and all parts of the streets and public alleys kept in good order; and shall also have made such of the repairs and improvements of the streets and alleys ordered by the committee on streets for the ward or by the committee on streets generally as may not be contracted for. The Superintendent shall see that the Overseer performs these duties in a proper manner, observing himself the directions of the committee on streets for the ward in which the work is done, so far as it may be practicable to do so, without neglecting what is required of him by the committee on streets generally or by the Council.

50. It shall be the duty of the respective Superintendents of the water and gas works to report in writing at least once in two weeks to the Superintendent of streets, all pavements, whether of stone or brick, taken up by either of them for the purpose of laying and repairing water and gas pipes, or any fixture or other thing in connection therewith; and upon such report it shall be the duty of the Superintendent of streets to proceed as early as practicable to cause the said pavements to be replaced, so that the replacing thereof shall be completed within fifteen days after such report.

51. Annually, as soon as practicable after the last day of January, the Engineer and Superintendent of streets shall respectively make to the committee on streets generally reports of their respective operations during the preceding fiscal year. The Engineer's report shall show the aggregate amount paid during the year on his estimates; how much of said amount was in each ward under his superintendence, the condition of said works, and what will have to be paid on or before the completion; and shall

contain such suggestions as he may deem proper in regard to the further improvement of the city. The Superintendent's report shall show the aggregate amount paid during said year in his department, showing separately the amount under each of the following heads, to wit: 1. Hire of hands. 2. Their food, clothing and lodging. 3. Purchase of horses and mules. 4. Stableage and provender. 5. Carts. 6. Tools. 7. Other materials. The report shall set forth what has been done for said aggregate amount; what work has been done in said year, under his superintendence, on contracts; showing separately as to each ward the amount paid for work contracted for in said ward. It shall also show the condition of any work contracted for under his supernitendence and not completed, and contain such suggestions as he may deem proper in regard to the keeping in order the streets and alleys of the city; which report the said committee shall examine and return to the Council, with such remarks as they may deem proper.

52. The committee on streets generally may allow a reasonable compensation for such chain carriers, books and implements as they may authorize to be employed or procured at the request of the Engineer or ths Superintendent of streets; and the same shall be paid for upon the draft of the Engineer or Superintendent, as the case may be, countersigned by the chairman of the committee on streets generally.

53. The Council shall designate a room or rooms in some building owned by the city, to be used as the office of the Engineer and of the Superintendent of streets. And each of them shall systematically arrange and keep in a fire-proof safe, to be provided by the city, in the room designated for him, the papers of his office not otherwise provided for. Except when leave of absence is granted him by the committee on streets generally, the Superintendent of streets shall, on every day, except Sunday, the fourth of July and Christmas day, be in his office from eight to nine o'clock in the morning, between the first of April and the first of October, and from nine to ten o'clock in the morning during the rest of the year.

54. The Engineer may, with the assent of the committee on streets generally, employ an assistant in his office, at a compen-

sation not exceeding five dollars a day, but such assistant shall only be employed when and as long as said committee shall think it necessary.

CHAPTER XXXV.

CONCERNING STREET RAILWAYS.

Contracts for the privilege of running railway passenger cars on the streets of the city of Richmond shall be subject to the following terms, provisions, conditions, restrictions and limitations, viz:

1. The contract shall prescribe specifically the streets in which the said railways may be laid down and the passenger cars may run, and the termini, in each street, of said railway, and to which the cars may run; and no part of the said work shall be changed without the consent of the Council. The said contracts shall state what part of the railways mentioned therein shall be with a single, and that with a double track, and if with a single track, where the sidings shall be located.

2. If after a single or double track has been prescribed for any part of a railway authorized to be constructed, the company or corporation shall desire to change it, or any part of it, in that respect, they may apply to the Council to be authorized to

make the said change. And upon such application the Council shall proceed as is prescribed in the first section; and their act shall, as to the subject to which it refers, have the same binding effect upon the company or corporation, upon their accepting the same, as is prescribed in said section.

3. The said railways and the track thereof shall be constructed on the most approved plan, and the same shall be approved by the Engineer of the city before the construction thereof is commenced. And the said railways and tracks shall be constructed under the supervision of the said Engineer, who shall see that the same is properly done; and if he shall be of the opinion that the same is not properly done according to the plan approved by him as aforesaid, he shall stop the construction thereof. But the said company or corporation may appeal from the decision of the Engineer to the Council, and the parties shall be governed by the decision of the Council upon the question. The said railways and tracks shall be so constructed and laid down as not to impede or obstruct the full flow of water across the streets or down the gutters thereof, and shall conform to the grades of the several streets through which they pass, as the said grades are now or may be hereafter established. And if the company or corporation shall afterwards desire to extend their railway and cars into another street, they shall apply to the Council, stating specially the streets or street into and along which they propose to extend their railway and cars, the points at which they propose to connect with their then existing railway, if the same shall connect therewith, and in any case the points in each street between which they propose to carry their railway and run their cars; and the Council at any of its regular meetings, or at a meeting adjourned or called for the purpose, and of which purpose the members shall have notice, may grant the application to extend the railway and run the cars as specified in the application, or may grant the application in part. But no such application shall be acted on without a reference thereof to the committee on streets generally, and until the same is reported upon by them, nor shall their report be finally acted on at the meeting of the Council at which it is made. And the Council may prescribe such additional terms, conditions and restrictions,

to the granting of the said application, as they may deem expedient; and the same shall be binding upon said company or corporation, if they shall accept the privilege of so extending their railways and running their cars.

4. The gauge of the said railway tracks shall be the same as that of ordinary street carriages in use in the city of Richmond, in order to admit of the passage of such carriages upon the tram-plate of said railway. But it shall not be lawful for any person or owner of any carriage, dray, cart or other vehicle whatever, to obstruct or impede the running of any car on any of said tracks, by occupying or driving on said tracks in front of said car, when by lawful increase of speed or turning out on either side of said tracks, such obstruction or impediments can be avoided, under a penalty of five dollars, recoverable as small debts out of court are recoverable, at the suit of said company or corporation; and all carriages, drays, carts or other vehicles, while running through any of the streets upon which said railway tracks may be laid, shall keep to the right in passing or turning out to permit the cars running on the same to pass, under a penalty of five dollars, recoverable as aforesaid. And it shall not be lawful, without the consent of the company or corporation, to establish any line of carriages, omnibuses or other vehicles of any description whatever (other than the cars of the proprietors of said railways), to be run upon the said railways for the purpose of carrying passengers for pay or hire.

5. The company or corporation in laying down the said railway tracks, shall restore all pavements and regrade all earth taken up or disturbed in said construction, and shall at all times, under the supervision of the Superintendent of streets of the city, at their own expense and charge, keep the streets and pavements upon which the tracks of the railways are laid, to the extent of the portion of said streets covered by said tracks, and for two feet on either side beyond the outside of said tracks, in good and complete repair; and should they refuse to do so for the space of ten days, after having been notified by the Superintendent of streets that any portion of their roads needs repairing, as herein provided, then the said company or corporation shall be liable to a fine of five dollars for each day they shall fail to

repair the same; and the Council may forbid the running of any car or cars upon said road until the same shall be fully complied with; and the city may in all such cases repair such streets when not done by the company or corporation as herein provided, and the expense thereof shall be a debt against the company or corporation, recoverable as debts are now recoverable by the city of Richmond.

6. Should the corporate authorities of the city hereafter determine to pave any street or streets in which such tracks may be laid, and which streets shall not have been paved at the time said tracks were laid, then the proprietors of said railways shall at the same time, at their own cost and expense, pave so much of said streets or street as may be covered by said tracks, and for two feet on either side beyond the outside of said tracks, for the same distance and to the same extent as the remaining portion of the street may be paved by the city.

7. The cars running upon the said railways shall be subject to all the police regulations which are now or may hereafter be contained in the ordinances of the city, in regard to railway cars or other vehicles, so far as they may be applicable thereto. The price of transporting passengers from one part of the city to any other, shall not exceed the sum agreed upon in the contract for each passenger; but if the passenger, without leaving the cars, shall return to any point nearer to that from which he started than a point which he has passed, he shall pay a second fare, unless this be occasioned by the line of the route on which he is passing being circuitous. And the said company or corporation shall pay to the proper officer of the city, in consideration of the privilege hereby granted, and in lieu of all charges by the city upon the property and capital stock of said company or corporation for taxes and assessments, ten per centum of the net profits made by them upon the transportation of passengers within the city limits, payable semi-annually from the time of opening the road to public travel, and that the aforesaid sum of ten per cent. of net profits shall be a preferred debt or claim against the road and property of said railway company. They shall also, before placing cars upon their roads pay into the office of the city Chamberlain, and annually thereafter, for the use of the city,

the sum of five dollars for each and every car intended to run on said railways.

8. The company or corporation shall use cars with suitable brakes thereto, and the cars shall be moved by horses or mules, and there shall not be more than four horses or mules to a car. And if from a want of sufficient brakes to any car or from the carelessness or incompetency of the conductor or driver of such car, the car shall run on said railway track or in the street at a greater speed than is authorized by this or any other ordinance, the said company shall be subject to a fine not exceeding twenty dollars, for the use of the city; and such careless conductor or driver may be subjected to a like fine. The said cars shall not incommode the crossings nor stop at corners of any street or elsewhere to solicit passengers. It shall also be the duty of conductors and drivers of the cars to give ample notice to drivers of vehicles and pedestrians of their approach, and also to afford all reasonable opportunity for them or either of them to avoid collision or accident; and any neglect by them to comply with the provisions of this section shall be punished by a fine of five dollars, to be recovered before the Mayor of the city, for the use of the city.

9. It shall be the duty of said company or corporation to employ careful, sober and prudent agents, conductors and drivers, to take charge of their car or cars when upon the road; and for violation of any act of assembly or ordinance of the city on the part of such officer or officers or employees upon said road, the company shall be liable to all fines, forfeitures or damages therefrom: provided, that this shall not be taken as an excuse or free any such officer or employee from penalties or responsibilities for any such violations or other acts committed.

10. Each car running upon the road shall be numbered, commencing at number one, and continuing in regular numerical order; which number shall be painted in some conspicuous place upon both sides of the car. For any neglect to comply with this provision the proprietors shall be punishable by a fine of ten dollars, to be recovered on complaint before the Mayor of the city, and for the use of the city; and in no case shall it be lawful to use the said railway cars for the accommodation of

passengers on the Sabbath day, under a penalty of fifty dollars for each car so run on the Sabbath day, to be collected as aforesaid.

11. After a company or corporation shall have been authorized to construct a railway and run their cars in any street of the city, said company or corporation shall not cease to run their cars therein as agreed on, without the consent of the Council, applied for and obtained in the manner prescribed in section three. And upon the failure of said company or corporation for six months to run their cars in any street as said company or corporation has been authorized to run its cars, said company shall forfeit so much of its railway on said streets as they have failed to run their cars upon, and the right of said company or corporation to run their cars in that part of the street shall cease; and the Council may grant the privilege to another company or corporation to run their cars therein or in any part thereof; or may have the railway taken up and the material thereof sold, and after paying all expenses arising therefrom, to pay the balance, if any, to said company or corporation.

12. The privilege granted to any company or corporation to construct railways and run cars in the streets, shall continue for such term of years, from the date of the grant, as shall be fixed by the Council, unless the same shall be forfeited under the preceding section. At the expiration of that period, the Council may extend the said privilege to said company or corporation for another period, to be fixed by the Council, upon such terms, conditions, restrictions and limitations as may be agreed upon by the Council and said company or corporation; and if the Council shall fail for one year to give notice to said company or corporation of its purpose to insist upon a new contract, the assent of the Council to the continuation of the privilege of said company or corporation for a period of fifteen years, upon the terms, conditions, restrictions and limitations on which they held said privileges at the expiration of the first period fixed, shall be presumed. But if the Council shall refuse to continue to said company or corporation the privileges held by them during the period fixed, upon the terms on which they were held during that period; or if the Council and said company or

corporation cannot agree upon the terms upon which the said company or corporation may continue to run their cars in the streets of the city, the Council shall have the right to take, and shall take the railways and fixtures thereto lying within the city, and the lots and buildings thereon and appurtenances owned by said company or corporation, and used and held as a part of its capital, and the cars of said company or corporation used upon its railways in the city; and the price to be paid therefor shall be fixed by arbitrators, one of whom shall be appointed by the Council and the other shall be appointed by the said company or corporation; and if they shall fail to agree, by an umpire mutually agreed upon by them. And in fixing the price of said property the same shall be valued as property, to be used for the purpose for which is was provided, and in its then place and condition; but the value of the privilege of running passenger cars in the streets of the city shall not be estimated as a part of the value of said property.

13. If the said company or corporation does not within two years from the date of the contract, construct the railways provided for in it, as agreed upon therein, the said contract shall be void and of no effect: and the Council may grant the privilege of laying down railways and running cars thereon in said streets to another company.

14. A grant to one company of the privilege of laying down railways and running cars thereon in one or more streets of the city, shall not prevent the Council from granting the like privilege to another company or companies in other streets. But the privilege shall not be given to two or more companies to run their cars in the same street, except at the crossing of streets, and only for the purpose of crossing a street. And when one company is authorized to lay their railways along a street, so that said railway will cross the railway of another company which has been first authorized to lay down its railway, the company crossing such railway shall at its own expense, and under the direction of the Engineer of the city, make the necessary alterations in the railway which is to be crossed.

CHAPTER XXXVI.

CONCERNING WAGONS, DRAYS, CARTS AND HACKS.

1. No wagon, dray, cart, hack or other wheel-carriage shall be kept or employed in the city for hire, directly or indirectly, unless the owner or keeper thereof obtain a license therefor, as hereinafter mentioned. The time for which the license is issued shall be until the first day of February next following the date thereof. Before such license is issued, the applicant shall give bond, in the sum of three hundred dollars, payable to the city of Richmond, with surety approved by the Chamberlain, conditioned that all articles entrusted to the owner, keeper or driver of any such vehicle, and all persons taken in or upon the same, shall be faithfully transported and delivered. On every such bond suits may be brought from time to time, in the name of the city, for the benefit of any person injured by any breach of the condition, as often as any such breach may be alleged, until damages shall be recovered for such breaches equal to the penalty of the bond. And a like license shall be taken out by the owner of any wagon, dray or cart which is employed on any streets of this city in the business, or for the private use or benefit of such owner, unless the same be exclusively employed in transporting fuel, provisions, manure or other things to be used, only at the owner's farm or dwelling.

2. Before issuing such license, there shall be paid to the

Chamberlain the following tax, to wit: seven dollars on a cart, dray or wagon, drawn by one horse or mule; ten dollars, if drawn by two horses or mules; fifteen dollars, if drawn by three horses or mules; and twenty dollars, if drawn by four horses or mules, unless the body of the four-horse wagon be on elliptic springs, or on wheels with tires not less than four inches wide; in which case the tax shall be seventeen and a half dollars. On a hack or any other wheel-carriage than those above named, the tax shall be fifteen dollars. And the Chamberlain may issue such licenses for the unexpired portion of the year, at a ratable proportion of the tax: provided that the same shall not be less than for a license for three months. But no such license shall be issued unless the applicant shall produce a certificate from the Inspector of carts and wagons, as provided in the seventh section of this ordinance.

3. The owner or keeper of every licensed vehicle shall have painted thereon its number and the initials of its owner's name, in figures and letters not less than one and a half inch in length, so that the same may be easily read. The same shall be painted, if the vehicle be a dray, on each shaft; and if a wagon or cart, on each side, unless the sides be movable, in which case they shall be painted on the frame on each side; and if a hack or other licensed vehicle for the transportation of passengers, in some conspicuous place on each side of said vehicle.

4. Any person who shall keep or employ in this city a wagon, cart, dray, hack or other wheeled-carriage, without a license therefor, when a license is required to be taken out for it, or who shall fail to have the number and initials painted thereon, as required by this ordinance, shall pay for every such offence a fine of not less than ten nor more than twenty dollars; and each day that the same shall be so kept or employed shall be a distinct and separate offence.

5. The unexpired term of any license granted under this chapter may be transferred, by assignment on the back thereof, by the person to whom it was issued, provided that the assignee of such license shall execute the like bond as was required of the assignor; and then a new license shall be issued to the assignee for the unexpired term of such license, who shall cause

the initials of his name and the number of the vehicle to be painted thereon, in the same manner and under the same penalty for failing so to do, as if the original license had been granted to him.

6. Whether a vehicle be licensed or not, neither coal nor dirt shall be transported therein, unless it be so tight and have such a tailboard thereon as will prevent the waste of the coal or dirt. For every violation of this section there shall be a fine of ten dollars.

7. The Council shall annually in the month of December, or as soon thereafter as convenient, appoint an Inspector of carts and wagons employed in transporting wood, coal or coke, who when applied to, shall examine such cart or wagon, and on examination, if he find himself justified in doing so, shall give a certificate that the vehicle is tight and in proper order to prevent the waste of coal or coke; and if it be a cart, that it contains twenty-five bushels when not loaded above, but leveled to the mark of full measure or loading. The said Inspector shall be paid fifty cents for each certificate.

8. The Inspector may at any time examine any cart or wagon, and if he shall find that its dimensions are not such as to contain the proper quantity when leveled to the mark of full measure or loading, he shall report the fact to the Mayor and the Chamberlain; and thenceforth the license for such cart or wagon shall be forfeited, and the owner or keeper thereof shall pay a fine of not less than ten nor more than twenty dollars. And if coal or coke be wasted on a street or public alley from a cart, wagon or other vehicle, whether the same be transported for consumption or not, the owner or keeper of such wagon, cart or other vehicle shall pay a fine of ten dollars.

9. The person for whom a load is carried shall be charged therefor no higher rates than are allowed by this chapter, and shall pay these rates, or sign a ticket expressing the place from which and to which the load is to be carried. Any person refusing to pay such rates or sign such ticket, and the owner or keeper of a vehicle who, or whose driver, charges a higher rate, shall for every such offence pay a fine of five dollars. A like fine shall be paid for refusing to carry a load or part of a load,

when not engaged; and the burden of proof of such engagement shall be upon the owner of the vehicle; but in such case the proper charge for carrying shall be paid, if demanded, before taking on the load.

10. The charge for a load on a wagon, dray or cart shall be as follows: for carrying it five squares or less, twenty-five cents, and for each square over five, two cents additional.

11. The charge for the use of a hack or other wheeled-carriage kept for hire shall be as follows: for carrying a person therein not more than ten squares, fifty cents, and for each additional square, five cents: provided, that the whole charge for carrying one person to any part of the city shall not exceed one dollar. The charge for carrying not more than four persons shall not for the whole exceed one dollar and fifty cents, unless more than one hour be employed, and shall then only be one dollar and fifty cents for the first hour, and fifty cents for each succeeding hour. The charge for a hack to attend a funeral procession shall not exceed three dollars and fifty cents; no charge shall be made for children under three years of age. For carrying persons between ten o'clock at night and daybreak, an additional charge of one-half the above rates may be made, and no more. For baggage the charge shall be twenty-five cents for each trunk carried outside, and nothing shall be charged for any article carried inside or for any carpet bag or basket.

12. The load for which the rates mentioned in the tenth section may be charged may be as follows, to wit: of tobacco, one hogshead; of flour, seven barrels; of imported salt, seven sacks; of sugar, one hogshead or six barrels; of liquids, one hogshead, or one pipe, or two half pipes or two tierces, or five barrels; of fish, six barrels; of wood, a half cord; of coal, coke or sand, twenty-five bushels; of brick or paving stone, the bulk of twenty-five bushels; of other articles, one thousand six hundred and fifty pounds; in the case of furniture, chairs, boxes, paper or light articles, the load shall be not according to weight, but according to bulk. When there is carried more than is hereby declared to be a load, there may be charged a proportionate rate for whatever is carried beyond such load; but no vehicle whatever supported on wheels shall, upon any public street or alley,

carry a greater weight than three thousand three hundred pounds, unless the tires around the wheels thereof be at the time at least four inches wide, when such vehicle may carry the weight of four thousand five hundred pounds and no more, unless the thing to be carried be a single piece of machinery or other indivisible article. The owner or keeper of a dray, cart or wagon, in or upon which there is carried, in any public street or alley, a greater weight than is allowed by this chapter, shall for every such offence be fined not less than ten nor more than twenty dollars

13. A copy of the rates for hacks and other wheeled-carriages shall be kept by the driver of every such hack or carriage, and he shall exhibit the same whenever called for by any person employing or using said hack or carriage. And if he shall fail to exhibit the same when so required, or if for carrying a person or baggage there be charged more than is allowed by this chapter, the owner or keeper of the vehicle, for every day of such failure or for every time of such charge, shall be fined not less than five nor more than twenty dollars.

14. If any person desiring the use of a hack or any public vehicle kept for the purpose of taking persons, for hire or compensation, from one place to another within this city, shall tender to the owner, keeper or driver of such hack or vehicle the proper charge, according to the rates established by this chapter, for the use and service thereof as required, and the owner, keeper or driver shall fail or refuse to render the service so required, he shall be fined not less than ten nor more than twenty dollars, unless the keeper, owner or driver of such hack or vehicle shall, upon summons or warrant, appear and by proof show good cause to the contrary; and no prior engagement of the use or service of such hack or other public vehicle shall be taken as good cause for such failure or refusal, unless upon the trial of the offender he shall make it manifestly appear with whom the prior engagement was made, and the place to which the said hack or such other vehicle was engaged to go, and that there was not, by the use of ordinary diligence, time to render both services: provided, however, that between the hours of ten o'clock P. M. and daylight, when his horses are put up in his stable, he shall

not be compelled to bring them out; but if he does consent to carry the person or persons calling upon him, he shall do so at the rates fixed in this chapter, under the penalty aforesaid.

CHAPTER XXXVII.

CONCERNING THE MEASURING OF LUMBER.

1. There shall be appointed by the Council at its regular meeting in May, or as soon thereafter as practicable, a Surveyor of lumber for the city, who shall hold his office until the next regular meeting of the Council in May, and until a successor is appointed and qualifies, unless sooner removed by the Council; who, before acting in his office, shall give bond in the penalty of two thousand dollars, with security approved by the Council, and with condition according to the ordinance on the subject; and said bond shall be filed in the Auditor's office A vacancy in the office may be filled at any time by the Council.

2. The said Surveyor may appoint one or more deputies, who shall be approved by the Council; and who after taking an oath faithfully to discharge his duties, and filing the same with the Auditor, may execute and discharge any of the duties or powers of his principal. Any such deputy may be removed at any time by his principal, as well as by the Council.

3. The Surveyor, after taking the oath of office and executing the bond required of him, shall faithfully measure and report to the proper parties all lumber arriving by railroad or water carriage in this market for sale; and, when required, mark legibly on every board or piece of lumber, the number of feet, board measure; and also, when required, inspect the same, making two qualities, viz: 1. Merchantable. 2. Cullings. All bark-edge, or worm-eaten, or wind-shaken or irregularly sawed lum-

ber shall be classed as cullings, and all other shall be classed as merchantable.

4. The Surveyor shall provide gauges for the use of himself and his deputies, and see that all lumber measured by him or them is of proper thickness; if cut for five-quarter boards, and will not fill the five-quarter gauge, it shall be considered as one inch or four-quarter boards; if cut for six-quarter plank, and it does not fill the six-quarter gauge, it shall be considered as five-quarter boards; if cut for two inches or eight-quarter plank, and does not fill the two-inch gauge, it shall be considered as seven-quarter plank: provided, however, that this and the preceding section shall not apply to lumber cut to order and brought to the city in fulfilment of such order.

5. The Surveyor shall provide the labor necessary to the performance of the services herein required of him, and for his services he shall receive thirty cents per thousand feet, board measure, one-half of which shall be paid by the purchaser and the other half by the vendor or his agent.

6. The Surveyor shall keep an account of all lumber measured by him, and make quarterly reports to the Council on the first of January, first of April, first of July and first of October of each year, showing the quantity of lumber measured; and he shall publish the same, at his own cost, in some daily newspaper published in this city. If he fail for ten days to report to the Council or leave it with the Chamberlain to be laid before the Council, and to make such publication, he shall be fined twenty dollars.

CHAPTER XXXVIII.

CONCERNING THE MEASURING OF WOOD.

1. Annually in the month of September there shall be appointed by the Council a Measurer of wood for the city of Richmond,

who shall be and is hereby authorized to employ a deputy, to be approved by the Council, to perform the duties required of him, whenever he may be unable to attend personally to the same. Said Measurer and his deputy shall, before they enter upon the duties required of them, take the following oath, which shall be certified to the Council, to wit: "I do solemnly swear that I will to the best of my skill and judgment render equal justice to all who may be interested in the discharge of the duties of my office." In case of a vacancy in the office of said Measurer by death, resignation or removal, a new appointment shall be made by the Council.

2. The said Measurer shall give bond with approved security for the faithful performance of the duties herein prescribed, in the penalty of one thousand dollars.

3. All wood brought to the city for sale by the railroads or water-carriage shall be measured, so as to insure the purchaser one hundred and twenty-eight solid feet to the cord; for which purpose said wood shall be four feet in width, piled four feet four inches in height, and at the rate of eight feet in length to the cord, excluding all that is rotten. Any person violating these conditions shall be fined twenty dollars for the first offence, and thirty for the second and every succeeding offence.

4. All retail vendors of wood other than those directly from their boats, shall be required to procure open standards or frames, to be four feet four inches in height, in which all wood sold by them shall be measured. Any person violating this section shall incur a fine of twenty dollars for the first offence and thirty for each succeeding one.

5. Any cartman or drayman hauling wood which has been sold to any citizen, upon any other kind of carriage than the frame or standards above prescribed, shall be fined ten dollars, to be collected by the Wood Measurer and paid over to the Chamberlain of the city; and all fines when imposed for violations of this ordinance shall be collected by the Measurer and paid to the City Chamberlain; but it is not intended hereby to interfere with any cart or carriage of any kind which is owned or hired by the person who has purchased the wood for his or her own consumption.

6. It shall be the duty of the Measurer or his deputy to visit all the wood yards in the city and see that they are supplied with the above described standards or frames, to measure all wood sold by retail vendors above referred to, including that sold directly from boats, for which the seller shall pay him fifteen cents per cord.

7. Should individuals offer to sell wood brought into the city other than by railroads or water-carriage, by the cord, it shall be optional with the purchaser if or not the City Measurer shall measure it. If he does, and the quantity shall be found to be less than that claimed by the vendor, the fee of fifteen cents per cord shall be paid to the Measurer by the vendor, otherwise the fee shall be paid by the purchaser.

CHAPTER XXXIX.

CONCERNING THE MEASURING OF GRAIN.

1. Annually at the regular meeting of the Council in May, or as soon thereafter as may be convenient, the Council shall appoint a Measurer of grain, who shall hold his office until the regular meeting of the Council in May of the next year, and until his successor is appointed, unless sooner removed by the Council.

2. Every person who shall bring to this city, for sale or barter, grain of any kind, potatoes, or any other article hereinafter mentioned, to be sold by solid measure (if over ten bushels), may apply to the Measurer of grain to weigh the same.

3. When any article is provided for in this chapter to be sold by solid measure (except Irish potatoes when sold by the barrel), if either the seller or buyer require the article sold to be weighed under the superintendence of said Measurer, and the other contracting party refuse to have the same so weighed, the party refusing shall pay a fine of twenty dollars.

4. When required by either the seller or buyer of any article mentioned in this chapter, the said Measurer shall weigh such article and ascertain the number of bushels according to the standard herein named; and his certificate shall be binding on both parties as to the number of bushels, to wit: Wheat, sixty pounds; corn, fifty-six pounds; rye, fifty-six pounds; oats, thirty pounds; meal, fifty pounds; peas, fifty-six pounds; beans, sixty pounds; potatoes, fifty-eight pounds; clover seed, sixty pounds; timothy seed, forty-two pounds; bran, eighteen pounds; shorts, twenty-eight pounds; brownstuff, thirty-four pounds; shipstuff, forty-six pounds; coal, seventy pounds. If either seller or buyer of any such article refuse to be governed by this ordinance, he or they shall pay a fine of twenty dollars. It shall be the duty of the said Measurer to test the scales used by him at least once a week, and oftener, if required.

5. The said Measurer may appoint one or more deputies, who (when approved by the Council) may, after taking an oath faithfully to discharge the duties of his office, discharge any duties of his principal, but the principal shall be liable therefor; and any such deputy may at any time be removed from office by the principal or by the Council.

6. The said Measurer shall receive for his services one-half cent per bushel; and the buyer and seller shall each pay one-half of the said fee.

7. The said Measurer shall quarterly, to wit, on the first day of January, first day of April, first day of July, and the first day of October in each year, return to the Chamberlain an account of the number of bushels of each article weighed, and the amount received by him, verified by oath. He shall also cause to be published, at his cost (in a newspaper of this city), a statement of the number of bushels of each article mentioned in said report. If he fail for ten days to return such account, and make such publication, he shall pay a fine of ten dollars; and each subsequent day shall be a distinct offence.

CHAPTER XL.

CONCERNING THE WEIGHING OF LONG FORAGE AND OTHER ARTICLES.

1. Annually, at the regular meeting of the Council in November, there shall be appointed by the Council a Weigh-master for each of the first and second markets, who, before acting in his office, shall give bond in the penalty of one thousand dollars, payable to the city of Richmond, with surety approved by the Council, and with condition for the faithful discharge by him of the duties of his office; which bond shall remain filed in the Chamberlain's office. A vacancy in either of said offices may at any time be filled by the Council.

2. The Weigh-master for each market shall have the care of the city scales and balances at or near the market for which he is appointed; and he shall keep the same for public use. In person, or by a deputy approved by the Council, he shall from sunrise to sunset of every day (except Sunday) attend the place at which the scales and balances under his care are kept, and weigh such articles as may be brought to the said place to be weighed.

3. The toll-gatherer of the James River and Kanawha Company may, with the assent of that company, act as Weigh-master near the basin of the James river canal, provided he shall before acting as such give bond in the penalty of one thousand dollars, payable to the city of Richmond, with surety approved by the Council, and with condition faithfully to account for and pay to the city such part of the fees received by him under this ordinance, and at such time and in such manner as is hereby required. If before said bond is given and approved,

the said toll-gatherer, or any person in the employment or under color of the authority of said company, shall weigh an article in any case in which the said company is not allowed by its charter to have such weighing done, such toll-gatherer or other person shall pay a fine of not less than two nor more than twenty dollars. After said bond is given and approved, there shall for weighing done by said Weigh-master be paid him fees in every case in which the said company is not allowed by its charter to have such weighing done.

4. Forage in bales or bundles, brought by water, may be weighed at a place other than is before mentioned, provided proper balances for the purpose and the necessary labor be furnished by the owner at such place. If such place be at the dock or in James river, the Weigh-master for either the first or second market may act; and the profits arising therefrom shall be equally divided between the said Weigh-masters.

5. When hay, fodder, oats, shucks or other long forage is brought to the city, the same shall be examined, weighed and certified by a Weigh-master, according to the provisions of this chapter. And if such hay be in bales, the Weigh-master, after a satisfactory inspection thereof, shall mark each bale with the quality of the hay contained therein, either as "number one," "number two," or "refused," and shall moreover mark it with the weight of the hay, exclusive of the wood or other wrapping around or about it. If the person offering such hay for inspection shall request it, the Weigh-master shall unpack it, and weigh the hay and the wood or other wrapping separately, and then repack the same, such person furnishing as many hands at his own charge to assist the Weigh-master as may be necessary; otherwise the Weigh-master shall make such deduction from the gross weight for the wood or other wrapping as he may deem reasonable. The Weigh-master's certificate in such case shall be special, stating the weight and quality of the hay. Moreover he shall carefully remove from the bale any marks of its weight or quality other than his own.

6. Any person who shall sell or store for sale such hay, fodder, oats, shucks or other long forage, before it is weighed and certified by a Weigh-master, and in case such hay be in

bales before it is inspected and marked as aforesaid, or shall when it is brought in a vessel remove it any greater distance than is necessary to have it weighed, shall pay a fine of not less than two nor more than twenty dollars per bale, unless it be a case in which the owner of the land upon which the article was grown has brought it to this city for his sole and exclusive use, or be such a case of hay sent to this city in bales by a farmer of the state as is contemplated by the act of assembly, passed the twenty-second of March eighteen hundred and forty-seven, and mentioned in the fifty-fifth section of the charter of the city.

7. Upon receiving the fee hereinafter mentioned, the Weigh-master shall grant a certificate of the article weighed, specifying the owner's name, at whose instance it is weighed, and its true weight, exclusive, when forage is weighed, of the wagon or other article containing it and of any wood around or about such forage. And he shall date and sign said certificate, and in a book, kept for the purpose, make an entry of the article, placing each species of long forage in separate columns, which entry shall correspond with the certificate. He shall also, when a bundle of hay is weighed by him, mark its weight upon the binding of such bundle. If any person alter said certificate or mark he shall pay a fine of twenty dollars.

8. When the Weigh-master on examining an article deems it not merchantable he shall so mark it, and his certificate shall be special, stating the quality and condition of the article, or what deduction will render the residue merchantable.

9. The fees to be paid the Weigh-master shall be for hay, whether loose or in bales, fodder, oats, shucks or other long forage, two and a half cents per hundred pounds, and for any other article a cent and a half per hundred pounds.

10. Every Weigh-master shall, quarterly, on the first day of every January, April, July and October, return to the Auditor an account, verified on oath, of his receipts for fees within the preceding three months, and after deducting three-fourths thereof as a compensation for his services, shall pay the residue to the Chamberlain. If a Weigh-master fail for five days to render such account or to make such payment, the Auditor shall report such default to the Council at its first meeting thereafter.

CHAPER XLI.

CONCERNING THE GAUGING OF LIQUORS.

1. Annually, at the regular meeting of the Council in the month of May, or as soon thereafter as may be convenient, the Council shall appoint a Gauger of liquors, who shall hold his office until the regular meeting of the Council in May of the next year, and until his successor is appointed, unless sooner removed by the Council. When spirituous liquors, wine, oil, molasses, vinegar, spirits of turpentine and burning fluid in casks are brought to or manufactured or rectified in this city to be sold therein, either by wholesale or retail, the same before being sold shall be submitted to the Gauger, who shall gauge and inspect each cask, ascertain the proof of the spirits, the capacity of each cask, and shall, with irons to be kept by him for the purpose, mark on each cask near the bung the capacity in gallons and fractions of gallons, and the proof of the spirits, and on the head, with chalk, the capacity and ullage. And if the Gauger deem it necessary, he shall stop up the bung of the cask, and make a new one in such part as shall appear to him most likely to obviate the malconstruction of the cask.

2. If any person violate the preceding section, or if any person shall alter the mark put on the cask by the Gauger, or shall, on any cask which has not been gauged and inspected, put a mark similar to or in imitation of the Gauger's mark, every such person shall for each offence pay a fine of not less than five nor more than twenty dollars.

3. This ordinance shall not prevent a merchant from selling in this city any of the said liquors as heretofore, after the same shall have been once gauged and inspected therein. But no person shall sell or refill any empty cask on which the Gauger

has put his mark, until the mark denoting the proof shall be completely obliterated. Any person violating this section shall pay a fine of not less than two nor more than ten dollars.

4. The Gauger shall not during his continuance in office vend any of the articles required by this chapter to be gauged.

5. The Gauger may appoint one or more deputies, who after being approved by the Council, and taking an oath faithfully to discharge the duties of the office, may discharge any of the duties of his principal. But the principal shall be liable therefor, and such deputy may be removed from office at any time by his principal or by the Council.

6. For the purpose of more accurately ascertaining the capacity of every cask containing the liquids enumerated in the first section, the Gauger and his deputies shall make use of the scale known as Gunter's scale.

7. The person submitting any cask of spirituous liquors, wine, oil, molasses, vinegar, spirits of turpentine or burning fluid, to the Gauger, shall pay him for ascertaining the proof or gauging and marking the cask twenty-five cents for each cask.

8. Semi-annually on the first day of January and the first day of July, the Gauger shall return to the Auditor an account, verified by his oath, of the number and description of casks gauged by him within the preceding six months, and of the fees charged or received by him within that time by virtue of his office. He shall also cause to be published, at his cost, in a newspaper, a statement of the number and description of casks mentioned in said account. If he fail for five days to return such account, and have such publication made, he shall pay a fine of twenty dollars; and every subsequent five days that the failure continues shall be a distinct offence.

CHAPTER XLII.

CONCERNING POWDER.

1. Not more than fifty pounds of powder shall be transported in the city at one time, except by a military company, or in a vehicle constructed as the Engineer of the city shall prescribe.

2. The master of a vessel or steamer arriving in the port of Richmond with more than fifty pounds of powder on board, shall forthwith report the fact to the Harbor-master, and take such berth as he shall assign.

3. The head man of a boat arriving in the city by the canal or river with more than fifty pounds of powder on board, shall forthwith report the fact to a police officer, and take such berth in the basin or canal as he shall direct. No fire shall be used on board of a boat having such quantity of powder on board.

4. When any person delivers more than fifty pounds of powder to a vessel, steamer or canal boat, he shall notify forthwith the Harbor-master of such delivery to a vessel or steamer, and a police officer of such delivery to a canal boat. And the Harbor-master shall assign a proper berth to the vessel or steamer, and the police officer shall do the same to the canal boat.

5. No person shall keep in the city longer than twenty-four hours more than two pounds of powder, except in tin canisters, or more than twenty-five pounds elsewhere than in a magazine, which shall be approved by the Council.

6. Violations of sections one, two, three, four and five by any person mentioned therein, shall be punished by a fine of not less than five nor more than fifty dollars.

7. The committee on public grounds and buildings shall have supervision of the powder kept in or near the city, and may prescribe such regulations for the reception, storage, delivery and transportation of powder as the public safety requires. The Engineer of the city shall inspect annually the vehicles used for the transportation of powder, and report their condition to the said committee, who may require such changes and repairs to be made in the same as they deem necessary.

CHAPTER XLIII.

CONCERNING PORT WARDENS, AND THE SPEED OF STEAMBOATS.

1. Annually, in July, or as soon thereafter as practicable, there shall be appointed for the port of this city four Port Wardens, each of whom, before acting in his office, shall give bond in the penalty of two thousand dollars, payable to the city of Richmond, with surety approved by the Council, and with condition for the faithful discharge by him of the duties of his office; which bonds shall remain filed in the Chamberlain's office. On any of said bonds suit may be prosecuted from time to time, in the name of the city, for the benefit of any person injured by any breach of the condition, as often as any such breach may be alleged, until there shall be recovered for the breaches damages equal to the penalty of the bond. The said Port Wardens shall continue in office until their successors are appointed.

2. Two of the Port Wardens, when called on by the owner or master of or any person interested in a vessel, which, or its sails or rigging, arrives in the port in a damaged state, shall inspect such vessel, sails and rigging, and assess the damage, and upon receiving for their services a fee of six dollars, grant a certificate of said damage.

3. If a captain or master of a vessel arriving in the port shall enter his protest before the hatches of his vessel shall have been removed, or if he shall, within twenty-four hours after his vessel shall have been moored to a wharf, give notice to two of the Port Wardens that he has entered his protest before removing the hatches, the two Port Wardens called on by said captain or master shall inspect the condition and storage of the cargo, and

on receiving for their services a fee of three dollars, grant a certificate stating whether, in their opinion, said cargo has been properly stowed and whether damaged or not.

4. When a captain or master of a vessel shall have removed the hatches of his vessel to land a cargo at Norfolk or any port on James river, and shall produce to two Port Wardens satisfactory evidence of his having at the time called for an inspection in regular manner, he shall be entitled to a further inspection; and the two Port Wardens shall proceed therewith.

5. When the two Port Wardens, on inspecting the cargo, find the same or any part thereof damagod, they shall immediately give notice to the consignee or the owner thereof, or person interested therein, and if requested by him, shall assess the damages to the cargo or such part of it as is damaged, and on receiving three dollars from the consignee, if there be but one, and one dollar from each consignee, if there be more than one, shall grant a certificate of their assessment to the consignee or owner of each separate shipment or the person interested therein.

6. When two Port Wardens disagree a third shall be called on, and of the two, that opinion to which the third approximates the nearest shall be taken as the judgment. The fees of Port Wardens shall be equally divided among those rendering the services.

7. When a cargo, or any part thereof, is abandoned to the underwriters, the Port Wardens shall take charge of the same, and after giving, in one or more of the newspapers of the city, such notice of the time and place of sale, as in reference to the nature and condition of the damaged articles they may deem advisable, shall sell what is so abandoned, at public auction, and after deducting the cost of advertising, necessary expenses for labor and for their services a commission of one and a quarter per centum, shall faithfully account for and pay the residue to the parties entitled.

8. The Port Wardens shall keep a record of their proceedings, and annually, at the regular meeting of the Council in July, return an account, on oath, of their receipts within the preceding year by virtue of their offices. If they fail to make such

return, neither of them shall be capable of being re-elected, unless he satisfies the Council of his inability to make it.

9. The captain or commander of every steamboat coming into or departing from the port of this city, shall, on its arriving within half a mile of the port, or while it is not more than half a mile from the port, retard its speed to one-half its usual rate, or fourteen revolutions of its wheels per minute. If he fail so to do, he shall pay a fine of ten dollars.

CHAPTER XLIV.

CONCERNING THE EMPLOYMENT OF PRISONERS IN THE CITY JAIL.

SEC.
1. Mayor may order persons in jail to be employed on public works.
2. May depute police or appoint others to attend prisoners whilst at work.

SEC.
3. Prisoner whilst at work shall have chain and ball attached to him.
4. Compensation to person not a police officer for attending prisoners.

1. The Mayor of the city may, by his warrant directed to the keeper of the jail of the city, order such persons as he may designate, and as are liable to be employed under the act of the general assembly, passed February 26th, 1856, and entitled "An act for establishing a workhouse in the city of Richmond," to be employed on the public work of the city, under the management of the Overseer of the public hands. In said warrant shall be specified the names of such persons, the number of days and the hours of the day during which such persons shall be so employed; and for sufficient cause to him appearing, the Mayor may supersede his said warrant, when the said employment of such persons shall cease. Such persons under the management of the Overseer shall be employed on the same works, and in like manner with the city hands under his control, but shall be furnished while so employed, by the keeper of the city jail, with proper food, clothing and lodging, in like manner with the other prisoners committed to the jail.

2. The Mayor may, by his order, depute any one or more of the police of the city, and should the refractory conduct of the prisoners make it necessary, may appoint other person or persons to attend the prisoners whilst at work, and passing and re-pass-

ing from the jail to the place of employment. It shall be the duty of such police or persons so appointed to enforce orderly behaviour and obedience of the prisoners to the Overseer when out of the custody of the jailor; and for this purpose they may command any person or persons to aid and assist in apprehending and securing such prisoners. Should any person, when required to aid and assist in apprehending and securing a prisoner as aforesaid, neglect or refuse so to aid and assist, such person shall pay a fine not exceeding ten dollars for every such offence.

3. For the more perfect security of the prisoners, the Superintendent of streets shall have provided a chain and ball for each prisoner that may be worked on the streets, to be affixed to his leg before leaving the jail, and not to be taken off until returned to jail.

4. Any person, other than a police officer, charged with and duly performing the police duty provided for in the first section of this ordinance, shall, on the Mayor's certificate that he is justly entitled thereto, be paid two dollars and fifty cents for every day that he is so employed.

TITLE 7.

NUISANCES.

CHAPTER XLV.

CONCERNING ANIMALS.

1. No hog or pig shall be kept on any lot or allowed to go at large within the limits of the city. Any person violating the provisions of this section shall pay a fine of not less than two nor more than twenty dollars; and such hog or pig shall be forfeited.

2. No dog or bitch shall be permitted to go at large in any street, lane or alley in this city, until the owner or keeper thereof shall have paid to the City Chamberlain one dollar and fifty cents, for the use of the city, for the first dog or bitch, and five dollars for every dog thereafter. And for any failure to comply with the provisions of this section, the owner of such dog or bitch shall pay a fine of not less than ten nor more than twenty dollars.

3. The Chamberlain shall grant a license to any person for his or her dog to go at large, on the payment to the City Chamberlain of one dollar and fifty cents for the first and five dollars for each dog over one; which license shall expire on the first day of February next after the same is given. He shall keep a record of all such licenses, and furnish each person taking such license with a medal with the number of such license stamped

thereon (the shape of the medal to be changed each year), which shall be kept about the neck of the dog attached to a collar, with the owner's name engraved or written thereon. If any person shall attach such medal to the collar of any dog without having obtained such license according to this ordinance, he shall pay a fine of not less than five nor more than twenty dollars, and said dog shall be killed.

4. Every unlicensed dog found going at large off the lot or premises of the owner or keeper of such dog, shall be taken and killed as directed by this ordinance: provided, that any unlicensed dog may be redeemed by his owner or any other person for him paying to the police officer having the custody of such dog five dollars, for the use of the city, at any time before sunset of the day on which said dog is taken.

5. If any person shall permit any dangerous or vicious animal owned or kept by him or her to go at large with or without a license, he shall be fined not less than one nor more than twenty dollars; and such animal may be killed by order of the Mayor, if after twenty-four hours' notice such animal is not removed beyond the limits of the corporation by the owner thereof. No butcher's dog shall appear or be brought into the markets on any account; and any such dog being found at or in any market house in this city shall be taken and considered within the meaning of this ordinance as a vicious animal going at large.

6. If any person shall unlawfully and without necessity kill a licensed dog, not vicious or dangerous, without authority from the owner of such dog, or shall steal or take away such dog with intent fraudulently to deprive the owner or keeper of the use of such dog, he shall be fined twenty dollars.

7. If any person shall suffer his cow or calf to be in any street or public alley of this city in the night time, he may be fined not less than one nor more than five dollars

8. If any owner or other person having the custody of any horse, mule, swine or goat, shall turn loose or permit the same to go at large in any public street or alley, he shall be fined not less than one nor more than five dollars, and every such hog or goat shall be taken and sold for the use of the city. But nothing

in this chapter shall be so construed as to subject any one visiting the city with his or her dog to any fine or forfeiture for ten days after their arrival; nor to prevent the owner or keeper of any animal (not vicious or dangerous) from driving it through the streets or alleys in coming into, going from or passing through the city. Nor shall this section apply to any goat, for which the owner thereof has obtained a license from the Chamberlain for keeping the same, for the time allowed by said license. But the said license shall only be obtained upon the certificate of the family physician, declaring that goat's milk is absolutely essential to the health of a member of said family; and fixing a period during which he conceives it will be so essential. A fee of one dollar shall be paid for every such license.

9. If any person shall cruelly beat or torture any horse, mule, dog or other animal, whether his own or that of another, he shall be fined not less than five nor more than twenty dollars.

10. The officers of police shall take up and secure hogs, dogs and goats going at large in violation of this ordinance. The Mayor may, as often as he sees occasion therefor, require the Overseer of the city hands to send through the city as many of the city hands, carts and horses as he may deem necessary, furnished with the fixtures and apparatus provided therefor, and put therein all hogs, dogs and goats so found at large. Such of the police officers as the Mayor may direct shall accompany said carts; and any person who shall prevent a hog, dog or goat from being taken under this ordinance by said officer, shall pay a fine of not less than one nor more than twenty dollars. Every hog, dog or goat taken up under this ordinance shall be removed to a place of deposit to be provided by the Mayor, and any such dog shall be kept until sunset of the day on which he was taken up, unless sooner redeemed. The owner of such dog so taken up, or on his failure until sunset, any other person may redeem such dog by paying to the police officer having such dog in charge, five dollars; but every dog not redeemed shall, under the direction of the Mayor, be conveyed beyond the corporate limits at least five hundred yards, and there put to death and buried; and every hog or goat taken up shall be sold at public auction by

a police officer, for the use of the city, at such time and place as the Mayor may direct.

11. Every police officer receiving money for dogs redeemed or for hogs or goats sold, under this ordinance, shall render to the Chamberlain an account thereof, verified by his oath, and shall pay the sum so received to the Chamberlain.

CHAPTER XLVI.

CONCERNING NUISANCES NOT IN STREETS.

1. If any person shall put or cause to be put into the canal, locks or dock, or any basin of the James River and Kanawha Company, or upon the margin of James river, within the corporate limits of this city, or the pond of the water works, the carcass of any animal, filth or nuisance of any kind, he shall be fined not less than five nor more than fifty dollars. And the like fine shall be imposed on the said company, if it shall suffer or permit any boat with offensive stagnant water or other nuisance therein to remain more than twenty-four hours in said canal, locks, dock or basin; and the captain or owner of such boat may also be fined not less than five nor more than twenty dollars. Every such nuisance when suffered to remain as aforesaid by the said company, shall be removed at the expense of the said company, by an officer of the police, or at the expense of the person so putting or causing it to be put, if he be known, otherwise at the expense of the city.

2. If any person shall put or cause to be put into any cellar or house, or upon any other private property not owned or occupied by him, any filth or nuisance of any kind, he shall be fined not less than one nor more than twenty dollars.

3. If any person shall employ any person other than those appointed by the Council to remove from any house or lot or any other place, any filth or other nuisance, and such person shall waste the same in the street or alley, or shall put or cause the same to be put into or upon any land or place mentioned in either of the preceding sections, the person so employing such person and the said person shall each be fined not less than two nor more than twenty dollars.

4. If any person shall have or suffer any noxious, unwholesome or offensive matter, stagnant water or nuisance of any kind, in any house or cellar, or upon any other private property owned or occupied by him, he shall be fined not less than one nor more than twenty dollars: provided, however, that if any such nuisance be caused or arise from the want of proper and sufficient draining, the occupier of any lot or tenement, if he be not the owner thereof, shall not be fined for such nuisance, if immediately after the existence of the same he give notice thereof to the owner; and unless, after such notice, the owner abate or remove such nuisance by proper and sufficient draining or otherwise, within such time as the Mayor or justice may prescribe, he shall be fined not less than ten nor more than fifty dollars.

5. Upon the complaint of any citizen or information given by any police officer to the Mayor or other justice, that a privy is so placed as to be offensive, he may, upon summons returned executed against the owner, order such privy to be removed.

6. If any person shall erect, have or keep any slaughter house or distillery in this city, he shall on proof thereof be held guilty of a nuisance, and be fined not less than twenty nor more than fifty dollars for each day the said nuisance shall continue.

7. If a person shall, within two hundred feet of a dwelling house, without permission of the owner or occupier thereof, burn any lime-kiln, brick-kiln or any other kiln, he shall pay a fine of not less than one nor more than five dollars for every hour the same may be burning.

8. On complaint to the Mayor that unslacked lime has been stored on premises within fifty feet of any house in this city, he shall issue a warrant, directed to three freeholders, to examine the said premises. If they deem it dangerous that the lime should be stored on said premises, the owner or occupier shall remove the same within twelve hours after being notified thereof. If he shall fail so to do he shall pay a fine not exceeding ten dollars; and for each hour thereafter that the same continues to be stored, he shall pay a fine of not less than two nor more than twenty dollars.

9. A stove pipe passing in or through a floor, partition, roof or side of a house, shall be enclosed the whole of such passage in earthenware or mortar or tin casing filled with sand, and if passing through a window, shall be enclosed with tin or sheet-iron; it shall extend two feet beyond the roof or side of the house, and if through the side of the house, it shall be capped with a cross pipe at least eighteen inches long; and no stove pipe shall project into a street. If any person put up, construct or use in any building in this city, any stove pipe otherwise than according to and in conformity with the foregoing directions and regulations, he shall be fined not less than five nor more than twenty dollars; and each day that the same shall continue shall be a distinct offence, and punishable as such by a fine of twenty dollars.

10. If any person shall put fire to a chimney to clean it, except in the day time, and whilst the roof of the house to which it is attached is well covered with snow, or whilst it is raining, and the roof thoroughly wet thereby; or if the chimney of any house shall take fire from not having been properly cleaned, the occupier of any such house shall be fined not less than two nor more than five dollars.

11. If any person shall sell or expose for sale in this city any torpedoes, popcrackers, squibs or other fireworks of any kind whatever, except in packages containing each at least one hundred, or shall without permission in writing from the Mayor, discharge or set off, in any street or alley of the city, any balloon, rocket, torpedo, popcracker, fireworks or any combination of gunpowder, or any other combustible or dangerous

material; or if any person shall, except under the forty-fourth section of the chapter concerning streets, without necessity, fire or discharge in this city any cannon, gun, pistol or other fire-arms of any kind, or shall make therein any unusual noise, whereby the inhabitants thereof may be alarmed, or raise or fly a kite in this city; or if any auctioneer shall use any bell or herald to notify the public of any sale, except of real property, every such person herein offending shall pay a fine of not less than one nor more than twenty dollars.

12. No person, firm or incorporated company shall keep in any house in the city any loaded shell or shot, or any explosive material of any sort, not authorized by ordinance. And any person, firm or incorporated company violating the provision of this section shall be fined not less than twenty nor more than one hundred dollars; and each day on which the same is so kept in the city shall be a distinct offence and punishable as such.

13. Every hotel keeper and keeper of a restaurant, lager beer saloon, or other place where ardent spirits, beer, cider or other drinks are sold or given away, shall close the bar where such drinks are sold or given away, every Sunday during the whole day. And any person violating the provision of this section shall be fined not less than twenty nor more than fifty dollars.

14. If any person shall by swimming, bathing, or in any otherwise, indirectly expose his person, or any part thereof, to the public view, or cause any person so to do within this city, or the river adjacent thereto, he shall be fined not less than one nor more than twenty dollars.

15. If after the Council, on the petition of the owners of not less than one-fourth of the ground included in any square in the city, shall have prohibited the erection in such square of any building or of any addition to any building more than ten feet high (unless the outer walls thereof be made of brick and mortar or stone and mortar), it be alleged by any officer of police or any citizen, to the Mayor or any other justice, that any person has erected any building or addition contrary to such prohibition, the said Mayor or justice shall have the said person summoned before him; and upon proof that a building or addition has been erected contrary to such prohibition, shall order him to remove

the same. And if it be alleged in like manner to the Mayor or any other justice that any building or wall of any kind hath become dangerous to citizens or to adjoining property by dilapidation or otherwise, he shall in like manner have the owner thereof or his agent summoned before him; and upon proof that the said building or wall, or any part thereof, is dangerous as aforesaid, shall order the said owner or agent to remove or repair the same or so much thereof as is dangerous as aforesaid.

16. Hereafter no wooden building shall be erected in the city, nor shall any wooden addition be made to any building already erected, without permission first had and obtained from the Council. Any person violating this section shall be fined not less than twenty nor more than fifty dollars; and for every day it shall remain after the first fine is imposed it shall be a distinct offence and punishable as such.

17. Upon its being alleged by a citizen or any officer of police, to the Mayor or any other justice, that ground in the city owned by a non-resident thereof, and not occupied by any person residing thereon, is subject to be covered by stagnant water, or that such owner permits or suffers any offensive or unwholesome substance to accumulate or remain thereon, reasonable notice of such allegation shall be given by the said Mayor or justice to the said owner or his agent, if any he has; and in case he has no such agent, by publication for not less than four weeks in a newspaper printed in said city. The said Mayor or justice shall communicate to the Council the fact of such allegation and notice, that they may cause such ground to be filled up, raised or drained, or to cause such substances to be covered or removed therefrom, and to collect the expense of so doing from the owner or owners, occupier or occupiers, or any of them, by distress and sale, in the same manner in which taxes levied upon real estate for the benefit of said city are authorized to be collected.

18. In every case arising under this ordinance, except under the seventeenth section, the Mayor, in addition to any fine he may impose, may in his discretion order the nuisance complained of to be abated or removed, whether specially so directed or not, and shall prescribe the time within which such order shall be

executed; and if any person shall, after notice of such order, fail or refuse to obey the same within the time prescribed (not in any case to exceed ten days), he shall be fined not less than ten nor more than twenty dollars for each day that such nuisance shall thereafter exist or remain; and he may moreover cause such nuisance to be abated at the cost of the person offending. If such cost shall not exceed one hundred dollars, he may issue execution therefor against the goods and chattels of the offender for the use of the city; and when such expense shall exceed one hundred dollars, an account thereof shall be filed by the Mayor with the Chamberlain, who shall proceed forthwith to collect the same by suit for the like use.

TITLE 8.

THE POOR.

CHAPTER XLVII.

CONCERNING THE POOR OF THE CITY.

1. The committee for the relief of the poor shall have the government, control and direction of the almshouse and grounds, and of any other buildings and grounds which may be acquired or used for the benefit of the poor of the city. It shall likewise have the government, control and direction of all the officers, agents, nurses and other employees connected with the institution, and of the poor receiving aid or relief from the city. And except the Superintendent of the almhouse, it shall appoint all such officers, agents and employees, prescribe their duties and fix their compensation. And it may prescribe the duties of the Superintendent.

2. To carry out the foregoing powers and duties, the committee shall prepare rules and regulations for the government, direction and control of the institution and of the officers, agents, employees and inmates connected with it, which shall be submitted to the Council; and when, or so far as they may be

approved by the Council, they shall have full force and effect as if embraced in this ordinance. And if at any time the committee shall be of opinion that other rules and regulations should be made, or those in force should be changed, such additions and changes shall be prepared and submitted to the Council, and when approved, shall have the same force and effect as if they had been originally adopted.

3. The officers of the institution shall be a Superintendent of the almshouse, who shall be elected by the Council at its regular term in the month of May, or as soon thereafter as may be; a physician, a matron of the almshouse and a matron of the hospital. And the salary of the Superintendent shall be fixed by the Council.

4. The committee may remove any officer, agent or employee engaged in the institution, except the Superintendent, and they may for any misconduct or neglect of duty, suspend him from the performance of his duties, and report the fact to the Council; and for this purpose shall call a meeting of the Council within three days. And the Council shall either restore him or dismiss him from his office as his conduct shall merit.

5. Any person who has lived in the city for one year at the time, may by himself or herself or another person, apply to one of the committee of the ward in which such applicant lives, for relief either for such applicant or his or her family; and if the said member of the committee shall be satisfied that the applicant or the family are proper subjects for the almshouse, he shall give to such applicant an order to the Superintendent directing him to receive the applicant, or the family, as may be, into the almshouse: and upon the presentation of such order to the Superintendent, he shall receive the person or persons who are embraced in it, and provide for them until the physician of the almshouse shall make his next visit. He shall then report the case to the physician, who shall examine the parties; and if he shall be of opinion that he or they are proper subjects for the almshouse, he shall endorse the order to that effect, and the party or parties shall be permitted to remain. But if the physician shall be of opinion that the party or parties are not proper subjects for the almshouse, he shall endorse the same on said order; and the

Superintendent shall thereupon dismiss them; and said party or parties shall not be again admitted to the almshouse for the same cause except by the order of the committee.

6. No out-door relief shall be given except in the most urgent cases, in which a physician attending on the person for whom application for relief is made, shall state in writing, or a member of the committee for the ward, upon his own view, shall be of opinion, that the person cannot be removed to the almshouse without endangering his life. In such case and upon such statement the members of the committee in that ward, acting together, may order such relief as they shall deem necessary; and shall report the case to the committee at its next meeting. And if in such case it is necessary to expend money immediately, they may give an order on the Auditor for the amount.

7. In cases in which a person who has not lived in the city for a year, is in the city sick and destitute, or not in a condition to provide for him or herself, or his or her children, he, she or they may be sent to and received and examined and treated at the almshouse in the mode provided in the fifth section of this chapter, but shall only remain there until he or she has recovered from his or her sickness, or is in a condition to provide for him or herself, or the children. But the Superintendent may, with the concurrence of the physician and the committee, discharge them at any time. And if any person is in the city sick and destitute, or if any destitute female or children, unable to provide for themselves, are in the city, and are likely to become chargeable to the city, the committee may send such persons to their homes; and the expense of so doing shall be paid by the Auditor upon the order of the chairman.

8. The committee shall hold monthly meetings at the almshouse, on such day as may be fixed by them. At these meetings the Superintendent and physician shall lay before the committee a statement of the supplies, and an estimate of their cost, which will be needed in their departments, respectively, up to the end of the second succeeding month; and the committee shall determine which and how much of said supplies shall be purchased, and may fix a price therefor, which shall not be exceeded; and the committee may authorize the purchase of

supplies for a longer period than one month, if they deem it expedient. When the committee have ascertained and entered on their journal the amount which will be necessary to be expended for the expenses of the institution during the next month, they may, if they shall deem it expedient, authorize the chairman to draw upon the Auditor, on a copy of the resolution, in favor of the Superintendent and physician, respectively, for the amount which the committee has fixed for expenses in their respective departments during the next month; and the clerk of the committee shall, immediately after the meeting, report to the Auditor the amount fixed upon for said expenses, and the resolution authorizing the chairman to draw upon him in favor of the Superintendent and physician.

9. At each monthly meeting of the committee, the Superintendent and any other officer or agent empowered by the committee to make any contract which involves the expenditure of money, shall present his accounts for the transactions of the previous month, with his vouchers, and after the same has been examined by the committee, and the committee is satisfied of its correctness, or so far as the same is ascertained to be correct, it shall be approved; and if any money is due thereon from the city it shall be paid by a draft of the chairman upon the Auditor; and in every case a copy of said account shall be returned to the Auditor: provided, that the expenses of the institution for the said previous month do not exceed the amount to which the Council may have restricted the expenditure, or which they may have appropriated for the relief of the poor, if a specific appropriation has been made for that purpose.

10. The committee shall keep a record of its proceedings, and for this purpose may employ a clerk, and make him a per diem allowance for his services. The clerk shall certify to the Auditor of the city the names of the several officers appointed by the committee under the first section, and the amount of compensation allowed to each. And the said officers may draw the same in monthly instalments upon application to the Auditor.

11. The committee shall report annually to the Council at its regular meeting in March; in which report they shall state the number of persons provided for in the year, showing how many

were white and how many colored, for what length of time and where each was provided for or assisted, the name of each, and the amount expended by the committee for the year for the support of the poor, distinguishing the amount expended for those at the almshouse or other building used for their lodging, from the amount expended for out-door relief; and whether any, and if any, how many, and which were kept at work, and for what length of time. They shall also state the amount expended in repairs of buildings or otherwise, not embraced in the amount expended for the support of the poor proper. They shall also make such recommendations, upon any or all of the objects included within the sphere of their powers and duties, as they shall be of opinion should be acted on by the Council.

12. In respect to all matters not provided for in this chapter, the committee shall have the power and perform the duties vested in and required of overseers of the poor by the fifty-first and one hundred and twenty-sixth chapters of the Code of eighteen hundred and forty-nine, so far as the same is not inconsistent with this ordinance. And if in executing any power or duty under the said chapters of the Code of eighteen hundred and forty-nine, it shall be necessary to act as overseers of the poor, they shall be such for that purpose, and they shall act with the organization they have as a committee, the chairman acting as president of the board.

CHAPTER XLVIII.

CONCERNING BEGGARS.

Police officers to inform committee for relief of the poor of persons begging.

It shall be one of the duties of the police officers of the city to give to some member of the committee for the relief of the poor such information in relation to every person going about begging, or staying in any street or other place to beg, as will enable such committeeman to proceed in the case, according to chapters fifty-one and one hundred and twenty-six of the Code of Virginia.

CHAPTER XLIX.

CONCERNING VAGRANTS.

1. Every railroad company and every captain or master of a steamboat or vessel, which or who shall bring to the city of Richmond or to the port thereof from another state or country any person not having ostensible means for his or her support, shall, before such person shall be permitted to leave the cars or the vessel, enter into bond to the city in the penalty of five hundred dollars, with condition to pay to the city any sum or sums of money which the city may expend during the next twelve months from the date of such bond for the support or care of such person. And if such railroad company, captain or master of a steamboat or vessel, shall fail or refuse to give such bond, such company, captain or master shall be required to keep such person in the depot of such company, or on board of his vessel, until such person shall be taken back beyond the limits of the state, by the company, captain or master who shall have brought him to the city.

2. If any railroad company, captain or master of a steamboat or vessel, shall fail to comply with the preceding section, or shall bring any such person as is therein mentioned near to the city, and permit him to leave the cars or his steamboat or vessel, and such person shall come into the city, such railroad company, captain or master shall be fined twenty dollars for each person; and every day that such person shall remain in the city shall be a separate offence.

3. It shall be the duty of the police of the city to arrest all persons having no ostensible means of support, who shall have come to the city within the preceding six months; and all persons known as robbers and pick-pockets, who have come from

other states within the same period, and to take them before the Mayor; and if the Mayor shall be satisfied that they are such persons as herein described, he shall commit them to jail until they can be sent back to the place from whence they came, if their former residence can be ascertained, and if not then to some place out of the state.

4. If the Mayor can ascertain by whose steamboat or vessel such persons were brought to the city or near it, he shall have them put on the cars of such railroad or on such steamboat or vessel; and it shall be the duty of such railroad company or captain or master of such steamboat or vessel to take back such person at their own expense or the expense of the persons themselves. And if such persons cannot be put on such car or vessel, they shall be sent out of the state at the expense of the city.

5. Any railroad company or captain or master of a steamboat or vessel, which or who shall refuse to receive such persons brought to the city or near thereto, upon their cars, steamboat or vessel, and to take them back, shall be fined twenty dollars for each person.

6. If any person described in the first or third sections of this chapter shall return to the city after having been sent away, he shall be placed in the chain gang of the city, and compelled to work upon the streets.

TITLE 9.

EDUCATION.

CHAPTER L.

CONCERNING THE EDUCATION OF INDIGENT CHILDREN.

Whereas, all the interest, rights, powers and duties enjoyed and exercised by the subscribers to the Richmond Lancasterian School, or by the board of trustees for said school, as organized under the act of incorporation, passed 22d of February 1816, were, by an act passed on the 10th day of January 1834, transferred to and vested in the Common Council of the city of Richmond, with power to the Council to pass laws, ordinances, rules and regulations for the proper government of said school: therefore,

1. The trustees which, under the second section of the said act and the forty-ninth section of the act to revise and amend the charter of the city, the Council has power to appoint for the management of the said school, shall be elected annually at the stated meeting of the Council in the month of May, or as soon thereafter as practicable, and continue in office until their successors are appointed; and at least three of said trustees shall be members of the Council.

2. A majority of the trustees shall constitute a quorum for the transaction of business. They shall appoint a president and secretary, and may allow the latter a compensation not

exceeding fifty dollars a year. They shall appoint a superintendent, assistant and other teachers, and fix their compensation, and report the names and compensation to the Council at its next regular meeting for approval; and they may authorize other disbursements. Such compensation and disbursements shall be paid by the Auditor upon the order of the board of trustees for such payment, attested by their secretary: provided the amount thereof does not exceed the annual appropriation to and other income of the said school; and that no payment of a salary of an officer or teacher shall be made until the report herein required has been made to and approved by the Council.

3. The rules and regulations for the management of the school which are now in force shall, so far as is consistent with this chapter, continue in force until altered, repealed or modified by the trustees, with the approbation of the Council.

4. There shall be paid annually to the order of the board of trustees of the Lancasterian School, the interest on the two thousand one hundred and fifty dollars of the stock purchased with the money received under a decree of the superior court of chancery for the Richmond circuit, made on the 27th day of February 1849, in the case of the Lancasterian School and the Mayor of Richmond v. Blair's executors and others, and two-thirds of the interest or dividends of the stock or certificates which have been purchased with the proceeds of the property devised by Whitaker Shadforth, and a further sum not exceeding sixteen hundred dollars. There shall be paid annually to the order of the trustees of the Female Humane Association of the city of Richmond one-third of the interest or dividends of the stock or certificates which have been purchased, with the proceeds of the property devised by Whitaker Shadforth, and the further sum of four hundred and twenty dollars; and there shall be paid annually to the Richmond Male Orphan Society five hundred dollars.

5. The sum of twenty-three hundred dollars is hereby annually appropriated as a fund for primary schools for the education of indigent children in the elementary branches of knowledge.

6. When the ward committees on primary schools are appointed, or as soon thereafter as may be, the Council shall apportion among the several wards the money appropriated to

primary schools for the year. The said committees may regulate for their respective wards the purchase and distribution of books, stationery and other things for the use of the schools, the selection of the teachers, the number of indigent children to be taught in each school, and the rate at which their tuition shall be paid for.

7. The committee for each ward may subscribe to schools in their ward for such tuition of indigent children as they shall think proper, at the rate allowed by the committee, so that the aggregate of what they subscribe, and the purchases of books, stationery and other things for the use of the schools in said wards, shall not together exceed said ward's portion of the fund.

8. Each of said ward committees shall choose a chairman and give notice thereof to the Auditor. Any member of the committee may call a meeting thereof. Payments may be made out of the treasury of the city, upon an order of said committee, signed by the chairman, or in his absence from the meeting by the member presiding, not exceeding the amount appropriated to said ward.

9. The committee for each ward shall at least once in every three months visit the primary schools therein, examine or inquire into the character and qualifications of the teachers, and the conduct and progress of the pupils, and note such as on account of their proficiency and good conduct should be educated in a high school.

10. The committee for each ward shall for each year make a report, showing, as far as practicable, the number of the indigent children within such ward, the number of schools, and names of the teachers therein for such children, and the number of children educated in each of said schools, and stating the committee's receipts, disbursements and proceedings.

11. The Richmond Lancasterian School shall be a high school for the education of those whom the committee for any ward may, under the ninth section, note on account of their proficiency and good conduct, and a school for the education of such other children as may be received therein, under the rules and regulations for its management which may hereafter be in force. Said committee shall cause information to be promptly given to the superintendent of the high school of all so noted.

12. The trustees of the Lancasterian school shall revise the rules and regulations for its management, and submit to the

Council for its approbation such rules and regulations as they may deem proper, to elevate the character of the school according to the intent of the preceding sections. The said trustees shall make report annually of the number of children educated in said school, showing the largest and the smallest number on any one day, and for each month the average number on each school-day of said month, stating the number of males separately from the number of females; the names of the teachers in said school; their compensation respectively; the branches of knowledge which they each teach; the condition of the school and what is wanted to make it operate more beneficially; the said report shall also show the receipts and disbursements for the year.

13. The trustees of the Lancasterian School shall have a public examination annually of the children taught in said school, and appoint to superintend said examination five citizens.

14. If of the scholars educated at the Lancasterian School (above the age of seventeen), there be any who, with reference to his character, capacity and the inability of the parent or pupil to furnish the means of education, ought, in the opinion of the superintendent or of the trustees, to be an applicant to be educated at the University of Virginia without charge, the superintendent, with the approbation of the trustees, shall cause testimonials on his behalf to be presented to the visitors and faculty of the University, according to the sixth section of the seventy-ninth chapter of the Code of Virginia. The names of those for whom application is so made to the visitors and faculty, shall be mentioned in the annual report of the trustees. If in any case the trustees should deem it proper that an appropriation should be made by the Council to obtain for any applicant the benefit contemplated by the said sixth section of chapter seventy-nine, they shall recommend to the Council in every such case such sum to be appropriated for this purpose as the said trustees shall deem advisable.

15. The annual reports required from said committees and from the trustees of the Lancasterian School, shall be for the year ending the thirtieth day of March, and shall be returned to the clerk of the Council annually before the stated meeting of the Council in April.

TITLE 10.

OFFICERS.

CHAPER LI.

CONCERNING THE CORONER OF THE CITY.

1. A room with the necessary furniture and fixtures shall be provided under the direction of the committee on police, to be under the control and management of the Coroner of the city, for the use of the said Coroner in taking inquests, and in the making of post mortem examinations, and discharging any other duties of his office.

2. The Coroner shall report semi-annually to the Council all cases in which he shall be called upon to examine a dead body, and shall examine the same, stating the nature of the case and the apparent cause of the death.

3. For all cases in which the Coroner shall be called upon to examine a dead body, and shall examine the same, but shall not consider it a proper subject for an inquest, he shall be entitled to a fee of five dollars for each case.

4. When an inquest is held over a dead body, in addition to the fee allowed by law, when the inquest is prolonged in consequence of the want of or search for witnesses, &c., he shall be allowed a per diem of five dollars while actually engaged in such inquest. And whenever the Coroner shall deem a post mortem examination necessary, and the same is made, he shall be allowed the sum of twenty-five dollars for such post mortem examination, whether made by himself, if he is a physician, or some other

physician; and this allowance shall be in full of any allowance by the Hustings Court of the city for this object; and any such allowance shall be paid by himself.

5. Where the Coroner is called to see a dead body, and there are no friends of the deceased who will bury the same, he shall have the body decently buried, and shall be allowed the reasonable expenses attending said burial. But this section shall not apply to cases provided for by the ninth section of chapter two hundred and two of the Code.

CHAPTER LII.

CONCERNING THE SURVEYOR OF THE CITY.

1. The duties of the City Surveyor shall be the same within the city as those of a county surveyor in a county, as prescribed by the laws of the state. For any service performed by him in the city, by virtue of his office, he may charge the party at whose instance such service is performed, at the rate, for each hour necessarily taken by him, of one dollar and fifty cents for the first hour, and of one dollar for each succeeding hour so taken; and when he performs a service, the whole fee for which, at this rate, would be less than one dollar, he may charge therefor one dollar, instead of at the rate aforesaid. What is allowed in this section to the Surveyor shall be deemed full compensation, not only for his own services, but also for the services of any chain carrier or assistants that he may employ.

2. The City Surveyor shall keep his office in such place in the city as the Council may designate. His books of record and other official papers shall be kept in his said office. He shall reside in the city, and be in his office at least one hour each day, Sundays, Christmas day, the first day of January, the fourth of July and twenty-second of February excepted.

3. The cost of any books procured by the Surveyor of the city shall be paid for by the Auditor when directed by the Council.

CHAPTER LIII.

CONCERNING THE ATTORNEY, CLERK AND SERGEANT.

1. There shall be paid to the Attorney appointed to prosecute for the commonwealth in the Court of Hustings for said city, what the said court, under any act of assembly authorizing the same, shall hereafter, from time to time, allow the said Attorney for his public services; and there shall be paid to the Clerk of said court and the Sergeant of said city what the said court may, from time to time, allow to them respectively under the like authority. Whenever the Sergeant, under any law of the state, appoints a deputy to hold an election or employs writers to enter names in the poll-books, the Sergeant, out of what is so allowed him for his services to the public and the city, shall pay such deputies and writers in like manner as the sheriff of a county, out of his allowance, pays deputies and writers employed by him.

2. Until it is otherwise provided, the Attorney so appointed to prosecute for the commonwealth, may act in other matters as Attorney and counsel for the city. As such he shall give his opinion and advice, in writing, when required to do so by the Council, or by any committee thereof, or by any officer appointed by the Council; and he shall appear as counsel for the city in any civil case in which it is interested, depending in any court in Richmond; and when the constitutionality or validity of an ordinance of the city is brought in issue in any penal prosecution, or when the Council shall direct a prosecution for a nuisance, he shall appear for the prosecution when the case shall come into the Court of Hustings; and if the Mayor shall require it he shall appear in such cases before him for the prosecution; and he shall perform such other duties as are or may be required of the Attorney for the city by any ordinance or resolution. Annually, on or before the thirty-first day of December, he shall deliver to the clerk of the Council, to be laid before the Council, a report of the state and condition of the civil cases in which the city is interested that are so depending. The said Attorney

shall, in every year, on the first day of January and first day of July, or as soon thereafter as practicable, render to the Chamberlain an account of his services, under this section, within the preceding six months, so stated as to show what he considers will be a reasonable compensation therefor; which account shall, without special order, stand referred to the committee on finance to report thereon. Whatever the Council, after the report of the commitee, may allow for said services shall be paid by the Auditor.

TITLE 11.

OFFENCES.

CHAPTER LIV.

CONCERNING INJURIES TO REAL ESTATE.

1. If any person shall wilfully destroy, injure or in any manner deface any church or other house of public worship, or other public building in this city, belonging to this city or state, the county of Henrico or the United States, or any enclosure thereof, or any tree or plant set on the outside of any such enclosure appurtenant thereto, or shall wilfully destroy, injure or deface any tree, shrub or other thing within any such enclosure, he shall be fined not less than two nor more than one hundred dollars. And if any person other than the owner shall wilfully destroy, injure or deface any other house or building not his own, or the enclosure around any other lot not his own, or any tree, shrub or flower within the same, he shall be punished by like fine; and this section, with the assent of the Governor, shall apply not only to the capitol square and the government house, but to all other enclosed grounds and buildings in this city belonging to the commonwealth, and to the enclosures thereof, and the trees, shrubbery and other things therein.*

2. If any person shall post or paste any bill or notice of any description whatever upon any wall, building, tree-box or en-

* Assented to by the Governor of Virginia, March 26th, 1859.

closure in the city, or paint or chalk or in any manner deface the same, without the consent of the owner or occupier of the premises, he shall be fined not less than five nor more than twenty dollars.

CHAPTER LV.

CONCERNING THE SALE OF LIQUORS AND GAMBLING.

SEC.
1. Penalty for selling liquors without a license.
2. Penalty on hotel keeper, &c., for allowing gambling or sale of liquors.
3. Penalty on other persons for allowing sale of liquors.

1. If any person shall sell by retail to a person in this city any wine, brandy, whiskey or other ardent spirits, or a mixture thereof, to be drunk at or in the house, or other place where sold, without a license to keep an ordinary or an eating house with license to sell liquors to his guests, at the said house or place, he shall be fined not less than five nor more than twenty dollars.

2. If any licensed keeper of a house of private entertainment or public boarding house, eating house, cook shop or lager beer saloon, shall allow any gambling or play of any kind for money or other valuable thing, or shall allow any wine, ardent spirits, or a mixture thereof, to be sold upon his or her premises, he, she or they shall be fined for each offence a sum not less than ten nor more than fifty dollars: provided, that this last prohibition shall not apply to the keeper of an eating house who has a license to sell liquors, to his guests, and sells it only as authorized by his license.

3. If any person not embraced in the next preceding section, shall allow any spirituous or fermented liquors to be sold upon his or her premises, he or she shall be fined fifty dollars for each offence. But this section shall not apply to keepers of ordinaries, or keepers of eating houses, or merchants having a license to sell such liquors, when the same are sold only as authorized by their licenses.

CHAPTER LVI.

CONCERNING INDECENT CONDUCT, ASSAULTS, &C., IN PUBLIC PLACES.

1. Any person who shall be guilty of lewd, indecent or disorderly conduct, or who shall exhibit any indecent representation of any subject or thing in the city, shall be fined not less than five nor more than one hundred dollars.

2. If any person shall fight or assault another in any place of public resort in the city of Richmond, or in the streets or public alleys of the city, he shall be fined not less than five nor more than one hundred dollars.

3. If any person shall appear in the streets or public alleys of the city intoxicated, or shall therein employ abusive or insulting languge to another person, or use obscene language or actions, he shall be fined not less than two nor more than fifty dollars.

CHAPTER LVII.

CONCERNING INJURIES TO THE PORT OF RICHMOND.

Deposits of stone, &c., in creeks or on margin of river; penalty.

If any person shall place or deposit or shall attempt to place or deposit any stone, ashes, dirt, rubbish or other thing in or near Gillie's creek or Shockoe creek, or upon the margin of the river or any island therein near the margin thereof, or between the southern limits of the city and the river, so that the same will or may be carried into the river at or below the port of Richmond, he shall be fined for each offence not less than twenty nor more than fifty dollars.

CHAPTER LVIII.

CONCERNING FINES AND PENALTIES.

1. Fines and penalties for the violation of any ordinance of the city, or any order of the Mayor or other justice, given in pursuance of any ordinance, shall be recoverable by prosecution before the Mayor, in the Mayor's court; and when recovered, shall inure to the use of the city and be paid to the Chamberlain, except in cases where it may be otherwise expressly provided.

2. Minors shall be prosecuted for breaches of ordinances in the same manner and to the same effect as adults; and if the minor be not an indentured apprentice, the fine may, in the discretion of the Mayor or other justice be imposed either on the minor or on his father or guardian; and if the offender be an indentured apprentice, upon the master or apprentice. For any violation of an ordinance by a married woman, the prosecution shall be against her husband, and the fine imposed on him.

3. When judgment shall be rendered for any fine under an ordinance, and the same be not immediately paid, the Mayor or other justice rendering the same shall issue execution thereon, to be levied of the goods and chattels of the person against whom such judgment is rendered, directed to any police officer of the city, returnable within fifteen days before the justice issuing the same. The officer who may levy such execution shall sell the property thereby taken, at public auction, for cash, at one of the market houses in the city, after three days' notice of the time and place of sale published in one of the daily papers printed in the city, to satisfy said execution, and all costs attending the levy and sale thereof.

4. On the first day of every month, the Mayor shall return to the Chamberlain an account of fines imposed by him within the preceding month. On the preceding day each officer of the police shall render to the Mayor an account of the fines collected by him within the said month, so made out as to show the date

of the judgment for each fine, whom against, and the amount thereof, with a statement subjoined of what the officer may have paid during the same month for supporting persons in the watch-house, or in the discharge of any official duty. And the said officer shall make oath before the Mayor that the account is correct. And the said officer shall within the first four days of every month pay the same into the treasury of the city. If the Mayor shall fail to make his said monthly reports, his salary shall be withheld until it is made.

TITLE 12.

ENACTING AND REPEALING STATUTE.

(Passed March 12, 1867.)

CHAPTER LIX.

TO FIX THE TIME FOR THE COMMENCEMENT OF THE FOREGOING ORDINANCES, AND TO REPEAL OTHERS.

1. The foregoing ordinances, as they have been hereinbefore printed and corrected, shall be in force from and after this day; and all ordinances and parts of ordinances, of a general nature, in force at the time of passing this ordinance, and not included in the foregoing ordinances, shall be repealed from and after this day, with such limitations and exceptions as are hereinafter expressed.

2. Such repeal shall not affect any offence or act committed or done, or any penalty or forfeiture incurred, or any right established, accrued or accruing, or any prosecution or proceeding pending, at or on this day, except that when any penalty, forfeiture or punishment is mitigated by the provisions of the foregoing ordinances, such provisions may, with the consent of the party affected, be applied to any judgment to be hereafter pronounced thereon.

APPENDIX.

AN ORDINANCE

TO ESTABLISH A CITY DISPENSARY.

[Passed March 19, 1867.]

1. *Be it ordained by the Council of the city of Richmond*, That for the purpose of establishing a City Dispensary three hundred dollars be and is hereby appropriated for the purchase of medicines. Said medicines to be purchased by the Board of Health, and to be paid for by the city, upon an order of the president of said board, approved by the chairman of the committee on health.

2. That the proposition of the Faculty of the Medical College of Virginia, to provide a room or rooms in the college building suitable for a dispensary, free of charge to the city, be for the present accepted.

3. That the Board of Health divide the city into six districts, and suggest the name or names of one or more suitable physicians, to be appointed by the Council, to attend the indigent white population in case of sickness, and supply them with medicines, free of charge. Hereafter the election of said physicians shall be made annually at the regular meeting of the Council in the month of March, and any vacancy occurring may be filled for the unexpired term, at any regular or called meeting.

4. That the six physicians so appointed shall each receive one hundred dollars per annum as compensation for their services, said salaries to be paid quarter-yearly.

5. That the distribution of said medicines shall be subject to such rules as the Board of Health may from time to time prescribe.

6. That the Board of Health shall report quarterly to the Council the condition of said dispensary, the amount of medicines used, that remaining on hand, and the amount required for the next quarter, and of any other matters pertinent to said dispensary.

7. The Council reserves the right to annul at any time the appointment of any or of all said physicians, for neglect of duty or other good cause, and to discontinue said dispensary and the services of said physicians, at their pleasure.

INDEX.

CLERKS OF COURTS.

COAL.

COLLECTOR.

COLLEGE.

COMMISSIONERS OF ELECTIONS.

COMMITTEES OF COUNCIL.

CONDUCTOR OF ELECTIONS.

CONSTABLES.

CONTESTED ELECTIONS.

COOK SHOPS AND EATING HOUSES.

CORONER.

CORPORATION.

COUNCIL OF THE CITY.

COURT OF HUSTINGS.

CONTESTED ELECTIONS.

ENACTING AND REPEALING STATUTE.

ENGINEER OF THE CITY.

ENGINES.

See *Railways*.

ESTATE.

See *Real and Personal Property*.

EXHIBITIONS.

See *Theatrical Exhibitions, &c.*

FIDUCIARY.

FIGHTING.

FINES AND PENALTIES.

HUCKSTERING, FORESTALLING, &c.

HUSTINGS COURT.

INCOMES.

INCORPORATED COMPANIES.

INDECENT AND DISORDERLY CONDUCT.

INJUNCTION.

INSPECTOR OF GAS.

INSURANCE AGENTS.

INSURANCE COMPANIES.

INSURRECTION OR INVASION.

INTERNAL IMPROVEMENT COMPANIES.

INTOXICATION.

IRON WORKS AND MILLS.

MAYOR'S COURT.

MEAL.

MEASURER OF GRAIN.

MERCHANTS, TRADERS, AND SHOPKEEPERS.

MESSENGER OF THE COUNCIL.

MILITARY.

MILLS AND IRONWORKS.

MINORS.

MOLASSES.

MORTGAGE AND DEED OF TRUST.

MUSICAL PERFORMANCE.

NIGHT WATCH.

NON-RESIDENT.

NUISANCES.

OATHS OF OFFICE.

OFFENCES.

OVERSEER OF CITY HANDS.

OVERSEERS OF THE POOR.

PAINTING, SCULPTURE, &c.

PATENT, &c., MEDICINES.

PAWN BROKERS.

PENALTIES.

PERSONAL PROPERTY.

PETITIONS.

PICKPOCKETS AND ROBBERS.

PISTOL GALLERY.

PLEDGE OF SECOND-HAND ARTICLES.

POLICE.

POOR.

PORT OF THE CITY.

PORT WARDENS.

POTATOES.

POWDER.

PRIMARY SCHOOLS.

PRIVIES.

PROFANITY.

PROSECUTIONS FOR FINES, &c.

PROXIES.

PUBLIC GROUNDS AND BUILDINGS.

TAVERNS.

PAGE.

TAXES.

www.ingramcontent.com/pod-product-compliance
Lightning Source LLC
LaVergne TN
LVHW010229110826
845151LV00004B/1238

* 9 7 8 1 4 2 5 5 2 5 9 4 1 *